One world, many knowledges

Regional experiences and cross-regional links in higher education

One world, many knowledges

Regional experiences and cross-regional links in higher education

Edited by Tor Halvorsen and Peter Vale

AFRICAN
MINDS

SANORD

Southern African-Nordic Centre

First published 2012 by the Southern African–Nordic Centre

University of the Western Cape
Private Bag X17, Bellville, 7535
Tel: +27 21 959 3802
http://sanord.net

ISBN: 978-0-620-55789-4 (print)
ISBN: 978-0-620-55788-7 (PDF)
ISBN: 978-0-620-55787-0 (ebook)

Copyediting and production management: Mary Ralphs
Design and typesetting: Scone-i
Cover artwork: Scone-i
Printing: Creda Communications (Pty) Ltd

Copies of this book are available for free download at
www.africanminds.org.za and http://sanord.net

ORDERS
For orders from Africa, please contact:
African Minds
Email: info@africanminds.org.za

For orders from outside Africa, please contact:
African Books Collective
PO Box 721, Oxford OX1 9EN, UK
Email: orders@africanbookscollective.com

Contents

Part IV: CRITICAL PERSPECTIVES

Frequently used acronyms and abbreviations

CHE	Council on Higher Education
CHET	Centre for Higher Education Transformation
DDRN	Danish Development Research Network
DEAFSA	Deaf Federation of South Africa
DHET	Department of Higher Education and Training
EHEA	European Higher Education Area
GATS	General Agreements on Trade in Services
HEMIS	Higher Education Management Information System
HSRC	Human Sciences Research Council
IAU	International Association of Universities
ICT	information and communication technologies
NATO	North Atlantic Treaty Organisation
NCHE	National Commission on Higher Education
NORAD	Norwegian Agency for Development Cooperation
NSFAS	National Student Financial Aid Scheme
SADC	Southern African Development Community
SANORD	Southern African–Nordic Centre
SAPSE	South African post-secondary education
SASL	South African Sign Language
SIDA	Swedish International Development Cooperation Agency
TBVC	Transkei, Bophutatswana, Venda and Ciskei
UK	United Kingdom
US/USA	United States of America
WTO	World Trade Organisation

Introduction: why this book, and what is it about?
Tor Halvorsen and Peter Vale

THIS BOOK BUILDS ON THE Southern African–Nordic Centre (SANORD) conference, held at Rhodes University, Grahamstown, in December 2009, on the theme 'Inclusion and Exclusion in Higher Education'. Its contents, however, do not simply replicate the proceedings of that event. Instead, although the bulk of the chapters were delivered as papers at the conference, one of the chapters derives from an earlier SANORD conference and others, including those written by Stanly Ridge and the two co-editors, were written especially for this book. This collection thus stands apart from, and gestures towards, the themes raised at the 2009 event.

Unsurprisingly, given its title, this book considers the value of academic co-operation – a notion that has been at the heart of conversations about higher education since the early 1990s. What is its purpose? Why is it necessary? What form should it take? And, central to the theme of the Grahamstown gathering, who benefits, and why?

These questions cannot be answered until it is understood that academic co-operation encompasses an array of interlinked networks that run from the minor to the meso. These criss-cross the modern university system in a bewildering number of ways: from the open exchange of ideas and knowledge; to the sharing of research results; frank discussions about research challenges; and (to pinpoint an increasingly threatened feature of university life) the creation of cross-regional academic communities, characterised by open dialogue about the challenges posed by the notion of the global 'knowledge society'. In other words, the contributors to this book are interested in the strategies that universities, in the North and the South, have adopted to deal with the time–space compression – to use David Harvey's helpful term – represented by the interconnected world that has been loosely (and recklessly) described as globalised.

Hovering in the background, during the three days of the 2009 conference as well as during the process of compiling this volume, is the question of whether a 'global template' for the management of both higher education and national research organisations emerged after the Cold War. And, if it did, must institutions slavishly follow its high-flown language or risk falling further and further behind in relation to its regime of 'excellence' and ubiquitous university ranking system? It is, therefore, not wholly surprising that these issues arise within the book, too.

The theme of how the global discourse of higher education and research is influenced by the concept of competitiveness appears again and again throughout these chapters. Competitiveness is said to be essential to the economic and social health of nations (and indeed the world), but are there alternatives that can achieve a better, more ethically inclined world than the supposedly endless growth required to feed the market? Are there other ways of recruiting students are to higher education? Can new governance systems be linked to the will of academics, rather than planners, as they work together across regions to shape alternative forms of knowledge? Will, for instance, alternative curricula produce different outcomes? Can these change our understandings of the challenges of growing global poverty? How can universities reach society beyond the formalised and increasingly institutionalised 'corporate social responsibility' model which, because it is copied from the business world, is preoccupied with the bottom line rather than with the emancipatory role of knowledge? Of course these, and many other questions, are captured within the idea of 'inclusion' and 'exclusion', the theme around which SANORD had convened its conference.

The book is organised into four sections, which we have called Background; the Dilemmas of Change; Inclusion and Exclusion; and Critical Perspectives.

Background

Veteran academic, and administrator of the University of the Western Cape, Stanley Ridge was central to the creation of SANORD. His lively chapter covers this story in unambiguous terms: SANORD was the product of a meeting of minds between old friends and their commitment to institutionalise their friendship anew. The network's goals are clearly discussed, and the personalities, including Ridge, who gave it shape are brought to life.

Danish academic, Anne Sørensen, takes the story forward by positioning SANORD within a series of debates on the role of higher education in development. This empirically rich chapter places the issue of SANORD membership within the framework of a loose cost-benefit analysis, and Sørensen uses this to report on recommendations made during her research into ways forward for SANORD.

Dilemmas of change

Nordic higher-education specialist, Risto Rinne, positions the post-Cold War changes in universities against the changes that took place during in the 1960s and 1970s. But his real purpose is to use the cumulative idea of change in higher education to report on the condition of higher education in Finland. Here, the university is caught between the professional responsibilities of academics and the meta-narratives of globalisation, which determine particular forms of control; it is an uncomfortable fit.

Rhodes University's Saleem Badat, policy-maker and university administrator, provides an account of the double whammy that South African universities have faced since the ending of apartheid. In a major key, he discusses the imperative of transformation in line with the country's constitution and shows how race, the issue that has dogged the country for so long, is intertwined with higher education. His minor key is provided by the concepts that drive global change.

Inclusion and exclusion

Musicologist, Bernard Bleibinger, highlights one of the many dilemmas raised by South Africa's transformation and by the utilitarian-inclined forces of globalisation. What is the role of music, and the arts in general, in education and society? Bleibinger's piece is a powerful plea for a new kind of 'struggle' – a struggle to free the mind from the prejudice of commodification. The reach of music, as his and his colleagues' experiences at the University of Fort Hare show, has the potential to fill the space between the local and the global, to offer skills and blur boundaries.

It is often said that migration has made the world what it is: Gabriel Tati, a statistician from the University of the Western Cape, uses his training to report on the findings of a study on students from other African countries who migrate to South Africa to further their education. Understandably, the reasons for coming are many and varied, integration is challenging and the decision as to whether to stay on or return home is often painful.

The University of the Witwatersrand is one of the few universities in the world that caters for deaf students. Lucas Magongwa points out that in terms of South Africa's 1996 Constitution, discrimination against the deaf cannot be tolerated and should be no hindrance to learning. Recording the experiences of 12 Deaf students at the university, he reveals that these students are strongly competitive, even if their social participation is low. But old issues, such as the resources required to provide interpreters and suitably trained tutors, continue to present major obstacles to their progress.

Tradition and modernity run through descriptions of southern Africa's troubled history: it is also the theme of a compelling paper on the management of the region's archaeological heritage by Zimbabwean and Mozambican scholars, Albino Jopela, Ancila Nhamo and Seke Katsamudanga. Their collaboration provides a fine example of the kinds of relationships that SANORD aims to foster, and why they matter, while revealing the complexities of preserving heritage within a complex triangular relationship – state, traditional authority, community – across a region which, effectively, has no boundaries.

But money matters, too, both in southern Africa and elsewhere and, to the concern of many, it may be the metaphor that matters most at this stage of the region's development. Two South Africans, economist, Peter le Roux, and higher-education specialist, Mignonne Breier, have this on their minds in the final chapter of this section. Driven by political (and even security) concerns, rather than by market interests, Le Roux and Breier suggest reasons for the poor performance of black students in South Africa: the wretched schooling system, the decline in government expenditure on higher education, inefficient planning in the sector, and the lack of sufficient incentives. They then propose changes to university funding formulas that have the potential to introduce far-reaching transformations in the South African context.

Critical perspectives
The three chapters in the final section open towards, if not fully embrace, what JJ Williams (in his February 2012 contribution to *The Chronicle of Higher Education*, entitled 'Deconstructing Academe') has called, 'critical university studies'. All three chapters deliver a critical perspective on the issues of higher education, its globalisation, its transformation in southern Africa, and the challenges these pose to networks like SANORD.

Anne Bang and Tore Sætersdal gesture towards the earlier chapter by Jopela, Nhamo and Katsamudanga, asking, what is the place of Africa's cultural heritage today? Using a Mozambican case study, they point West, East, and North, and their canvas seems wider than the southern African region. The argument they make is, however, clear and unambiguous: preserving the past secures the future, and higher education and sustainable research have a responsibility, whatever the funding regime and current organisational fashions, to preserve it.

Tor Halvorsen, co-editor of this volume, explores how shifting priorities have changed the way that higher education and research have been organised since the fall of the Berlin Wall. The disciplining of the sector was seen to be essential and governments were persuaded to do this by a series of discourses and tools developed and advanced by the Organisation for Economic Co-operation and Development. Thus, knowledge became a commodity and the professoriate was brought to heel by various regimes of control. Halvorsen considers the role of SANORD in this context.

Halvorsen's co-editor, Peter Vale, suggests that the meta-narrative of globalisation is anchored in what he calls 'weasel words' – words emptied of real meaning. He uses this to suggest that the word, 'innovation', which is central to the lexicon of university reform at a global level, has become a cipher for the neo-liberal economics that has so deeply divided the world between rich and poor. Since we live in such a little-known world, Vale argues, imagination, rather than weasel words such as innovation, should guide the work of organisations such as SANORD.

Like life itself, editing is a community effort: this book is no exception to the rule that all our labour is built on the work of others. Our thanks are due to all the participants in the Grahamstown conference, not only for presenting on that occasion but also for submitting their papers for inclusion here. The selection process was long – no, too long – for which we apologise. In the process, several papers were lost, and some even withdrawn. While this is a pity, we nevertheless feel that this book is a good reflection of the interests and concerns that drove the conference.

Out thanks are especially due to those whose papers appear between these covers. We are also grateful to the staff at the SANORD office in South Africa, Leolyn Jackson and Maureen Davies. Brian O'Connell, chair of the SANORD board and rector at the University of the Western Cape (UWC), supported the project throughout, as did Asri Andersen, vice-rector at the University of Bergen and vice-chair of the SANORD board. We thank UiB Global for providing an enabling environment, and Professor Steinar Askvik in the Department of Administration and Organisation Theory for his continual efforts to make SANORD work. We are also grateful for Estelle H Prinsloo's editorial and administrative support. Finally, this book would not have been possible without the skills and imagination of freelance editor and project manager, Mary Ralphs.

PART I: BACKGROUND

Chapter 1

The Southern African–Nordic Centre: from conception to realisation

Stanley GM Ridge

IN ONE SENSE, the Southern African–Nordic Centre (SANORD) had to happen. Nordic countries had developed distinct relationships with movements for liberation and national development long before southern African countries won their independence and apartheid was finally abolished. For universities in these two regions not to develop new forms of co-operation would have been a kind of betrayal. Yet finding new forms of co-operation was by no means certain. The world changed fast in the final decades of the last century: liberation movements became governments that could be expected to make their own way in the world, and the fall of the Soviet Union demanded a massive reorientation in the kinds of development relationships required within Europe. Neo-liberal economic thinking also came to challenge a great deal of what had characterised Nordic–southern African relationships. For example, Nordic universities came under pressure to cultivate relationships that might prove prestigious in terms of the international-ratings systems introduced in the early 2000s. On reflection, then, it might be truer to say that SANORD could not have happened without visionary leadership, strong ties of friendship, and a lively sense of possibility.

Setting up

From the late 1990s, some years before SANORD's formation, there were conversations about the need to put the relationships between Nordic and southern African universities on a new footing. Peter Vale – who was at the University of the Western Cape (UWC) at the time – and Tor Halvorsen – at the University of Bergen (UiB) – were saying this, as were colleagues at the

University of Oslo, Linköping University and elsewhere. In the end, it took the particular vision and bonds of trust and friendship between Sigmund Grønmo, rector of UiB, and Brian O'Connell, rector of UWC to set the ball rolling and keep it in play.

In the initial discussions that took place in 2006, three major reasons were put forward in favour of the initiative. First, global challenges require the flexibility and variety of perspectives that diversity offers, and neither North nor South can afford to be locked into a received mindset. Second, however useful individual projects may be, their fixed time frames tend to encourage partnerships that last only until the funds are spent. Besides, if they are not mutually intellectually profitable, they promote patronisation rather than partnership. Sustainable, longer-term and mutually beneficial relationships require both multilateral engagements and the careful alignment of activities with the strategic plans of the institutions involved. Third, institutional leadership is usually marginal to project-based international relationships, but university leaders need to be centrally involved in building partnerships, so as to enhance the vision for what is possible and to help achieve institutional alignment.

Thus, Sigmund Grønmo and Brian O'Connell agreed to approach six other universities, all in different countries, to form the initial membership of an organisation to promote collaboration between southern African and Nordic research institutions. In the meantime, the Nordic ambassadors to South Africa were briefed and proved very supportive. South Africa's foreign affairs and education departments also expressed interest and were kept in the picture. At the invitation of the Norwegian ambassador, Tor Chr. Hildan, the ambassadors of Denmark, Finland and Sweden met with UWC's Brian O'Connell, Larry Pokpas and myself to discuss the possibilities. Since it was deemed highly desirable that the initiative have strong political support, Larry Pokpas and I included meetings with university and government leaders in Norway and Sweden on our next trip to Europe.[1] In the meantime, through the initiative of Sigmund Grønmo, Norway's state-funded Fredskorpset offered to provide funding to enable a senior retired Norwegian university administrator to be sent to South Africa to get the initiative moving, and also to send a South African to spend a year in the North, making appropriate contacts and preparing to run the central office. Accordingly, Kjetil Flatin, who had recently retired from the University of Oslo, agreed to spend time in South Africa, and Leolyn Jackson was appointed as director of the new organisation, and his first mission was to spend a year in the North.

The universities of Aarhus (in Denmark), Malawi, Namibia, Turku (in Finland), Uppsala (in Sweden) and Zambia agreed to join UiB and UWC at a first meeting in January. In the event, the University of Namibia did not attend and eventually withdrew from participation for internal reasons. Senior representatives of all the other institutions were present, however, as well as Tor Halvorsen from UiB, as well as Larry Pokpas and me from UWC. Kjetil Flatin contributed a great deal to setting up the meeting and preparing the founding documents. After extensive discussion, drafts of a statute, a mission statement and a value statement were accepted, and the groundwork for establishing a web portal was prepared, with UiB spearheading the project.

It was agreed that a council would be set up consisting of rectors/vice-chancellors/heads (or their mandated alternates) of all member institutions, and that they would appoint an executive board (hereafter referred to as the board). It was agreed that the founding members would constitute the board until such time as the organisation was fully established, and that the chair and vice-chair could jointly act for the board when necessary. Brian O'Connell was elected chair, with Sigmund Grønmo vice-chair. The council undertook to meet face to face on an annual basis, with this meeting coinciding with a conference or symposium to emphasise the primacy of the intellectual nature of the project. In-between, the board would meet (at least) quarterly by conference call.

In terms of the statute, it was decided that the organisation's central office would be at UWC, and a special agreement was reached with the university in this regard. The board, which met immediately after the founding meeting, mandated UWC to 'set in motion the appropriate action for hiring' a director. It was envisaged that the initial funding for the centre would be from voluntary contributions by members, but a committee was established to make proposals on membership fees. At the next board meeting, a two-level fee structure was approved. This was initially set at R35 000 for institutions in the South and R50 000 for institutions in the North.

The organisation's mission statement went through a number of drafts before it was finalised. It reads as follows:

The Southern African–Nordic Centre is a non-profit, membership organisation of institutions of higher education and research, committed to advancing strategic, multilateral academic collaboration between institutions in the two regions, as they seek to address new local and global challenges of innovation and development. Its activities are based on shared fundamental values of democracy, social equity, and academic engagement, and on the deep relationships of trust built up between the regions over many years.

The corresponding value statement and list of goals explore the implications of the mission statement, emphasising the values of mutuality, leadership, strategic development, and sustained engagement, as well as announcing the organisation's particular concern with multilateral partnerships. Semiotics received a good deal of attention. The name of the organisation was hyphenated as the Southern African–Nordic Centre to emphasise the mutuality between the two regions: it is not a Nordic Centre located in southern Africa. The acronym SANORD was chosen as it immediately conveys the connection between the two regions. Soon the web portal had been commissioned, and at its first virtual meeting, the board approved a striking logo.

At the board's September 2007 meeting, Leolyn Jackson was appointed as SANORD's director, and he spent a year in Bergen from April 2008. This experience was of immense value, enabling him to tune in to the Nordic ethos, to visit many universities and to establish personal relationships with key people in the region, especially those directly involved in SANORD. The UiB leadership, and those active in SANORD at UiB, advised Leolyn on the kinds of the issues he might have to deal with as director, and gave him crucial insights into Nordic life and practices so that he could approach issues with a deeper understanding of the dynamics relevant to institutions in both the North and the South.

The wisdom of Fredskorpset in proposing and supporting this exchange has been demonstrated repeatedly and their vision did not stop there. After having helped to lay sound foundations, Kjetil Flatin returned to Norway in September 2007. Fredskorpset then sponsored Poul Wisborg, a Norwegian researcher with South African experience, to be based at UWC from September 2008 to March 2010. Wisborg was there when Jackson returned to the central office and when SANORD's first administrator, Maureen Davis, was appointed. Wisborg's energy and collegiality was critical in building the capacity of the central office, and in making SANORD known across the southern African region. Membership grew and active academic partnerships increased substantially as a result. Fredskorpset's sustained contribution thus amounted to approximately 50 person-months.

Membership

Issues around increasing membership were an early challenge. Indeed, the University of Iceland indicated a strong desire to join at the outset, and was happily added to the founding group *ex post facto*. In fact, Iceland's recently appointed ambassador to South Africa joined the founding meeting for one session. However, in January 2007, the board, aware of the range of issues that still needed to be resolved, decided that initial growth should be on the basis of classic universities concerned with teaching and research in a dynamic relationship with their own communities. This provided important space for resolving difficulties, building capacity, increasing mutual understanding and building a sense of potential. At the September 2007 meeting, seven new members were accepted: Bergen University College, Oslo University College, Mzuzu University (in Malawi), as well as the universities of Johannesburg, Jyväskylä (in Finland), Southern Denmark and the Witwatersrand (in South Africa). By March 2008, there were three more members: the Cape Peninsula University of Technology and the University of Cape Town (both in South Africa), and Lund University (in Sweden). Others followed, and by September 2011, SANORD had 42 members: 17 institutions from the Nordic region and 25 institutions from six southern African countries.

Soon, other membership possibilities emerged. What about independent research institutes? What about tertiary institutions focused almost exclusively on teaching? And what about sub-regional university consortia? In March 2008, a nominations committee was established to make recommendations to the SANORD board on criteria for membership and on specific applications. On the recommendation of the nominations committee, it was agreed to accept as members all institutions likely to benefit and to further the purposes for which SANORD was founded. Relationships with consortia are, however, governed by specific memoranda of agreement.

Local and international events

Organisations thrive when they are perceived to be serving a useful purpose, so from an early stage, members undertook to organise SANORD events on their campuses and to promote participation in joint events, both regional and international. The first major event involving all members was a conference held at UWC in December 2007. Its theme, 'Higher Education, Research and Development: Shifting Challenges and Opportunities', invited reflection on SANORD's founding concerns. Setting a pattern for the future, the conference committee, drawn from both North and South, developed the programme and vetted proposals for papers and seminars. Nico Cloete, Extraordinary Professor of Higher Education at UWC, played a critical role in the first conference, but inputs from all institutions were testimony to the commitment of imagination and intelligence that characterises SANORD's membership. The opening speaker, Nobel laureate and UWC's chancellor at the time, Desmond Tutu, set the context superbly. Plenaries were held on issues such as: the implications of information and communication technologies for North–South co-operation; the International Foundation for Science's approach to capacity building; and the roles played by funding agencies. The major part of the conference took place via a range of sessions on key topics for research co-operation such as poverty, the environment, sustainable societies, biodiversity, land reform, and the politics of higher education. A unique feature of these sessions was that they reported back both to the full conference and to the SANORD council on issues that delegates believed would benefit from leadership intervention. These details are provided as an indication of the ways in which SANORD's distinctive strategic focus shaped the programme.

Holding an annual conference proved impractical and a biennial conference was agreed upon. However, the annual face-to-face meeting of rectors/vice-chancellors proved so valuable that it was decided to persist with those meetings. Thus, instead of a full-scale conference, it was agreed that a symposium would accompany these meetings, again emphasising the primacy of the organisation's intellectual concerns. The second meeting also took place at UWC in December 2008. That year's symposium was organised around the theme 'Innovation and Development', and drew in leading figures from Denmark, Finland, Norway and Sweden along with representatives of government, business and universities in southern Africa. So strong was the call from research groups, however, that space had to be made in the programme for some of these to share their findings and attract more participants.

The global challenge of the knowledge economy was the major focus of the symposium. To meet it, mindset adjustments and new partnerships were called for in all countries. Four aspects were raised for ongoing attention of the kind that SANORD is well placed to give:

- The importance of ambitious, long-term thinking on the part of leadership, as opposed to the quick-fixes often demanded in institutional and national politics;
- The interests of government, industry and universities in scientific excellence, and the responsibility shared by these sectors to find ways of promoting it, through, for example, fostering new and co-operative relationships;
- The fact that truly co-operative relationships are fundamental to success and to achieving appropriate scale, and that achieving such relationships can require significant shifts in mindset for all parties; and
- The crucial importance for sustained development of being able to attract and retain talent – an ability that can be significantly enhanced by committed partnerships.

SANORD has run a number of successful conferences and symposia at Rhodes University, the University of Johannesburg, and the University of the Witwatersrand, and in 2012 the first such event to be held outside Africa took place in Aarhus, Denmark. Future events include a conference in Malawi in 2013, a symposium in Karlstad, Sweden in 2014, a conference in Windhoek, Namibia in 2015, and a symposium at Uppsala, Norway in 2016.

Stimulating research and innovation

One of SANORD's main objectives is to stimulate research and innovation by researchers and students who team up across institutional, disciplinary and national boundaries. With some cash in hand after the 2007 conference, the SANORD board approved modest support grants to some of the theme groups and to others interested in developing links within SANORD. In 2008, SANORD funded six projects to organise seminars, conferences and other activities directly related to the North–South multilateral co-operation in the fields of social development, water-resource management, Islamic education, climate change and environmental security, archaeology, and literacy education in Zambia. Students formed an integral part of these research networks, and master's and PhD candidates were exposed to international academic experts.

Of the 22 interesting applications received in 2009, ten were recommended for financial support. Since the SANORD board had the funds to support just four of these, SANORD's secretariat requested permission from the board to seek additional funding. Funding for four additional projects involving Swedish university partners was obtained through a joint application from SANORD and Uppsala University to the Swedish International Development Cooperation Agency (SIDA). One of the Swedish-funded research groups (led by researchers at the University of the Witwatersrand and the University of Johannesburg in South Africa and Uppsala University in Sweden) was later granted extra funds to allow selected researchers from southern Africa an opportunity to discuss and interact with peers in Uppsala, as a means of strengthening research capacity and facilitating staff mobility.

SANORD has grown steadily since it began. This expansion means that there are many more opportunities for research partnerships. Over the first two years, 14 research groups received seed funding totalling R740 000. In 2011, the board mandated the SANORD secretariat to source expertise to develop strategies and guiding principles for the monitoring and evaluation of research projects funded. Meanwhile, discussions are underway with various research teams at the universities of Bergen (Norway), Botswana, Jyväskylä (Finland) and Karlstad (Sweden) who want to register their research networks and academic activities with SANORD.

The growing membership also means a larger pool of potential hosts for joint events. While various South African universities hosted events between 2008 and 2011, the 2012 symposium took place at Aarhus University in Denmark and there have been offers to host the 2013 conference in Malawi and the 2014 symposium in Karlstad, Sweden. This can only be to the good.

Taking stock

With its vital signs looking strong, it is possible to take stock of SANORD's achievements, as of mid-2012, in relation to its initial goals.

- *To promote strategic co-operation by stimulating discussion and planning of joint endeavours by leaders at institutions of higher education and research.* This goal is predicated on the need to align institutional co-operation with the strategic thinking within such institutions and thus increase the probability of partnerships being sustained beyond project boundaries. Many institutional leaders have been active in SANORD; they have benefited from the annual meetings, and have made valuable contributions. However, there is a growing tendency for SANORD membership to fall under institutions' international offices, and thus find themselves at one remove from their institution's core leadership. Clearly, there are practical advantages to an alignment with the institutions' international goals, but the need for creative leadership in response to rapidly changing circumstances is one of SANORD's founding motives. It is gratifying that rectors and vice-chancellors of member institutions often consult one another informally, and have often taken the initiative in proposing new ideas for the support and development of major initiatives. The distinctive thrust of this book is a case in point. Although based on papers presented at the 2009 conference at Rhodes University, it is not simply a record of those proceedings. Its purpose is to examine the global developments that frame the academic enterprise, and to explore fruitful responses. The prevailing global academic climate is characterised by competition for knowledge resources, the search for knowledge influence for the sake of political and economic domination, and, linked to this, competition for students, for star professors, and for control over the topics considered relevant for research priority. In exploring modes of co-operation that lie at the heart of the SANORD enterprise, this book provides a basis for rethinking these issues and for considering alternatives. It also engages with an initiative taken at the June 2012 Aarhus symposium, which established three working groups with the aim of strengthening and expanding co-operation. The first group was tasked with developing goals and an action plan for the organisation, thus shifting the onus from the central office to the members when it comes to shaping the framework for activities. The second group was charged with mapping SANORD's research environment and developing research focus areas to strengthen the partnerships between members. And the third group was mandated to give detailed attention to a compiling a portfolio of funding models suited to developing research capacity and output and increasing student and staff mobility.

- *To provide opportunities for staff and students to meet around issues relevant to the SANORD mission.*
The core conferences and symposia, as well as activities within projects and SANORD-linked events on individual campuses, have provided lively opportunities for interaction. In addition, this goal has informed the conceptualisation of major activities such as the SIDA-funded Uppsala–SANORD project. Beyond facilitating the organisation's core purpose of supporting research groups, these events have made possible the increasing participation of researchers, even supporting delegates from two southern African universities that were not yet members – the University of Botswana and the University of Namibia, which have since joined SANORD.

- *To offer resources and information services, including virtual and physical meeting places to facilitate co-operation.*
SANORD's central office has been established, a regular newsletter is published, and a web portal has been developed. The latter two are used to profile SANORD and its member institutions, to provide a forum for the exchange of research news and information, and to share announcements of scholarships and other opportunities that might support exchange and networks. Students have been identified as a distinct user group, and the portal is being expanded to further meet student needs. One advantage of having SANORD fall under the international relations offices at some institutions is that this provides clear institutional spaces for meetings and channels, through which co-operation can be facilitated.

- *To promote cultural exchange for the strengthening of academic life.*
The importance of cultural exchange in enriching educational environments has been recognised from the start. While some activities

have taken place, its potential to enhance capacity and build long-term relationships has not yet been systematically exploited. Existing bilateral and multilateral cultural agreements between countries in which members are based provide a promising basis for addressing this challenge in future.

- *To build relationships with the donor community, commerce, industry and the media.*
Significant progress has been made in developing relationships with the donor community. As of 2012, partnerships have been established with SIDA and Norway's Fredskorpset, as already mentioned. Having noted progress thus far, Fredskorpset has indicated that it is willing to consider a long-term agreement to support staff exchanges between Norway and southern members of SANORD, and an application for such an agreement is being developed and was developed for submission by the end of 2012. With the full support of its board, SANORD is engaging with these groups, as well as with the European Union's Erasmus Mundus and Intra-ACP programmes, with a view to promoting core multilateral interests. In addition, SANORD is itself an associate partner in the EUROSA consortium, helping it implement, promote and monitor the project, disseminate scholarship opportunities, and attract applicants through the other educational networks with which it is engaged. However, SANORD has no room for complacency about donor support. Securing funding requires constant attention and alertness to the shifting focuses of donor agencies and the possibilities of finding synergies with others. A major challenge lies in gaining backing for initiatives from a wider group of donors, including national research foundations and national and international development agencies. In addition, mutually beneficial relationships with commerce and industry have still to be developed, and there is room for much wider media involvement.

- *To strengthen the SANORD central office and the SANORD network by improving the modes of operation, access to resources and efficiency.* The SANORD secretariat has worked consistently with member institutions in establishing fruitful modes of operation, and the structural arrangements made to date testify to the shared desire to realise the potential of this unique partnership. Yet there is much more to do. While it is important to keep the operation lean, ways will have to be found to expand what the central office is able to do in the way of supporting emerging partnerships and making the significance of what is being achieved more widely known. For example, the visits to various centres by

Leolyn Jackson and Poul Wisborg in 2008 and 2009 proved very fruitful in attracting new members and in building on existing relationships and facilitating increased participation in projects. It is important that such personal contact occur on an ongoing basis. While virtual contact is no substitute for face-to-face engagement, it has a vital role of its own. SANORD must also be proactive about the possibilities of personal and group teleconferencing, particularly as broadband access becomes a reality in many parts of Africa.

It takes a great deal to build a new organisation; visionary leadership, strong ties of friendship, and a lively sense of possibility inspired the founding of SANORD and continue to inform its activities. The long-term vision of its founders has been crucial in sustaining the organisation's development. In addition, members have supported one another through a number of crises, and have both given and received resources for projects and for building sustainable, multilateral partnerships well beyond their minimum commitments. For example, when some member institutions (in both the North and the South) were severely affected by the global financial crisis, others (from both the North and the South) quietly paid their fees in order to keep them within the partnership. This kind of thing happens only when there is genuine enthusiasm and unequivocal commitment. With a sound organisational basis, leadership engagement in setting the agenda and an ethos of warm and generous collegiality, SANORD is well placed to respond to the exciting challenges and opportunities that lie ahead.

Note
1   We owe much to Lena Wallensteen (Sweden) and Inger Stoll (Norway) for opening doors to us and helping to organise our programme.

Chapter 2

Drivers and challenges in the internationalisation of higher education and research: the case of the Southern African–Nordic Centre

Anne Sørensen

THE GLOBAL CONTEXT FOR INTERNATIONAL collaboration on research and development is changing rapidly. It is no longer easy to confine problems associated with issues such as environmental degradation, migration and climate change to developing countries. These problems affect people worldwide, and it is now widely acknowledged that higher education and research are key, if sustainable development is to be achieved. Furthermore, it is no longer sensible to work in isolation in our globalised world, and the internationalisation[1] of higher education, combined with international research partnerships and networks, is playing a bigger role than ever in strengthening education for sustainable development. Consequently, much is expected from the science- and knowledge-producing communities, in terms of finding solutions to the problems of development and growth in developing countries, and offering guidance to decision- and policy-makers. Science journalist David Dickson (2009) summed this up as follows:

> Anyone seeking to tackle the problems facing the developing world must remember two simple facts of life. First, none of these problems – from food shortages and the spread of disease, to achieving sustainable economic growth – can be addressed without the use of science and technology. Second, harnessing science for development depends on the skills of a country's people. And that in turn requires a robust and effective higher education system – the only mechanism that can produce and sustain these skills.

This situation also means that governments have to deploy their national budgets to mainstream capacity development in the areas of higher education and research. Yet, many governments still seem to overlook the important information contained in Dickson's observation, and many poverty-reduction strategies do not refer either to science or to strengthening the tertiary education sector. These are serious omissions as these strategies are meant to guide investment priorities for decision-makers and donors. In the first decade of the twenty-first century, policy-makers and governments in the North have made some progress in this regard. In Scandinavia, for example, the Norwegian government has prioritised the education sector in its development policy. And Denmark's Africa Commission has listed the promotion of 'post-primary education and research' among its five priority areas. This shift has led to increased support for several higher education initiatives in Africa, including the UniBRAIN programme, which aims to co-ordinate the efforts of university educators, researchers and business leaders in the field of agricultural innovation (see Africa Commission 2009; UniBRAIN n.d.).

In this chapter, I focus on the internationalisation of higher education as a key instrument and strategy for capacity development in higher education and research in the North and the South. I first outline the wider context of the internationalisation of higher education and research, focusing on changes in the donor support for capacity development in the higher education sector in developing countries. Second, I present and discuss the findings of a survey on the internationalisation of higher education and research carried out in collaboration with the secretariat of the Southern African–Nordic Centre (SANORD),[2] among its member institutions. The rationale for SANORD institutions' engagement in internationalisation is analysed and the challenges explored. Focus is directed towards those challenges that are specific to developing countries. Finally, recommendations and ideas on possible ways forward conclude the chapter, and I highlight some of the key issues that need to be addressed for institutions like SANORD to fully benefit from internationalisation.

The context: is higher education back on the development agenda?
In 1994, the World Bank announced that higher education should not be prioritised in development strategies; from being allocated 17 per cent of its education budget between 1985 and 1989, higher education received a mere 7 per cent of the organisation's education budget between 1995 and 1999. Following this period of drastic cuts during the late 1990s, several factors

combined to get higher education back on the agenda of major development donors (including the World Bank) by the beginning of the twenty-first century. Table 2.1 shows the distribution of World Bank education lending by sub-sector during the period 2005 to 2009. The Bank's focus on post-basic education was especially strong in 2008, with lending to tertiary education accounting for 25.9 per cent of total World Bank lending to the sector. However, World Bank support for tertiary education decreased drastically in 2009, returning back to lows seen in the late 1990s. Figure 2.1 illustrates the funds allocated by the top ten Organisation for Economic Co-operation and Development (OECD) donors to the higher-education sector between 1995 and 2007. With the exception of Japan, the graph confirms a general increase in donor funding to higher education during the first decade of the twenty-first century.

TABLE 2.1   World Bank education lending by sub-sector, 2005–2009

Sector	2005 Million US$	2005 % of total	2006 Million US$	2006 % of total	2007 Million US$	2007 % of total	2008 Million US$	2008 % of total	2009 Million US$	2009 % of total
Adult/ non-formal education	5.0	0.3	39.6	2.0	37.0	1.8	19.0	1.0	0.4	0.1
General education	506.5	26.0	456.6	22.9	627.0	31.0	504.0	26.1	1 036.0	37.6
Pre-primary education	88.0	4.5	147.3	7.4	14.0	0.7	36.0	1.9	185.0	1.2
Primary education	565.2	29.0	552.3	27.7	414.0	20.5	702.0	36.5	998.0	28.0
Secondary education	375.6	19.2	449.3	22.6	253.0	12.5	99.0	5.1	944.0	24.8
Tertiary education	360.8	18.5	263.4	13.2	260.0	12.9	499.0	25.9	208.0	7.5
Vocational training	50.1	2.6	81.9	4.1	415.0	20.6	69.0	3.6	74.0	0.9
Total	1 951.1	100	1 991	100	2 022	100	1 927	100	3 445	100

Source: World Bank (2012).

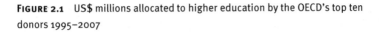

FIGURE 2.1 US$ millions allocated to higher education by the OECD's top ten donors 1995–2007

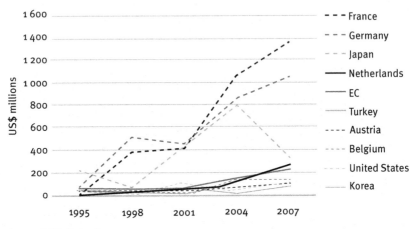

Legend:
- - - France
- - - Germany
- - - Japan
— Netherlands
— EC
— Turkey
- - - - Austria
- - - - Belgium
- - - United States
.... Korea

Y-axis: US$ millions — 0, 200, 400, 600, 800, 1 000, 1 200, 1 400, 1 600

X-axis: 1995, 1998, 2001, 2004, 2007

Source: OECD (Various).

A report published by the World Bank and UNESCO in 2000 indicated that higher education in developing countries was in a 'perilous' state and, while higher education could not guarantee rapid development, sustained progress would be impossible without it (Bloom and Rosovsky 2000).

Capacity building in higher education has, since, been on the agenda of several international meetings. For example, UNESCO's 2009 World Conference issued a strong recommendation on the need to pay greater attention to higher education and research in the fight against under-development and poverty in Africa (UNESCO 2009).

SANORD members and the internationalisation of higher education

The data and findings presented in this section are based on a survey conducted among member universities of SANORD, and on presentations made at SANORD's 2009 conference in Grahamstown, South Africa, on the theme 'Inclusion and Exclusion in Higher Education'. I draw particularly on the session entitled 'Higher Education and Research Collaboration in a Globalised World', which was organised by the Danish Development Research Network (DDRN)[3] with Danish SANORD member universities. The following extract from an African member university's internationalisation policy captures the essence of internationalisation in SANORD very well; it defines internationalisation as: 'The process of developing, implementing and integrating an international, intercultural and global dimension into the purpose, functions and delivery of higher education'. Of the 20 SANORD institutions that responded to the survey, 18 have an internationalisation policy, and although these differ in format and focus, the overall understanding of the internationalisation is basically the same for all institutions. All emphasise issues of *process,* and the need for the *integration* of international and intercultural dimensions into the teaching methods, research and service functions of the institutions is reflected in most of the respondents' descriptions of their respective internationalisation policies.

Likewise, all the institutions see globalisation as having profoundly affected the way in which countries, institutions and businesses operate. Accordingly, internationalisation is recognised as an essential element of quality higher education and research. As expressed by one of the survey respondents, 'internationalisation is essential and affects everything'. Furthermore, all SANORD members seem to agree that a key characteristic of excellent higher education anywhere in the world is its global relevance.

Drivers of internationalisation

The increasingly competitive environment in which universities operate is reflected in the internationalisation objectives of both Northern and Southern universities. Nordic universities expressed the need to secure their institution's position of strength in the global market, to sharpen their competitive edge and to strive to become the 'premier university in EU' by, for example, 'improving co-operation opportunities with the best international higher education institutions'. The position and reputation of universities is also seen as vital in the South. Thus the University of Cape Town's internationalisation policy aims to: 'to assist the university in growing its global profile with an Afropolitan niche', and recognises its location in the Southern African Development Community, in Africa and globally as central to its mission. Institutional culture, intercultural understanding and the promotion of multiculturalism were rated highly by many of the respondents and seen as key principles of internationalisation. However, acute concerns about economic survival, and securing a strong institutional position in the region and/or globally, were seen to pose a threat to the principles of solidarity and equity.

In order to better understand the reasons why institutions engage in internationalisation, respondents were asked to rank a list of pre-defined

TABLE 2.2 SANORD institutions' ranking of reasons for engaging in internationalisation

Reasons	Unimportant	Of little importance	Of some importance	Of great importance	No response
Contribute to academic quality	0	0	2	18	0
Create international profile and reputation	0	0	5	15	0
Increase student and faculty international knowledge, capacity and production	0	0	5	15	0
Strengthen research and knowledge capacity production	0	0	0	20	0
Promote curriculum development and innovation	0	0	7	13	0
Diversify income generation	0	6	8	6	0
Broaden and diversify source of faculty and students	0	1	9	10	0

reasons for engaging in internationalisation process. The results of the ranking are shown in Table 2.2.

Institutional motivations

The primary motive for SANORD members engaging in internationalisation is to 'strengthen the research and knowledge capacity production' of staff and students. Many respondents also saw the creation of an 'international profile and reputation' and its precondition, 'academic quality', as key motivations. It is important to note that internationalisation, combined with collaboration through strategic alliances and networks, promotes changes in curriculae and in educational and research methodologies. Approximately a third of respondents indicated that 'diversification of income' was of little importance. This was quite surprising, considering the tough economic climate, budget cuts and increasing competition for funds and projects that many universities were facing. However, one respondent added 'employability' as a very important rationale for engaging in internationalisation.

Instruments

All members agreed that 'alliances', 'agreements', 'networks' and 'mobility opportunities' were key instruments in SANORD's and their own institutions' internationalisation strategies. Other exchange and collaboration mechanisms that many respondents rated as important were 'visits from international scholars' and 'international development programmes'.

No one rated instruments, such as establishing 'campuses and delivery of educational programmes abroad' highly, but several respondents indicated that 'South–South collaboration' should be added to the list of important instruments. Some respondents also found it necessary to qualify some of the options given in the questionnaire, and one respondent noted that 'joint degrees' were especially important at doctoral level. Another respondent commented that 'distance education' was a high priority in certain fields, such as development studies.

Benefits

By engaging in the internationalisation of higher education and research, SANORD institutions expect to obtain benefits, such as improved academic quality, increased capacity, etc. Respondents were therefore asked to indicate the priority given to a number of pre-defined potential institutional results and benefits, focusing on benefits *actually* achieved.

As shown in Figure 2.2 the top score was 'strengthened research' with 17 out of 18 respondents indicating that this was an actual benefit achieved (two respondents did not reply to this question). Among other benefits that scored highly were 'academic quality' and 'internationalise staff/students' and 'brain gain', including brain gain in Europe.

As pointed out by one of the respondents, the specific benefits proved to be difficult for the respondents to rate at institutional level, given the range of different faculties involved. One respondent also drew attention to the fact that the importance of a benefit like 'innovation in curriculum' varies depending on the field in question. Further investigation of this issue at faculty or departmental level may be useful in future.

What this does indicate, however, is that the top three priorities in terms of achieved benefits, correspond very well with the key principles and reasons for engaging in internationalisation, namely: to 'strengthen research', improve 'academic quality' and 'internationalise staff and students'. There is no doubt that collaborations can have huge returns in terms of knowledge creation, circulation, development of capacity, networking, etc. To document these returns is beyond the scope of this paper, but it is hoped that further ways of measuring the actual benefits of collaborations fostered by SANORD will be explored. The policy on internationalisation developed by Rhodes University (in South Africa) mentions that the international office, among other things, does research on the process of internationalisation. The results of such research could, perhaps, be a starting point for the further sharing of knowledge and experience on the process of internationalisation across SANORD institutions.

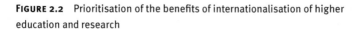

FIGURE 2.2 Prioritisation of the benefits of internationalisation of higher education and research

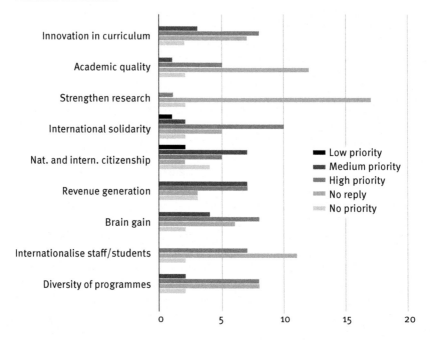

Information about the institutional collaborations that SANORD members are involved in was collected by asking the respondents to describe the two most important programmes at their respective institutions – one in higher education and one in research. We obtained 24 descriptions of programmes from 12 institutions in seven different countries in SANORD (three from southern Africa and four in the North).[4] The brief descriptions of programmes included the title of programme, the purpose, contact person and websites.

The main purpose of this aspect of the survey was to get an idea of the types of collaboration SANORD institutions were engaged in;[5] it does not give a full picture of the collaboration programmes within SANORD.

In the higher education field, most collaborative programmes outlined by respondents seemed to try to bridge the traditional North-South divide, but some also focused on enhancing regional co-operation such as the programme described by the University of Witwatersrand, and student exchanges such as those run by Bergen University College. On the whole, the higher-education collaborations described form a fairly heterogeneous group of programmes, and differ in both scope and content. They include long-term collaborations at institutional and personnel levels, twinning agreements, and capacity building in relation to post-secondary education and training. Some institutions have scholarship programmes specifically targeting master's and PhD students within specific areas. For example, there are post-graduate training programmes aimed at promoting women's legal rights in east and southern Africa, and several institutions have student-mobility schemes or student-exchange programmes in health, technology and other areas.

Collaborative programmes focused on research include larger strategic programmes, including long-term capacity building within research programmes. Two such examples are the Norwegian Programme for Development, Research and Education and the international science programme at Sweden's Uppsala University, which aimed to strengthen basic sciences in developing countries through building South–South networks. On a smaller scale, specific exchange programmes and smaller research projects linked to key themes identified by SANORD were in place. Common to most of these programmes was a strong element of capacity development and exchange.

Challenges – funding, dependency and marginalisation

The positive trend in the international development community with regard to funding higher education and research (discussed earlier) was not reflected in SANORD institutions' responses on this issue. Generally, it was felt that internationalisation is given a lot of 'political' attention at institutional level, but only half of the respondents indicated that internationalisation was given high priority in terms of the allocation of funds and other resources. The same discrepancy between political and economic support was revealed in the priorities of national governments. Only four respondents found that their respective governments accorded a high priority to internationalisation in terms of the allocation of funds. The positive exception here is Norway, which has included higher education and research as a sector in its development aid policy.

In many developing countries, the fiscal crisis that began in 2009 has caused a reduction in social investment and, consequently, a decline in financial support for universities. Under these circumstances, universities and research institutions have to deal with increasing pressures to obtain external funding to help to cover the high costs of educational programmes, research projects, and technology upgrades.

With regard to the international donor community, the picture is less clear. No respondents indicated that the international donor community sees internationalisation as a high priority, either politically, or economically. On the other hand, only a few seemed to think that donors give higher education a low priority. Quite a number of respondents chose to skip the question. This may be partly because it is difficult to give a general answer without discussing specific organisations and donors.

Respondents were also asked to prioritise a given list of barriers and challenges with the possibility of adding others. The results indicated that there are five main challenges preventing SANORD institutions from engaging fully in internationalisation. These are listed below and then discussed in more detail:

- a lack of capital and issues of resource shortfalls, such as poor ICT capacity and connectivity; enrolment explosions, but low participation rates etc;
- the commercialisation of internationalisation;
- the exclusion or marginalisation of weaker institutions from collaborative programmes;
- the dominance of North–South relations and dependence on Northern financial support means that South–South exchanges are too rare; and
- structural barriers.

The marginalisation of weaker institutions is closely linked to capacity issues, resource shortfalls and the increasing competition to be counted among the top ten (or even top hundred) institutions in a field, a region or the world. Weaker institutions in developing countries become less attractive when partners in the North seek partners and long-term collaborations. Emerging countries in Asia are often favoured, and Africa is at risk of losing out in the scramble for funds and minds. One of the respondents in the SANORD survey drew attention to the negative aspects of the 'ranking culture' that prevails in the higher education sector, noting that it was a major challenge to 'locate the institution in the global configuration where rankings become important and the institutional profile and programme offerings are immersed in criteria that apply to particular elite institutions and dismiss institutional areas of excellence'.

The prominence given to the issue of exclusion and marginalisation underlines the relevance of SANORD's 2009 conference theme, 'Inclusion and Exclusion in Higher Education'. It also points to the importance of seeing internationalisation as a 'tool in national integration policy' as mentioned by one of the southern African universities. This is not to say that marginalisation is not an issue for the Nordic countries, where the small size of the region, language barriers, etc. also play a role. A respondent from a Nordic institution illustrated this, stressing that 'internationalisation and knowledge of international development are the lifelines of small nations'.

Insufficient funding for higher education and research is a general problem across institutions and countries, both North and South. There is no doubt, however, that universities and researchers in developing countries are worse off, and are thus particularly vulnerable in the struggle for resources and collaboration partners. Dependence on resources from the North is almost absolute. Furthermore, insufficient funding and unequal access to resources lead to imbalances in the partnerships that do exist.

Structural barriers and bureaucratic inflexibility are another barrier to internationalisation. Institutional policies and funding mechanisms are often not conducive to collaboration across countries and regions, and can prevent student and staff mobility. Respondents cited heavy institutional management burdens – that is, bureaucracy, delay in disbursement of funds, etc. as severe barriers to collaboration. In this regard, Finland's efforts to adjust the funding instruments of its Ministry of Foreign Affairs and Ministry of Education to enable polytechnics and universities to participate in publicly funded development partnerships, provides a positive example of a way of addressing such structural inflexibilities. There are institutional challenges too. According to Gerald Ouma, a senior lecturer at the University of the Western Cape, and member of the South African Higher Education Funding Review Committee, collaborative work is, at times, not seen as official work when it comes to allocating workloads. He argues that this is mainly because collaborative ventures are generally not institutionalised. Instead they are are seen as revolving around individuals. Another challenge mentioned by Ouma is that most funding is short term, but there is need for long-term perspectives. In other words, strategic interests can shift before capacity is adequately entrenched. Such challenges have severe implications for academic freedom and institutional autonomy. For example, funding is meant to benefit students from particular countries that are considered to be of strategic interest to the funding country. But who makes decisions about which students to enrol and which ones to exclude?

Another challenge that emerged from the presentations at SANORD's 2009 conference was the way in which cultural differences and language problems can lead to misunderstandings, particularly in relation to credit-transfer systems and intellectual-property issues. In his presentation to the DDRN session on drivers and challenges in higher education, Ouma also raised the issue of North–South collaboration being considered or perceived as development aid. The implication of this is that the Northern partner is viewed as the 'giver'. The 'stranger' or the weaker partner in the network – usually a Southern institution – is often brought in to meet funding requirements, and is easily marginalised. Such researchers are expected to show gratitude because their capacity is being 'developed', and they are often ignored in decision making related to the allocation of funds, curriculum development, research design and the development of research tools, etc. In practice, they are reduced from being collaborators to being research assistants.

According to Ouma, collaborations in networks also include power relations. Pant (2009) affirms this view, noting that networks have become one of the most significant social trends of our time, and help to channel efforts towards achieving specific agendas.

Recommendations for SANORD

Recommendations made by respondents in the SANORD survey fall into two broad categories, namely resources and practices. Both stress the issue of capacity building. Funding for student and staff exchange programmes, and for research collaboration, was a major concern. Recommendations linked to funding, structural and other issues are listed below:-

Funding

- Review funding practices to increase the number of staff and student exchanges.
- Secure additional financial support for African students to study in the North.
- Explore funding possibilities for joint programmes.
- Secure sustainable funding for activities.
- Lobby donors to provide seed grants for collaborative projects.
- Establish a university consortium to target EU funding.
- Lobby donors to provide more assistance without dictating terms.

Structure
- Remove barriers related to language, credit-transfer systems and mobility.
- Enhance student and teacher mobility.

Co-operation and partnerships
- Develop relations between academia and the private sector.
- Establish 'sandwich model' exchange programmes at PhD level; these are multi-phased schemes in which candidates carry out their coursework and research in, for example, both South Africa and Denmark under the supervision of a mentor from universities in both countries.
- Increase reciprocity and build long-term relationships.
- Provide active support for the Southern partners.
- Develop/support multilateral partnerships within Southern Africa.
- Encourage joint research between and among Northern and Southern universities.

Capacity building and training
- Ensure long-term capacity development through giving support to training and infrastructure.
- Develop and offer joint degree programmes.
- Identify and communicate institutional research priorities.
- Provide support related to proposal writing.

Networking and knowledge sharing
- Strengthen and support South–South networking.
- Prioritise multi-disciplinary and multi-institutional research.
- Support and give time to participation in networks.
- Give members opportunities to develop contacts and deeper knowledge of different institutions.

Conclusions

The demand for higher education in Africa is rapidly increasing. This opens up new opportunities for SANORD-linked institutions, in relation to agenda setting and putting research and knowledge to use. However, as the survey findings showed, it also poses a number of new challenges and increases the pressures on universities to increase their relevance and responsiveness, both globally and locally.

The internationalisation of higher education and research, both in relation to SANORD and more generally, is characterised by a push-pull mechanism. On the one hand, SANORD member universities are pushed into the internationalisation and globalisation process as they have to provide quality and prove their relevance. But in pursuing these aims, they are also pulled into competing with each other for funds and minds in an environment where competition is continuously getting stronger. On the other hand, internationalisation is attractive to universities as a means for universities to become active members of the global village. Moreover, it can be an efficient tool in integration of the diverse communities across the university and assist in creating a multi-cultural and international learning environment.

SANORD members called for differentiated institutions and diversified programmes within each institution to cater for different types of learners. This clearly shows that the process of transformation and adaptation to change is ongoing. There is a need for greater collaboration at institutional, national and regional levels, and for collaboration to be meaningful and mutually beneficial – 'real' involvement of all partners is necessary. Furthermore, the institutionalisation of collaborative ventures is important for their long-term success.

The issue of inadequate funding for international collaboration in higher-education and research cuts across all institutions and remains a major challenge for SANORD, and especially for its southern African partners. The findings of the survey confirmed the need for additional funds. Efforts to diversify and extend the funding base thus need to be enhanced. At the same time, lobbying parliamentarians and policy-makers to increase government allocations to higher education must continue. Links with the private sector should also be strengthened, and innovative practices, such as public–private partnerships, need to be explored. Many academic institutions seem to be insufficiently prepared for innovation within this area, and this has negative consequences for both university development and for society.

SANORD faces a major task in encouraging researchers from several institutions to collaborate around key issues such as the improvement of policies and practices related to: research and teaching; ensuring student access and admission; curriculum development; and promotion of strategic interdisciplinary programs including multi-, inter- and trans-disciplinary research projects.

Notes

1   Internationalisation is understood as a mechanism for institutions to enter, influence and expand strategic relationships with other universities internationally. It can involve institutional and individual collaborations, South–South, North–South, North–North, etc. Collaboration between universities, a key feature of internationalisation, typically includes: collaborative research and publications; joint programmes and training; student and staff exchanges etc.

2   SANORD is a collaboration of Southern African and Nordic academic institutions that have sought to promote research for development in Africa by consolidating their independent research projects towards one common goal. With over 30 members, the association has organised conferences on topics such as economic development, environmentally friendly technologies and education.

3   DDRN is a network linking research-based knowledge and development. The network has around 2 300 members drawn from universities, the private sector, NGOs and development organisations. Around a third of the members are from developing countries. The main purpose of the network is to contribute to integration of research-based knowledge in development through the promotion, production, dissemination and exchange of research-based knowledge. DDRN's activities include: publishing newsletters, research overviews and briefs, as well as running workshops and conferences. DDRN has a strong focus on multi-disciplinarity and North–South and North–North collaboration. Thematic focal areas include research communication, climate change and food security. For more information, see http://ddrn.dk/.

4   Eight institutions did not complete this part of the questionnaire.

5   The full descriptions of programmes are annexed to the working paper presented at the DDRN session that formed part of the 2009 SANORD conference. See Sørensen (2009).

References

Africa Commission (Danish Ministry of Foreign Affairs) (2009) *Realising the Potential of Africa's Youth: Report of the Africa Commission*. Copenhagen.

Bloom D and H Rosovsky (2000) *Higher Education in Developing Countries: Peril and Promise*. Washington DC: World Bank Task Force on Higher Education and Society. Available online.

Dickson D (2009) 'What role for higher education in development?' *SciDEV.Net*, 11 March. Available online.

OECD (Organisation for Economic Co-operation and Development) (Various) OECD Statistical Databases: iLibrary. Available online.

Pant LP (2009) *Learning Networks for Bridging Knowledge Divides in International Development: Aligning Approaches and Initiatives.* IKM Working Paper 4, IKM Emergent Research Programme, European Association of Development Research and Training Institutes, Bonn, Germany.

Sørensen A (2009) 'Internationalisation of Higher Education and Research: The Case of SANORD'. Copenhagen: Danish Development Research Network. Available online.

UniBRAIN (Universities, Business and Research in Agricultural Innovation) (n.d.) 'Realising the potential of Africa's youth: Linking university education, research and business in sustainable agriculture', Forum for Agricultural Research in Africa. Available online.

UNESCO (2009) *UNESCO World Conference on Education for Sustainable Development: Proceedings.* Paris. Available online.

World Bank (Various) 'Education Lending in FY 2009'. Available online.

PART II: DILEMMAS OF CHANGE

Chapter 3
Changes in higher education policy and the Nordic model

Risto Rinne

FOLLOWING THE MASSIVE EXPANSION in primary and secondary education worldwide, the higher education sector has followed suit. In 25 years the number of tertiary education students in the world almost tripled (from around 52 million students in 1981 to some 140 million students in 2006) (Rinne and Järvinen 2010). The meaning of higher education – its social and cultural place, role and functions, as well as the economic costs and outcomes – has changed radically, in what I see as a new era of global higher learning. The whole concept of higher education has been redefined.

Historically, different regions developed different models of higher education. In Europe, for instance, the Anglo-Saxon market-oriented model, the continental state-centred Napoleonic or Humboldtian model, and the Nordic egalitarian models emerged. By the late twentieth century and on into the present, mainstream higher education policy seems to mostly follow the market-oriented model, placing much emphasis on economic success, effectiveness, competition and new public management, and less on the public governance of universities. This new paradigm has been dubbed the 'enterprise university' or the 'academic capitalism'.

In this chapter, I examine the historical roots of higher education and consider how these have changed. I then look at the core characteristics of the new university and, taking the case of Finland as an example, I ask how the old Nordic university model, which was quite the opposite of the market-oriented model, has reacted to the challenges and pressures posed by the new paradigm.

Historical roots

If we try to trace the basic notion of the university as institution we may come to various conclusions. Torsten Husèn (1993) sums these up, noting that traditional universities, at least from a Western perspective, were established on the basis of the following four core presumptions:

- Universities make a more-or-less sharp distinction between theory and practice.
- Universities put a premium on autonomy and aloofness, even to the extent of complete irrelevance.
- Universities have been elitist institutions, both socially and intellectually.
- Universities have tried to be 'ivory towers', seeing their main purpose as 'seeking truth'.

Most of these core presumptions have been questioned ever since and the concept of the university is now different in almost every aspect. The number of universities have expanded enormously and have become one of the most central social, economic and cultural institutions in societies everywhere. They have differentiated and segregated along many trajectories, assuming ever more duties and functions along the way.

In the 1930s, Abraham Flexner (1930) stated that development had brought more and more new departments and schools to universities. According to him, a gamut of educational schools, vocational schools, teacher-training institutions, research centres, supplementary education and business operations was developing inside the walls of traditional science universities. As a result of academic drift (Clark 1983), more and more new professions emerged within university education. This line of development may be tellingly called a change from the traditional university to the multiversity of a new era.

It is almost forty years since Martin Trow (1974) launched the concept of mass higher education – a concept that has long been a reality in many parts of the world. The diversification of higher education, and the constant generation of new sectors within higher education explain a great deal of the growth. These include, for example, private and business based higher-education institutions as well as open and virtual distance-learning universities. The higher-education system has become an increasingly significant social focus point because larger numbers of children have participated in it, and its costs have multiplied. As Phillip Altbach (1999: 110) notes, 'Higher education has moved from the periphery of society to its centre'.

Until the mid-twentieth century, studying at a university was a privilege reserved for members of the upper class. After the Second World War, and the transition made by some nations from industrial to service and welfare societies, higher education became increasingly accessible. Universities had to answer the demand for a highly trained work force in an ever-growing range of occupations. When two out of three members of an age cohort are reserved a place in the higher-education system, staying outside of that system becomes a 'sign of failing or character that needs to be specially explained, justified or excused', at least in middle-class circles (Trow 1974: 63).

According to Halsey (2006: 857–858), behind this (at least the European-wide) educational movement, three drivers and at least three obstacles can be detected. He sees the drivers as primarily social and economic. The first and most obvious, was the resuscitation of the Western European economy and the need for labour-force efficiency. This was quite strongly initiated and pushed by pressure from the Organisation for Economic Co-operation and Development (OECD). The second driver was the strong confidence and trust in the capacity of universities to improve technical and technological efficiency. It is true that the academy has 'produced the atomic bomb, penicillin and the map of human genome'. The third and perhaps the most powerful driver, according to Halsey, was the push within the nation states to enlarge access to tertiary education. At first, this initiative aimed to redress some of the inequality of the pre-war period; later, it took the form of widening access to women, ethnic minorities, the lower classes and mature students.

For Halsey (2006), the anchors or obstacles preventing change can be listed as follows:

- Existing institutions tended to cling to their autonomy and remain attached to Humboldtian and Newmanesque conceptions.
- The upper classes tried to defend the class divisions and status associated with a university education, wishing to pass on their advantages to their own children via the universities.
- The state showed reluctance to spend money on higher education; this was linked to the claims of warfare over welfare, the unwillingness of electorates to vote for higher taxes, and the liberal economic doctrines of minimal government.
- There was resistance from the anti-market, guild, or public-service orientation of staff within schools, colleges and faculties; although the voices of teachers' and researchers' organisations were powerful, in the end they were impotent to stem the reorganisation of education.

Becoming market-driven enterprise institutions

One of the more striking features of the postmodern global world is 'the educational gospel', the amazing continuity of belief in the strong connection between economic development and the growing role of education. In this way of thinking, especially in the developed countries, the idea is that we have entered a new 'knowledge economy' and a kind of 'age of human capital'. This policy mantra forecasts a world in which most people are highly skilled, highly paid employees. The repetition of this mantra has changed little since the 1960s, when human-capital theory was first glorified within education and economic policy (Brown et al. 2007; Rinne 2010).

Supranational organisations, such as the OECD, have developed various ways of measuring the academic quality and performance of nations, ranking their educational systems and their universities in order of human capital. The competition for human knowhow and capital between nation states has become ever more intense. As, for example, Britain's prime minister has suggested: 'if we are to succeed in a world where off shoring can be an opportunity...our mission [is] to make the British people the best educated, most skilled, best trained country in the world' (Brown et al. 2007: 193).

The ascendancy of neo-liberal theory in policy-making has emphasised particular ways of looking at the higher education system as an engine for economic growth, producing prime human capital for private rather than public good, and as a new service sector within the economy. These ideas also lie behind the concept of the 'New Europe' as a 'Europe of Knowledge' and the development of the European Higher Education Area (EHEA) and the European Research Area (Robertson 2009). Thus, throughout the post-industrialised societies, the trend towards more market-oriented 'enterprise universities' is growing stronger. Supranational organisations, such as the OECD, the World Bank and the European Union (EU) are applying tremendous pressure to promote this kind of unifying university politics and growing competition.

In the name of internationalisation, accountability and assessment, universities have been given new social responsibilities and, in the tumult of change, their traditional tasks and values have been questioned. A new paradigm is taking the stage, with universities being depicted as 'entrepreneurial' or 'managerial' and analysed using concepts such as 'academic capitalism' or the 'MacDonaldisation of higher education' (the 'McUniversity'). These terms have been coined to refer to the changing nature of the tasks carried out by universities: the production of knowledge for those outside the university; the competition for funding; the emphasis on risk-taking and innovation;

and the ever-increasing demand for (cost) effectiveness, profit-seeking and immediate benefit to be evident in all activities (see, for example, Clark 1998; Kivinen et al. 1993; Rinne 2010; Rinne and Koivula 2005; Ritzer 2002; Slaughter and Leslie 1997). Figure 3.1 illustrates the pressures typically exerted on the 'enterprise university'.

FIGURE 3.1 The entrepreneurial university in context

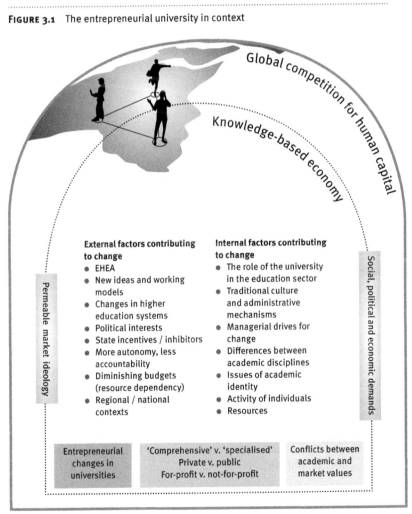

Source: See Rinne and Koivula (2005).

Universities today are expected to do more and obtain better results with fewer and fewer resources. They have to try to maintain their cultural and academic heritage, but, simultaneously, hastily and flexibly respond to every new demand. They have to retain some common features, while constantly responding to thousands of new voices, because everyone may be a stakeholder. As Burton Clark says, the modern research university has become 'overextended, underfocused, overstressed and underfunded' (Clark 1998: xiii-xiv).

The changes that have occurred between the late 1980s and the time of writing in 2012 may be traced by listing the factors presented first by Guy Neave (1985) and Frans van Vught (1990):

- Cuts in public funding.
- Pressures for efficiency, that is, more throughput using fewer funds.
- Pressures for reducing student fees.
- Conditional contracting, that is, funding tied to objectives and results.
- The introduction of evaluation systems.
- Managerialism, involving the introduction of strategic management within universities, with an emphasis on the values of enterprise culture.
- Massification, that is, competition between universities for students.
- Despite increased autonomy, restricted freedom of universities because of accountability and market competition.
- The need for more professional management and governance structures.
- Increased expectations and pressures to deliver innovation and provide services.
- The need for harmonisation among degree structures.

Since the mid-1980s, universities around the world have been under exogenous pressures to change. Social uncertainty has created growing controversies about the changing nature of the university. Nowadays the *raison d'être* of universities tends to mostly be defended by pragmatic and utilitarian arguments, such as to improve the competitive power of a nation in world markets or to produce an effective work force for the labour market. Universities are involved in a new level of instrumentalising knowledge and have developed a new relationship with the state as a principal stakeholder (see Dale 2007; Husèn 1993; Nedeva 2007).

Massification and structural change in Finnish higher education

Arild Tjeldwoll, in his introduction to the book *Education and Scandinavian Welfare State in 2000: Equality, Policy, and Reform* (1998), claims that all five Scandinavian countries share the characteristics of a similar kind of welfare-state model. At the core of this model is a striving for social justice and the ideal of creating a democratic society; goals that have been historically progressed by means of social and educational policies. Central to Scandinavian welfare states is an egalitarian education policy and, in the field of higher education, the Nordic higher-education (university) model.

Until the late 1980's, the main characteristics of the Nordic university model have been listed a follows (see Rinne 2010):

- Relatively small, with restricted markets.
- Strict centralisation and control of resources.
- Formal institutional uniformity, with, ostensibly, almost no recognised hierarchy.
- Restricted competition with respect, not to markets, students, or business, but to state resources.
- Low institutional initiative, as conditions of strict centralisation inhibited the taking of initiative, challenges to the bureaucratic rule in the universities and the development of an entrepreneurial culture.
- The right to free higher education.
- A strong belief in fostering social equality by removing obstacles that prevented equality of opportunity in higher education.
- Higher-education policy as a vital part of the wider regional and social policies.

But after the 1980s, and especially the 1990s, the Nordic university model also changed dramatically. As in other Western nations, the expansion of university education began in the Nordic countries, including Finland after the Second World War, and especially as the baby-boom generation emerged from secondary schooling in the 1960s and 1970s. Figure 3.2 illustrates the transformations of Finnish universities as an example of the changes in the Nordic countries more generally. In less than a hundred years, our institutions transformed from elite universities via mass universities to universal multiversities, and from cultural universities via research universities to enterprise university.

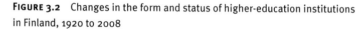

FIGURE 3.2   Changes in the form and status of higher-education institutions in Finland, 1920 to 2008

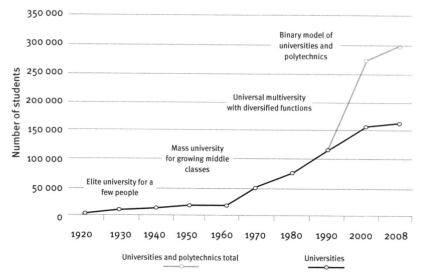

Sources: Antikainen et al. (2006); Clark (1983); Flexner (1930); KOTA (2009); Rinne (1999; 2002; 2004); Ritzer (1993; 1999); Slaughter and Leslie (1997); Tilastokeskus (2009); Williams (1978); Wittrock (1985).

Over the same time period, great structural changes have occurred in the higher-education sector. Finland has moved from the unitary university model to the new binary model of higher education, whereby universities are no longer the only higher-education institutions. There are now two tiers in Finnish higher education, although these are officially kept apart. Applying Clark's classic 'triangle of co-ordination' model to the two-tier system, Finland's universities have been moving strongly towards the 'market' and 'market drift' corners, and the old 'academic oligarchy' has had to give up its historical position and power. At the same time, the new polytechnics (Fachhochschule) are evidence of a strong 'academic drift' on the part of lower educational institutions in the educational and labour market. Under pressure from the global market and supranational organisations, Finland has adopted the new paradigms of effectiveness, competition and assessment. Finnish universities no longer breathe the same air that they traditionally did in the old days.

By further elaborating Clark's 'triangle of co-ordination' and his ideas of 'academic drift', we arrive at the quadrilateral image shown in Figure 3.3.

In addition to the state, market and academic oligarchy we can add the fourth element, namely civil society with its mass of potential students and their families. Supranational organisations and globalisation are included to indicate their growing power over nation states. And, in addition to academic drift, three more drifts have been added. The first is market drift, which is strongly linked to the market orientation of the universities and polytechnics, and to their contest in the labour market. The second is efficiency drift, which is evident in the rapidly growing assessment and evaluation machinery that looms above the higher education sector. The third is individual drift, which denotes the massification of higher education and pressures towards diversification from students and their families.

FIGURE 3.3   Finland's binary system of higher education (from the 1980s onwards) showing external pressures and internal drifts

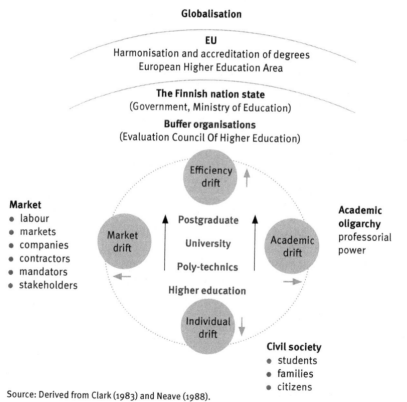

Source: Derived from Clark (1983) and Neave (1988).

From academy to neo-liberal university

According to various more or less speculative and spectacular rankings and assessments, Finland has been celebrated as, for example: the Nordic welfare state, an alternative model for the information society (Castells and Himanen 2002); as economically one of the most competitive and innovative societies in the world (World Economic Forum 2005); and as an example of an excellent education system, combining both quality and equality (OECD 2001; 2004; 2007; 2010). In spite of this global commotion, Finnish universities have, in many respects, remained relatively traditional in their doctrines when compared to most other countries. While countries in the vanguard of university reform (such as the UK, the US, the Netherlands, and Australia) have faced issues such as the (new) wave of managerialism, the quality revolution, and the launch of the institutional evaluation industry since the early 1980s, the Finnish university only really confronted these changes nearly two decades later.

In fact, it took a considerable amount of time before the Nordic university system was grafted onto the wider education system and began to be affected by social, economic, welfare and educational policy. It lived a long life as almost the typical ivory tower, dominated by an 'academic oligarchy', the elite professoriate. Thus, in Finland, for example, it was not until the 1960s that the growing welfare state, through the rising Ministry of Education, started more powerfully to legislate, regulate and plan the functions of a massifying higher-education system. Since then, and during the later period of the 'state regime of the development doctrine', it was literally forbidden for the surrounding market and economic life to make any efforts to influence the decisions of the autonomous (but state-driven) universities. Even private donations, for example, were virtually forbidden as irrelevant interference with the principles of academic freedom and autonomy.

Up until the 1990s, Finnish welfare policy clearly followed the Nordic social-democratic model, strongly stressing universal and comprehensive social security, strong state control, significant income transfers, full employment and a high level of equality. Educational policy has been considered one of the most important elements spearheading the removal of all types of social inequality (Rinne 2004).

The country's higher-education policy strongly supported the removal of all hindrances and inequalities preventing citizens from moving up the educational ladder. This was intended to strengthen the equality of educational opportunity in higher education and ensure that socio-economic and cultural background, gender, religious or ethnic backgrounds played no role in preventing students from gaining access to higher education. Thus, the higher education system was rapidly expanded and regionally broadened to cover the whole country.

Prior to this, university expansion in Finland occurred after the Second World War, and was carried out by relying heavily on the ability and the will of the academic elite to steer the rather autonomous and independent university sector. The aim of that phase of expansion was mainly to guarantee the freedom of teaching and research in universities and to provide an elite education mostly related to the needs of the country's civil service, and it lasted in Finland until the 1960s.

The decades from the 1960s until the late 1980s can be termed the period of 'the social-democratic Nordic state development doctrine' and it formed a kind of watershed between the old, more Humboldtian 'traditional academic doctrine' and the rising, more liberal 'managing by results and competition doctrine', which, in turn, has been evolving into the 'neo-liberal new public management doctrine', since the early 2000s.

We can therefore, quite justifiably, divide the history of the Finnish higher education sector into four periods, each with their corresponding doctrines, as shown in Table 3.1 (see also Rinne 2004; 2010).

A new and quite radical University Law was passed in Finland in 2009. Under this law, universities are no longer state institutions, but have a stronger financial and administrative status as 'independent legal persons' supplied with starting capital. This does not imply the total privatisation of universities, however. Instead, it is said that as 'legal persons' (rather than as 'state accounting offices', as they were designated before) the universities will be better equipped to respond to their own needs, as well as to the expectations of society and the market. The composition of university boards is changing radically though, with representatives of different kinds of stakeholders and market agents outside the university taking more powerful roles, and even occupying the position of chair.

Changes driven by economic, ideological and pragmatic motives have steadily modified the forms and mechanisms of university governance and policy making, even in Finland, the country that formerly upheld the Nordic university model. Thus, Finland's older and more traditional frameworks which accommodated 'collegial organisation', 'professional bureaucracy', 'organised anarchy' or 'loosely coupled organisations' have been replaced by alternative perspectives and paradigms such as 'the corporate university', 'the entrepreneurial model', 'the service model' or 'the McUniversity model'. Common to both the older and the newer models, however, is the

TABLE 3.1 The phases of and doctrines behind Finnish university development since 1960

Policy dimensions	'Traditional academic' (until the 1960s)	'State development' (late 1960s – late 1980s)	'Managing by results and competition' (late 1980s onwards)	'Neo-liberal new public management' (since 2009, New University Law)
The aims of teaching and research:	Freedom in teaching and research. Focus on the provision of education for the elite. Professional power.	Production of adequate supply of trained manpower. Allocation of training quotas by labour market needs. Science as a factor of production.	Response to demand from many sources. Focus on productivity. Orientation to EU and EHEA policy.	Elastic and flexible. Europeanisation of Finnish higher education. Full quality assessment and evaluation.
The nature of political influences and relations with the state:	University autonomy.	Subordination of education to social, regional and labour market policy. State dirigismé in education. University democracy in inner governance.	Flexible and innovative service of societal needs. University steered on basis of achieved results. Innovation policy. Evaluative state.	Non-state institutions. Process of restructuring the university field. Amalgamation of universities. Strong innovation policy and the 'third function'. New public management.
Economic role:	No expectations of immediate economic benefit but an awareness of long-term benefits	Higher education as a crucial factor in economic development.	The promotion of international competitiveness and industrial diversification. Market driven university.	Extensive external private funding. Diminished public funding. Economic stakeholders involved in governance.
Equality:	Training students for leading positions in society, especially in the civil service.	Full utilisation of potential talent requiring egalitarian educational access. Rapid expansion leading to levelling out of social and regional inequality.	Observance of gender and regional equality. Promotion of state-led competition. Equity.	Full free profit-seeking competition. Excellence above all. Top units. Equity as individual performance and competition.
University type:	Elite university.	State mass university.	State-driven mixed universal university.	Quasi-market-driven enterprise university.
Higher education model:	Nordic model with a relatively weak state.	Nordic model with a strong state.	Liberal quasi-market model.	Neo-liberal quasi-market model.

Sources: Derived from Kivinen et al. (1993) and Rinne (2004; 2010).

perception of universities as peculiarly bottom-heavy organisations with weak organisational governance (De Boer et al. 2007; Rinne and Koivula 2005; 2009). And that is also why, at least in Finland, a kind of battle is looming between an approach which values cultural heritage versus the new public management approach.

Concluding words

The Nordic countries, following the mainstream, are trying to increase competitiveness between universities by diminishing funding and establishing extensive assessment procedures aimed at guaranteeing and improving efficiency and quality. The expectations placed on universities are enormous. Forces in favour of common global (or at least European market-oriented) higher-education policies are strong even in Finland, which has become a member of the EU and part of the EHEA and which has tried to behave as a kind of 'model pupil' in Europe's educational class.

However, in the most recent stage of university development, the historical and cultural roots of the nation states and different university models are beginning to reassert some of their traditions and characteristics. The Nordic model still has some key features of its own, although many of its distinguishing characteristics have vanished. Some traditional educational principles of social democracy, such as the right to free higher education and the effort to keep all the country's regions under the university system, are still alive. This does not, however, mean that Finland is not moving towards the more uniform higher-education policies common to the market-driven approach.

References

Altbach PG (1999) 'The logic of mass higher education', in I Fägerlind, I Holmesland and G Strömqvist (eds) *Higher Education at the Crossroads* (Studies in Comparative and International Education 48). Stockholm: Institute of International Education, Stockholm University.

Antikainen A, R Rinne and L Koski (2006) *Kasvatussosiologia*. Helsinki: WSOY.

Brown P, H Lauder and D Ashton, (2007) 'Towards a high-skills economy: Higher education and the new realities of global capitalism', in D Epstein, R Boden, R Deem, F Rizvi and S Wright (eds): *Geographies of Knowledge, Geometries of Power: Framing the Future of Higher Education* (World Yearbook of Education 2008). New York and London: Routledge.

Castells M and P Himanen (2002). *The Information Society and the Welfare State: The Finnish Model*. Oxford: Oxford University Press.

Clark B (1983). *The Higher Education System: Academic Organisation in Cross-National Perspective*. Berkeley: University of California Press.

Clark B (1998) *Creating Enterpreneurial Universities: Organisational Pathways of Transformation*. Paris: IAU Press.

Dale R (2007) 'Repairing the deficits of modernity: The emergence of parallel discourses in higher education in Europe', in D Epstein, R Boden, R Deem, F Rizvi and S Wright (eds) *Geographies of Knowledge, Geometries of Power: Framing the Future of Higher Education* (World Yearbook of Education 2008). New York and London: Routledge.

De Boer H, J Enders and L Leišytė (2007) 'Public sector reform in Dutch higher education: The Organisational transformation of the university. *Public Administration* 85 (1): 27–46.

Flexner A (1930) *Universities*. London: Oxford University Press.

Halsey AH (2006) 'The European university', in H Lauder, P Brown, J-A Dillabough and AH Halsey (eds) *Education, Globalization and Social Change*. Oxford: Oxford University Press.

Husèn T (1993) 'The idea of the university: Changing roles, current crisis and future challenges', in Z Morsy and PG Altbach (eds) *Higher Education in International Perspective: Toward the 21ˢᵗ Century*. Paris: UNESCO.

Kivinen O, K Rinne Rand Ketonen (1993) *Yliopiston huomen*. Tampere: Hanki ja jää.

KOTA (2009) *Opetusministeriön KOTA-tietokanta*. Helsinki: Opetusministeriö. Available online.

Neave G (1985) 'The university and state in western Europe', in D Jaques and J Richardson (eds) *The Future of Higher Education*. Milton Keynes: Open University Press.

Neave G (1988) 'On the cultivation of quality, efficiency and enterprise: An overview of recent trends in higher education in Western Europe, 1986–1988', *European Journal of Education* 23 (1/2): 7–22.

Nedeva M (2007) 'New tricks and old dogs? The "third mission" and the reproduction of the university', in D Epstein, R Boden, R Deem, F Rizvi and S Wright (eds) *Geographies of Knowledge, Geometries of Power: Framing the Future of Higher Education* (World Yearbook of Education 2008). New York and London: Routledge.

OECD (2001) *Knowledge and Skills for Life: First Results from PISA 2000*. Paris.

OECD (2004) *Learning for Tomorrow's World: First results from PISA 2003*. Paris.

OECD (2007) *PISA 2006: Science Competencies for Tomorrow's World*. Paris.

OECD (2010) *PISA 2009: Results: What Students Know and Can Do: Student Performance in Reading, Mathematics and Science*. Paris.

Rinne R (1999) 'The Rise of the McUniversity', in I. Fägerlind, I Holmesland and G Strömqvist (eds) *Higher Education at the Crossroads* (Studies in Comparative and International Education 48). Stockholm: Institute of International Education, Stockholm University.

Rinne R (2002) 'Binaarimallista Bolognan tielle: Erilliset ammattikorkeakoulut tulevat ja menevät', teoksessa J-P Liljander (toim.) *Omalla tiellä. Ammattikorkeakoulut kymmenen vuotta.* Helsinki: Edita.

Rinne R (2004) 'Searching for the rainbow: Changing the course of Finnish higher education', in I Fägerlind and G Strömqvist (eds) *Reforming Higher Education in the Nordic Countries: Studies of Change in Denmark, Finland, Iceland, Norway and Sweden.* Paris: International Institute for Educational Planning.

Rinne R (2010) 'The Nordic university model from a comparative and historical perspective', in J Kauko, R Rinne and H Kynkäänniemi (eds) *Restructuring the Truth of Schooling: Essays on Discursive Practices in Sociology and the Politics of Education. A Festschrift for Hannu Simola* (Research in Educational Sciences 48). Jyväskylä: Jyväskylä University Press and Finnish Educational Research Association.

Rinne R and T Järvinen (2010) 'Frafall og videregående opplæring i Finland: En gjennomgang av nyere studier og tiltak for å holde flere i utdanning', in E Markussen (ed.) Frafall i utdanning for 16–20-åringer i Norden. TemaNord 2010: 517. København: Nordisk ministerråd.

Rinne R and J Koivula (2005). The changing place of higher education and a clash of values: The entrepreneurial university in the European knowledge society, *Higher Education Management and Policy* 17 (3): 91–124.

Rinne, R and J Koivula (2009) 'The dilemmas of the changing university', in M Shattock (ed.) *Entrepreneurialism in Universities and the Knowledge Economy: Diversification and Organisational Change in European Higher Education.* London: Open University Press and Paris: IIEP, UNESCO.

Ritzer G (1993) *The McDonaldization of Society.* Thousand Oaks: Pine Forge Press.

Ritzer G (1999) *The McDonaldization Thesis.* London: Sage.

Ritzer G (2002) 'Enchanting McUniversity: Toward a spectacularly irrational university quotidian', in D Hayes and R Wynyard (eds) *The McDonaldization of Higher Education.* Westport, CT and London: Bergin and Garvey.

Robertson S (2009) 'Europe, competitiveness and higher education: An evolving project', in R Dale and S Robertson (eds) *Globalisation and Europeanisation in Education.* Oxford: Symposium.

Slaughter S and L Leslie (1997) *Academic Capitalism.* Baltimore: Johns Hopkins University Press.

Tilastokeskus (2009) Ammattikorkeakoulujen uudet opiskelijat ja opiskelijat ammattikorkeakouluittain 2008. Helsinki: Tilastokeskus. Available online.

Tjeldvoll A (1998) 'Introduction', in A Tjeldvoll (ed.) *Education and the Scandinavian Welfare State in the Year 2000: Equality, Policy, and Reform*. New York and London: Garland.

Trow M (1974) 'Problems in the transition from elite to mass higher education. Policies for higher education', in *General Report on the Conference on Future Structures of Post-Secondary Education*. Paris: OECD.

Van Vught F (1990) 'Recent developments in higher education governance', paper presented at the Conference on Policy Change in Higher Education, University of Turku, Finland, 4 June 1990.

Williams B (1978) *Systems of Higher Education*. New York: International Council for Educational Development.

Wittrock B (1985) 'Dinosaurs or Dolphins?' in B Wittrock and A Elzinga (eds) *The University Research System* (Studies in Higher Education in Sweden 5). Stockholm: University of Stockholm.

World Economic Forum (2005) *Global Competitiveness Report 2005/06*. Available online

Chapter 4

University transformation: a crisis for the social sciences and the humanities

Tor Halvorsen

It was always a bit of a lie that universities were self-governing institutions. Nevertheless, what universities suffered during the 1980s and 1990s was pretty shameful, as under threat of having their funding cut they allowed themselves to be turned into business enterprises, in which professors who had previously carried on their enquiries in sovereign freedom were transformed into hurried employees required to fulfil quotas under the scrutiny of professional managers. Whether the old power of the professoriate will ever be restored is much to be doubted.

JM Coetzee, Diary of a Bad Year, p. 35.

WHEN A RESEARCH UNIVERSITY IS TRANSFORMED, relations between its faculties and disciplines are transformed, too. The reverse is also true: when the relative importance of disciplines and faculties shift, the nature of a university as an institution changes.

In this chapter, I discuss how the European Union (EU) led by the Organisation for Economic Co-operation and Development (OECD) seeks to reform both its universities and the relations between disciplines and faculties. I focus, in particular, on how these university reforms seek to make tertiary institutions useful as sites of 'innovation'.

Knowledge and society

In recent decades western nations have been labelled as 'post-industrial' society (Bell 1973), the 'technological society' (Berger et al. 1974; Habermas 1968), the 'knowledge society' (Stehr 1994), the 'risk society' (Beck 1985), and the 'reflexive society' (Giddens 1990). All the OECD countries have experienced the development of 'expert systems' in both the public and private sectors (Weingart 2010). The social sciences have also developed theories of modern organisations, analysing how knowledge and power shape our collective behaviour and institutions. In the modern world, it seems that only organisations that can learn seem to thrive (Wagner 1994). Society is becoming increasingly formal and differentiated, and knowledge is becoming a driving force behind both the internalisation and the institutionalisation of the values of the modern world.

The main slogan, however, does not focus on organisational or societal learning related to the internalisation of values, but rather on narrower ideas about economic change. The most frequently used descriptors of the relationship between society and knowledge are terms such as the 'knowledge economy' and 'innovation'. In other words, the terminology has shifted in focus from *society* to the *economy*, from *learning* to *innovation*. The consequences of this shift for the social sciences and the humanities (and particularly for the latter) have already been dramatic at a number of universities in several countries. Some of these consequences are potentially very negative, not only for the societies served by the affected universities but also for a variety of economic actors. But the primary concern is the threat to the role that universities have played in the past proponents of democracy within and beyond nation states.

Developing an alternative to the rhetoric of innovation

I argue that we need to hold on to the idea of modern society as a learning society. More controversially, I also argue that this means we have to defend the old-fashioned Humboldtian-inspired university. By this I mean universities that value academic autonomy, interfaculty interaction and research-based teaching, while they focus on producing students, and ultimately PhD candidates, of high calibre; universities that study and teach both the humanities and the sciences, and, that, as time goes by, absorb new disciplines in the image of the old, as new *faculties* of knowledge.

Today's universities of *innovation* seem to be universities of engineering, with this faculty transforming all the other disciplines and faculties in its own image. As John Higgins, a prominent scholar in South Africa has argued, this 'entrepreneurial' kind of university may lead to a one-sided focus on the so-called STEM disciplines (science, technology, engineering and mathematics), and thus to a neglect for the disciplines that promote the knowledge necessary for a learning society: namely, narrative, analysis, interpretation and literacy (NAIL).[1] In line with Higgins's argument, I would also suggest that it is time to turn the old debate started by CP Snow in 1959 on its head, but also (more than the Snow debate allowed) to focus on the interplay between various faculties.

From a learning society to an innovating economy

The change in use of terminology about how knowledge and society shape each other indicates a shift in reality that has a bearing on the position of the research university in society, and thus on how society gives support to and tries to reform this. For example, if Jürgen Habermas (1981/1984) feared that the life-world would be suppressed by universal cognitive and technical rationalities (but that this could be counterbalanced by a strengthening of the 'discourse democracy'), such fears seem to be less prevalent today. Another change is the tremendous growth in the number of 'experts' and 'expert systems'. No longer do these necessarily emerge from universities. They are often shaped and created by large organisations within the economy and the public administration sector. Sometimes they are later formalised as disciplines within higher education. Examples are 'financial management', 'computer programming', 'environmental studies', and even 'gen tech laboratories' – all of which first emerged within organisations that produced their own specialties. Knorr-Cetina (2001) talks of epistemic cultures across different kinds of organisations including, but no longer prioritising, universities. A third change, linked to the previous one, is what Helga Nowotny and her colleagues named as the transformation from Mode 1-type to Mode 2-type knowledge production. Universities must understand that knowledge and ideas now develop in epistemic cultures, to which research universities contribute but no longer have a monopoly on creating or even necessarily dominating. The focus has shifted to innovation. Innovation is change driven by the users of knowledge. Knowledge is demand driven, and therefore best supported by a cross-disciplinary expert system. According to this view, the old academic disciplines tend to resist change, since change crosses disciplines. From this perspective, the role of a university is to be part of growing an expert system, and the role of the social sciences and humanities is to support such knowledge development, and *focus on the social/human implications and consequences of innovation* (Nowotny 2010).

Innovation versus the educated person

The much-debated Berlin university (of 1810 and onwards) united what, at that time, were the research activities of the natural sciences with those of the humanities, for the sake of giving the new leadership (and the growing bureaucracy) a degree of independence as academics. Clark (2006) highlights Schleiermacher's anti-French attitudes by referring to his description of the French 'evil of specialisation' as being 'infected by an un-German, corrupting spirit, who recommended to us a reconstruction and dispersal of universities into special schools'. It was at this time that it was decided that the highest degree in both the arts and the sciences should be the doctor of philosophy – the general title expressing the unity of the faculty of knowledge.

It was also at this time that it became accepted that only graduates from such universities would occupy the higher echelons of the civil service. In other words, a particular link was intentionally created between knowledge and politics through the idea that a bureaucrat who arrived at a top civil-service position should act in accordance with *Bildung*; that is, having entered the sanctuary of academic knowledge through a holistic process of self-cultivation, self-discipline, and skills acquisition and being dedicated to ongoing philosophical development and growth. This idea of how knowledge and the authority of office merge has shaped much of the current debate about the relationship between higher education knowledge and organisational leadership.[2]

The idealist university tradition has been modified but, so far, not fully undermined. The 'innovation' paradigm discussed below is perhaps the final attack on this historical tradition. It represents a fundamental shift in European culture, which has so far been marked by a belief in the value of independent knowledge as truth telling. In particular, Schleiermacher, and building on his ideas, Humboldt, created a productive link between idealism and positivism, thus producing knowledge which is neither transcendental, nor positivist/ empiricist, nor split between the two (as, it is often argued, is the case in other cultures such as those in India or China). Today however, the innovation paradigm seems to be reducing this particular European knowledge culture to a kind of empirical positivism that excludes the humanities.

In Europe we are used to arguing, within the sociology of science, that knowledge is part idealism and part positivism, but reducible to neither. It is theoretical and empirical at the same time. Thus, more than other cultures, Europeans have made idealism (both the rational and romantic) and positivism (both logical and empirical) constantly confront one another in a productive although often conflictual manner (Münch 1982). This has given us an ability to ask, not only what to innovate and change, but also *why* change is necessary, and what the meaning is behind it all.

Within the universities, this means that the different faculties must speak to each other; we have to be able to question general societal development under capitalism (Habermas 1968). The focus on innovation, however, has the potential to reduce Europe's cultural heritage to a one-sided affair, leaving us with a theory of knowledge that supports the empirical positivism needed to promote innovation, but very little else. Many no longer question why this or that capitalist development is taking place, but are interested only in how.

From universities to specialised functional schools?

The university as an organisation of departments, that specialise in research but also integrate with other disciplines and faculties, is to be transformed into a specialised organisation for certain societal functions and actors. The so-called *differentiation* policy, and the supposed urgency for universities to find a niche in the knowledge market follows from the innovation paradigm. In other words, universities are being asked to contribute to the differentiation of the sector both *horizontally* and *vertically*, as if they were competitive organisations in a market for and about knowledge.

The shift in focus from educating a 'whole person' (*Bildung*) to innovation has, in Germany, led to universities adopting this differentiation policy, and thereby breaking with the core values of their own and most of Europe's university history. In his much debated book, *Die akademische Elite*, Richard Münch (2007) describes how the so-called excellence initiative has undermined the academy's ability to renew knowledge on a broad basis due to the kinds of differentiation policies that guide the selection of elite universities and research programmes.

This undermining of the links between research and teaching, so as to make research more receptive to demands from actors in society, confronts the basic idea of the Humboldtian university head on. As noted, Humboldt's basic idea was that the universities should keep the faculties together, and engaged in constant interaction, for the sake of '*Bildung*'. The development of the person through research was seen as more important than the development of the 'products' of research. The innovation paradigm reverses this focus. The humanities, in particular, are threatened by this shift. The role of the humanities (and now sociology and the other social sciences) is not only to educate its own candidates, but to give meaning to the world and society as it is transformed through science.

As Münch shows, Germany's Excellence Initiative is an example of how elite universities, of some specialisation or other, are to be drawn out of the grey masses of the total population of universities. While the majority of these institutions remain bogged down by the massive growth in the student numbers, the elite universities will, instead, become allied with the elites of society, for whom the rhetoric of innovation has become almost like a secular religion. This differentiation is justified by 'knowledge arguments', but such 'arguments' have meaning only for politicians. Excellence is an empty category that gains substance through the political privileging of certain kinds of knowledge at the cost of others.[3] Political tools that promote excellence are the same tools that promote differentiation *through* competition, socially constructed *through* the practice of ratings, rankings and evaluations which are linked to particular rewards. But these tools do not promote the fair competition that the liberal ideology of the market once dreamed of. Rather they create a concentration of resources around big projects, big programmes and well-established research groups that already have a lot, but which, as Münch convincingly shows, also have low productivity and low creativity levels. When productivity is measured against the number of employees or resources utilised per research hour, universities other than the elite universities often prove superior. And when comparing faculties and disciplines, this is particularly the case for the humanities. While the tendency to create oligopolies and even monopolies (centres of excellence) for the sake of 'elite competition' (which so far has given priority to medicine, engineering and biotechnology – the kinds of sciences that apparently embody the values of innovation) the kind of productivity seen in the humanities is not recognised, as John Higgins (2010) shows so well in his contribution to the South African debate.

But the dramatic fall in creativity, linked to the undermining of the social sciences and humanities faculties, fails to excite the politicians. Germany's Excellence Initiative (and the now about 12 universities under its wing, also known as 'Elite unis') illustrates that the social sciences and the humanities are of little value to universities that wish to compete for the 'excellence' label. These disciplines and faculties carry little weight in the selection process that the politicians have created. Admittedly, it is difficult to measure their value, particularly when it comes to measuring their contribution to 'innovation'.

Germany is not unique. The hype around the notions of excellence and innovation is global. A global policy is being developed for the creation of hierarchies that can compete in different niches to supply specialised knowledge to different kinds of users. Germany may have driven this policy to the most extreme level, but most European countries have adopted a similar approach, in line with the EU's drive to transform Europe's university landscape according to the degree to which universities contribute to innovation.

It is not surprising, then, that one of the most important people shaping European higher education and research policies, Helga Nowotny, is a strong advocate of innovation. She seems to perceive it as the saviour of our time, and to envisage the social sciences and humanities as providing supply and support, driven by the needs of the 'hard science' disciplines mentioned above. In a paper published in *World Social Science Report* with the catchy title 'Out of science: Out of sync?' (Nowotny 2010), the emeritus professor and president of the European Research Council put forward these arguments. Innovation has a social side, she argues, and the humanities and social sciences should see it as their duty to analyse this for the sake of understanding change as defined by innovation. An analysis of continuity, stability, cultural identities and circles of human experience through history seem to have less value for her and her colleagues.

The EU and rhetoric around innovation

Higher education and research have become burning issues for the EU despite the lack of any formal or legal basis for the promotion of policies linked to these two areas. The Bologna Process, despite including a number of countries outside the EU, has become a tool for the co-ordination of policies on higher education and led to the establishment of the European Higher Education Area (EHEA).

Research co-operation has a long history between European states and university researchers, and has been gradually drawn into the EU's policy sphere. The Lisbon Declaration of 2000 strongly linked university-based research and the need to reform the universities with the growth and innovation strategy. The declaration proposed that Europe should be the world's foremost knowledge economy, driven by innovation and the renewal of knowledge that innovation presupposes. For this purpose, universities needed new policies, but only after 2004 did the universities become responsible for these changes. It was at this point that neo-liberal policies were articulated particularly clearly (Mirowski and Plehwe 2009, Plehwe 2011).

After 2004, it became clear that the processes that drive innovation must also drive university reforms. In other words, for higher education institutions to be more useful for innovation, they need to be oriented towards the users of innovation, differentiated by competition and rewarded by results. By 2010, this policy had been articulated to perfection in the EU's growth strategy known as 'Europe 2020'. In terms of this strategy, research universities are characterised by how useful they make themselves in relation to innovation, and preferably by being organised as entrepreneurial universities. Thus a research university should, as the EU sees it, view itself as part of a global competitive environment, if it is to be supportive of the new programme for European economic growth. Furthermore, the EU's adoption of the OECD's knowledge-based economic policies is seen as compulsory, and the strengthening of co-operation with the OECD around the concept of the knowledge economy is highly recommended. Thus by 2010, if not before, universities had been shaped into tools for new ends, and primarily as a means for ensuring the growth of Europe as a regional economy and expanding its global influence.

For the Europe 2020 strategy to work, universities will have to reform.

Most are not yet good enough at contributing to the innovation process. All activities, from 'blue sky' to applied research need to be streamlined to fit this new purpose. To make this happen, both more management and more of a market is needed. As the OECD argues, only competition can overcome the inertia of the traditional and obsolete Humboldtian universities. Tradition, not functionality, prevents institutions from being useful for the innovation economy (OECD 2008). For OECD policy-makers, exposing the universities to 'the rhythm of the market' will provide the strategies for change, and managerialism can bring this about. The Europe 2020 policy document on innovation (EU 2010) has a tagline which reads: 'A strategy for smart, sustainable and inclusive growth'. In this document, the biggest challenge to the EU is defined as its ability to 'adopt a much more strategic approach to innovation', as an 'overarching policy objective' (EU 2010: 2). The fact that universities must transform to make this possible is taken as truism: only then can the necessary co-operation between the world of science and the world of business be enhanced, only then can obstacles such as old Humboldtian influences be removed, and incentives be put in place in accordance with the necessary ratings, rankings and evaluations. The consequences of this policy for the EU's financial and organisational tool, research policies and budget allocation (namely, Framework Programme 8) are already evident. While the humanities and social sciences were weakly supported in Framework Programme 7, which is the co-ordinating tool for EU research funding for 2007 to 2013,[4] in Framework Programme 8 they seem set to survive only as support disciplines within programmes, and will not be supported as disciplines in themselves. An initiative from Freie Universität, Berlin, to mobilse against such a development may, as the somehow defensive arguments in their call for action indicated, be too late.[5]

Thus, strategy taken by Framework Programme 7, and the ongoing debate about the Framework Programme 8, promises growth for those disciplines that directly contribute to innovation in Europe, but few resources and no future for the disciplines that interpret the world differently from that proposed by the innovation paradigm. If this strategy continues to dominate university policy and funding, it goes without saying that the humanities and social sciences have a future only in so far as they support the knowledge needs defined by 'innovation', and that only those actors in society who are able to express their knowledge needs will decide whether and how the social sciences and humanities shall be allowed to contribute.

The marriage between the EU and the OECD

The shift in focus within academic institutions, from the time when the first university was founded in Bologna at end of the eleventh century, until public values were replaced with the pursuit of 'innovation', also represents a shift in levels of identification from the nation state to the region (EU) and latterly the globe (OECD). This transformation is primarily a transformation of the long-term relationship between knowledge, polity and economics. The relations between a state and an academic sector protected by the state that allowed scholars to express independent knowledge (more and more as a democratic right and duty), is, in the neo-liberal phase (post 1983), being dissolved and rendered suspect. How these relations will be reassembled at the global level, and how a new public space for the protection of academic freedom will emerge is a crucial issue in these times. This is the future to which all scholars in the social sciences and the humanities need to direct their attention. As I suggested at the outset, a defence of Humboldtian values beyond the nation state is required.

For now, however, the uniting idea of governance at a global level is still a rather monolithic fixation on innovation. The central idea of the knowledge economy, for which innovation is the engine, has been developed by the OECD since 1996, in response to the ongoing debate about the role of knowledge for economic development (see OECD 1996; 1998; 2004; 2005; 2006a; 2006b; 2008; and Santiago et al. 2008). According to these documents, a learning organisation learns less of value from experience than before, and more from its well-trained academics and their ability to link into and adapt knowledge linked to innovation. The shift from a learning society to an innovation economy has become the OECD's mantra. This new economy, where learning in a broad sense of the word is replaced with the notion of an innovation economy, also presupposes a national innovation system oriented towards the global competition between economic actors and competitive states.

This is also how the policy of university differentiation may be seen as a contribution of the state to the innovation paradigm: some universities may be elevated to international institutions promoting the interests of actors in the global economy, and the quality of the competitive state may be linked to their support for these actors. The role of OECD – as a membership organisation – in promoting this system has been to develop quantitative indicators for knowledge-based economies, and thus to guide the governance of such a development (a soft method of co-ordination). When states apply the OECD's tools to their higher education and research policies, the logic of differentiation and competition (that again promotes further differentiation) emerges systematically.

As in Germany, these indicators downgrade the social sciences and humanities, while upgrading other kinds of academic achievements and disciplines within a world of internationalised comparisons. The indicators are used to highlight best practice and to reveal deviations from best practice. Four main areas where indicators needed to be developed, according to the OECD's 1996 document, were: knowledge stocks and flows, knowledge rates of return, knowledge networks, and knowledge and learning. The last area holds a primary position as an indicator, but is understood as *human capital development* – that is, a new kind of capital that brings the highest social and personal/private returns. Soon 'knowledge and learning' was exchanged with 'innovation', and *Bildung*, the process of learning to behave in a communicative and public society vanished from the value system.

The integration of universities into the 'innovation economy' has been streamlined by the quantitative measurements developed since 1996 onwards. As argued, the key driver in the transformation from a qualitative to a quantitative understanding of knowledge, or from human development and nation-state identities to human capital and global capitalism, has been a moving target called 'best practice' (Martens and Weymann 2007), or more generally, the soft 'guidance' of activities driven by comparisons between 'competing units'. EU policies for both research and education are now driven by these so-called 'soft methods of co-ordination'. 'Best practice' transcends references to a social unit – or nation state – and is linked to economic units whose competitive advantage depends on their ability to mobilise resources in their near or far surroundings, and primarily their human-capital resources. Best practice thus also creates uniformity and convergence that only an entrepreneurial university dismissive of the humanities and social sciences can live up to.[6]

After a long decade, the OECD concluded in a two-volume report (Santiago et al. 2008) that its policy has been accepted, as far as the role and organisation of universities is concerned. The question now is implementation. How does OECD make local authorities adjust to the global regime of best practice? The answer seems to be via competition, as this can be promoted by delinking universities from their nation states and reassembling them as providers of human capital (as measured by OECD) to users who themselves are actors in and creators of the knowledge market.

> First and foremost, the external pressures for reform are weak in tertiary education. Different from unsound macroeconomic policies which may quickly trigger capital outflow and force governments to greater

discipline, tertiary education does not face similar sanctions for failing to deliver services of the highest quality. The advent of the knowledge economy and acceleration of the pace of technological progress are now increasing the cost of inaction, *but the imperfect international competition in tertiary education* still hinders the long-term commitment of policy-makers to tertiary education improvements. (Santiago et al. Vol. 2: 327, emphasis added)

Conclusion

The basic idea of the humanities – that society is and can be shaped by new knowledge that evolves out of a research process – has little space in the reasoning underpinning the concept of knowledge for innovation. Similarly, the understanding that such knowledge is inter-subjective and that it is the duty and the privilege of the university to grow this inter-subjectivity through interfaculty interaction now has little traction. Achieving this, would require universities to keep their independence and distance from specific societal interests and to constantly expand their interactions with society in general.

The ideology of innovation and the knowledge economy works to counter this. The links between faculties are broken down by a differentiation according to competitive criteria. The paradox is that this leads to less creativity and a general loss of knowledge within academic culture as a whole. In the end, it leads to less knowledge and less innovation. Generally it has proven difficult to plan knowledge development for innovation (Weingart 2010). Had universities been allowed to develop more broadly, and with academic 'honour' (the acceptance of best among equals) as a 'competitive' criterion, more knowledge would be available to society, and more creativity would be at our disposal.

When some universities have to specialise and occupy specific niches, and others monopolise a disproportionate amount of resources in order to develop as elite universities, the resulting concentration and specialisation of knowledge undermines society's general knowledge base. The consequences of this are dramatic, primarily for the humanities, but also for some (if not all) of the social sciences. The transformation of the nation state escalates this process. The development of nation states shaped the humanities in their own image and vice versa. No such shaping is evident in the processes of regionalisation and globalisation – apart from the debates that university researchers themselves generate about these issues, that is.

As the ideology of innovation penetrates research councils and regional research funding organisations, such as the EU framework programmes, it is no wonder that the defenders of the humanities and the social sciences are found among academics themselves. As the Berlin initiative indicates, and SANORD is another important example of this, a broad mobilisation of a global magnitude is necessary. Many of Humboldt's values must, in my view, be writ large in such a mobilisation – a modernised Humboldt, of course, one befitting a time of democratisation. This is where the debate among academics should focus in the future, as an alternative to the idea that the role of the social sciences and the humanities is to support the 'innovation' process.

Knowledge in the social sciences and humanities is mediated by language, and its meanings shape our identities and our social relations. If these disciplines are to have an independent future in line with their past, they need to regain their old scholarly independence, to demonstrate the value of the knowledge that emanates from universities as a contribution to society, whether or not it is useful to certain users, and as necessary to public debates underpinning democracy, identity and culture. Of course, this means stepping beyond the innovation paradigm and entering the broader debate about the future of democracy. Democracy, today, is part of the nation state and the world is moving towards regionalisation and globalisation. Thus the future of the social sciences and humanities is both to save (and improve) the democracies we have and to raise the debate about regional and global democracy. What kinds of identities and institutions can promote the communicative and inter-subjective stability of nation-state democracies, while enhancing the development of democracy on a regional and global level?

Notes

1   At the time of writing, John Higgins was the Andrew W Mellon Research Professor of Archives and Public Culture at the University of Cape Town. His views appeared in *Business Day*, 28 December 2010, p. 5 under the headline, 'Narrow focus on science and technology leaves South Africa poorer'.

2   Clark (2006: 444) refers to Fichte's *Deduzierter Plan einer zu Berlin zu errichten höhern Lehranstalt* (1807), in which he outlined his idea that the academic life was to be one's 'home', absorbing the whole person, an end in itself. Fichte set academic life against the utilitarian, commercial demands of civil society and civil service. An instructor must be an autonomous artist (*Freier Künstler*). Clark argues that Schleiermacher's *Gelegentliche Gedanken über Universitäten in deutchen Sinn* (1808) marvellously reflects the Romantic notion of research. Schleiermacher spoke of the necessary inner unity of learning, and strongly emphasised the artistic – almost to the detriment of *Wissenschaft* (science) – although he also argued that a university should teach both the sciences and self-development (*Bildung*), even in the specialised disciplines.

3   Jürgen Kaube (2009) has edited a book with the title *Die Illusion der Exzellenz. Lebenslügen der Wissenschaftspolitik* in which a number of prominent German scholars outline the irrationalities of this policy and the destructive effects it has for the 'knowledge society' as a whole.

4   In Framework Programme 7, *less than 2 per cent* (€0.6 billion) of the budget was allocated to the humanities and the social sciences while €9.1 billion was allocated for ICT.

5   In a paper called 'European Funding for Social Science and Humanities Research beyond 2014', academics at the Freie Universität in Berlin argue that: researchers in the humanities and social sciences engage already in *multiple collaborations* with public authorities and policy-makers, international organisations, think tanks, media, NGOs, churches, business and employee's organisations, companies, museums, citizen fora, etc. They note that researchers (and the collaborative groups they work with) fulfil *different tasks in society*. Researchers are more independent and offer a differentiated analysis. They are able to take a medium-term view and look beyond current situations. They note that *all other spheres use research as a basis for their own contributions.* Without social science research, there is a risk that contributions of other spheres of society will become superficial. They note further that politics is complicated and contested by various actors. Researchers cannot give simple answers, but can highlight sound criteria according to which decisions should be taken and clarify the likely consequences of particular policies. *They enable policy-makers to make decisions based on scientific evidence.*

6   The entrepreneurial university cannot be fully discussed here, although its organisational model fits the innovation ideology most precisely. Its development is however seen as an expression of a revolutionary shift (of same magnitude as when research became as guiding force in 1810 (see Etzkowitz 2004 and in numerous other articles). This kind of university is well described in Kor Grit's (1997) analysis of the University of Twente's transformation into an 'entrepreneurial university'. In fact, the University of Twente has become prototypical in influencing the EU's ideas of university reform. The six 'ideal typical' traits to which the Twente university tried to adjust and promote as 'entrepreneurial' were: (i) productivity as a norm, (ii) a market orientation, (iii) an entrepreneurial attitude, (iv) management through quantification and quantification as surveillance, (v) linked to the previous point, steering at a distance, and (vi) managerialism. Grit rightly asks if this university is a child of the European Enlightenment. While a return to German idealism is not possible, in many debates the 'entrepreneurial university' (or the German elite university) is seen as having reformed Humboldtian university values.

References

Beck U (1985) *Risikogesellschaft.* Frankfurt am Main.

Bell D (1973) *The Coming of Post-industrial Society: A Venture in Social Forecasting.* New York: Basic Books.

Berger P, Berger B and Kellner H. (1974) *The Homeless Mind: Modernization and Consciousness.* New York: Vintage Books.

Clark W (2006) *Academic Charisma and the Origins of the Research University.* Chicago and London: University of Chicago Press.

Coetzee JM (2008) *Diary of a Bad Year.* London: Vintage.

Etzkowitz H (2004) 'The evolution of the entrepreneurial university', *International Journal of Technology and Globalisation* 1 (1): 64–77.

EU (European Commision) (2010). *The Innovation Union.* SEC (2010) 1161. Brussels.

Giddens A (1990) *The Consequences of Modernity.* Stanford: Stanford University Press.

Grit K (1997) 'The rise of the entrepreneurial university: A heritage of the Enlightenment?' *Science Studies* 10 (2): 3–22.

Habermas J (1968) *Technik und Wissenschaft als Ideologie.* Frankfurt am Main: Suhrkamp.

Habermas J (1981/1984) *The Theory of Communicative Action, Volume 1: Reason and the Rationalization of Society.* London: Polity Press.

Higgins J (2010) Narrow focus on science and education leaves South Africa poorer', *Business Day,* 28 December, p. 5.

Kaube J (2009) *Die Illusion der Excellence. Lebenslügen der Wissenschaftspolitik.* Berlin: Verlag Klaus Wagenbach.

Knorr-Cetina K (2001) 'Transparency regimes and management by content in global Organisations', *Journal of Knowledge Management* 5 (2): 180–184.

Martens K and A Weyman (2007) 'The intenationalization of education policy: Towards a convergence of national paths?' In S Liebfried, K Martens, P Mayer and A Hurrelmanm (eds) *Transforming the Golden Age Nation State.* New York: Palgrave.

Mirowski P and D Plehwe (2009) *The Making of the Neoliberal Thought Collective.* Cambridge MA: Harvard University Press.

Münch R (1982) *Theorie des Handelens: Zur Rekonstruktion der Beiträge von Talcott Parsons, Emile Durkheim und Max Weber.* Frankfurt am Main: Suhrkamp Taschenbuch Wissenschaft.

Münch R (2007) *Die Academische Elite.* Frankfurt am Main: Suhrkamp.

Nowotny H (2010) *Out of Science, Out of Sync?* World Social Science Report. Paris: International Social Science Council UNESCO.

OECD (Organisation for Economic Co-operation and Development) (1996) *The Knowledge-Based Economy.* Paris

OECD (1998) *Redefining Tertiary Education.* Paris.

OECD (2004) *On the Edge: Securing a Sustainable Future for Higher Education.* Paris.

OECD (2005) *Six Scenarios for Universities: OECD/CERI Experts Meeting on University Futures and New Technologies.* Washington: World Bank.

OECD (2006a) *Four Future Scenarios for Higher Education: Higher Education: Quality, Equity and Efficiency.* Meeting of OECD Ministers of Education, Athens.

OECD (2006b) *Guidelines for Quality Provision in Cross-border Higher Education.* Paris. Also published as the *OECD-UNESCO Guidelines on Quality Provision in Cross-border Higher Education* (Available online).

OECD (2008) *The Global Competition for Talent. Mobility of the Highly Skilled.* Paris.

Plehwe D (2007) 'A global knowledge bank? The World Bank and bottom-up efforts to reinforce neoliberal development perspectives in the post-Washington Consensus era', *Globalizations* 4 (4): 514–528.

Plehwe D (2011) Who cares about excellence? Commercialization, competition, and the transnational promotion of neoliberal expertise', in T Halvorsen, A Nyhagen (eds) *Academic identities, academic challenges? American and European experiences of the transformation of higher education and research.* Newcastle upon Tyne: Cambridge Scholars.

Santiago P, K Tremblay, E Basri and E Arnal (2008) *Tertiary Education for the Knowledge Society: Volume 1, Governance, Funding, Quality; Volume 2, Equity, Innovation, Labour Market Internationalisation.* Paris: OECD.

Stehr N (1994) *Arbeit, Eigentum und wissen: Zur Theorie von Wissengesellschaften.* Suhrkamp. Frankfurt am Main.

Wagner P (1994) *A Sociology of Modernity, Liberty and Discipline.* Routledge. London.

Weingart P (2010) Wissenschaftssoziologie. In D Simon, A Knie and S Hornbostel (eds) *Handbuch Wissenschaftspolitik.* Wiesbaden: VS Verlag.

Chapter 5

Redressing apartheid's legacy of social exclusion: social equity, redress and admission to higher education in South Africa

Saleem Badat

In South Africa, social inequalities were embedded and reflected in all spheres of social life, as a product of the systemic exclusion of blacks and women under colonialism and apartheid. The higher education system was no exception. Social, political and economic discrimination and inequalities of a class, race, gender, institutional and spatial nature profoundly shaped, and continue to shape, South African higher education. In 1994, South Africa's new democratic government committed itself to transforming higher education, as well as the inherited apartheid social and economic structure, and institutionalising a new social order.

Indeed, since the advent of democracy, virtually no domain of higher education has escaped scrutiny and been left untouched, and there has been a wide array of 'transformation-oriented' initiatives.[1] These have included: the definition of the purposes and goals of higher education; extensive policy research, formulation, adoption and implementation in the areas of governance, funding, academic structures, academic programmes, and quality assurance; the enactment of new laws and regulations; and major restructuring and reconfiguration of the institutional landscape and of institutions themselves.

The realisation of social equity and redress for historically disadvantaged social groups in higher education, and therefore the issue of admissions, has necessarily also loomed large in policy discourse. In this chapter, I undertake the following:

- to briefly analyse the colonial and apartheid legacy in so far as the provision of higher education and the participation of black South Africans are concerned;[2]

- to advance a number of propositions with respect to the erosion of the apartheid legacy in higher education and the realisation of social equity and redress for students from historically disadvantaged social groups. These propositions relate to equity and excellence or quality, equity of access and opportunity or outcomes, diversity, affirmative action and admissions policy and practice;
- to describe the approach adopted towards social equity and admissions under democracy, and its outcomes to date; and
- to identify the critical challenges that continue to confront the state and higher education institutions, if constitutional and legislated values and goals related to social equity and redress are to be realised.

It should be noted that in this chapter I confine myself to the issues of equity, redress and admissions for *students* from historically disadvantaged social classes and groups. The important issue of equity and redress with respect to the *employment* of members of historically disadvantaged social classes and groups is not addressed, beyond noting that there has been limited progress in this regard and that employment equity in higher education remains a key challenge. Furthermore, while institutional redress to enhance the academic capabilities of historically black institutions remains an important issue and the arguable lack of state support for institutional redress continues to make the government's policy related to the promotion of institutional differentiation and diversity controversial, this issue is outside the scope of this chapter.

It is necessary to make three observations with respect to the context of social equity, redress and admissions in higher education in South Africa.

First, higher education institutions were profoundly shaped by apartheid ideology and planning, in that they were reserved for different 'race' groups and allocated different ideological, economic and social functions in relation to the reproduction of the apartheid social order. The fundamental differences in allocated roles constituted the key axis of differentiation and the principal basis of inequalities between the historically white and black institutions. Inherited patterns of advantage and disadvantage continue to condition the capabilities and capacities of institutions to pursue excellence, engage in knowledge production, provide high-quality teaching and learning experiences, ensure equity of opportunity and outcomes, and contribute to economic and social development.

Second, research and teaching were extensively shaped by the socio-economic and political priorities of apartheid's separate-development programme. Post-1994, higher education has been called upon to address and respond to the development needs of a democratic South Africa. These needs have been formulated in various ways. The 1994 Reconstruction and Development Programme speaks of 'meeting basic needs of people'; 'developing our human resources';[3] 'building the economy' and 'democratising the state and society' (Ministry in the Office of the President 1994). The Higher Education White Paper of 1997 calls on higher education to contribute to South Africa achieving 'political democratisation, economic reconstruction and development, and redistributive social policies aimed at equity' (DoE 1997: 1.7).

Third, the attempt to transform higher education occurs within the context of a formidable overall challenge of *simultaneously* pursuing economic development (including restructuring economic relations to address inequitable historical patterns of ownership, wealth and income distribution), social equity and the extension and deepening of democracy.

For good political and social reasons, no element of this triad can be eliminated, postponed or tackled after any other. They all have to be pursued simultaneously.

The colonial/apartheid legacy

Under colonialism and apartheid, separate institutions existed for black and white students. During the early twentieth century, the twin concerns of the colonial state were guaranteeing capitalist development on the basis of cheap unskilled black labour and consolidating the structures of white political domination and privilege. As a result, the higher education of black people was not a priority for the state. By 1948, black university students numbered only 950, a mere 4.6% of total enrolments (Malherbe 1977: 731), and by 1959 black students constituted some 10.7% of total enrolments. Black students mainly studied under sufferance at white English-language universities. State policies ensured that higher education was essentially restricted to certain sections of the dominant white classes (Badat 1999).

From the 1960s onwards, provision of higher education for black South Africans expanded. This was intimately linked with apartheid's separate-development programme and the project of geographical segregation and the consolidation of ethnically structured territorial units known as bantustans (or previously as 'native reserves'). The linkage between the establishment of universities for Africans and the launching of the bantustan system was unambiguous, the intention being to restrict the economic advancement, social mobility and political rights of Africans to the bantustans, which were where the products of the 'African' universities were also expected to find employment. Universities for black students were thus intended to produce the professional and administrative corps for the separate development of black bureaucracies, and to assist in the formation of a black middle class that would, it was hoped, collaborate in the separate-development project.

Following the 1976 and 1977 political uprisings, the reformist objectives of the corporate sector and the apartheid state gained currency, and black higher education expanded tremendously. Now, as part of a 'winning the hearts and minds strategy', the goal was to foster a black middle class through the expansion of the higher education system. The hope was that this new middle class would seek accommodation with the state and with the predominantly white corporate sector, and also act as a buffer against rising black and especially worker political militancy (Badat 1991). New higher education institutions were established for blacks, and black student enrolments increased dramatically from 25 104 students in 1977 to 140 604 by 1990, although only 11.9% of these students were permitted to enrol at 'white' institutions (Badat 1999).

At the close of the apartheid period, the gross participation rate in higher education was about 17%.[4] However, participation rates were highly skewed by 'race': approximately 9% for Africans, 13% for coloureds, 40% for Indians and 70% for whites (CHE 2004: 62). While black South Africans (that is, Indians, coloureds and Africans) constituted 89% of the population in 1993, black students constituted only 52% of the total student body of 473 000. African students, although constituting 77% of the population, made up only 40% of enrolments. On the other hand, white students, although only 11% of the population, constituted 48% of enrolments. Of total student enrolment, 43% of students were women. These statistics, taken together with the patterns of enrolment by fields of study, qualification levels, and mode of study, highlight well the relative exclusion of black and women South Africans from higher education.

Eroding the apartheid legacy and advancing social equity

I wish to approach the issues of eroding apartheid's legacy in higher education and providing social equity and redress for students from disadvantaged social classes and groups by advancing six propositions that I consider key to the pursuit and achievement of a substantive social justice agenda.

Equity and redress

For much of their history, progressive political movements in South Africa have advanced a *politics of equal recognition*, whether in relation to 'race', gender or ethnicity. The *Freedom Charter* statement that 'South Africa belongs to all', and its declaration that 'All national groups shall have equal rights', is one manifestation of this commitment to a politics of equal recognition.

With the advent of democracy, this politics of equal recognition was translated into a constitution that guarantees equality in all spheres of society. The Constitution of the Republic of South Africa set out the character of the society that was envisaged, proclaiming the values of 'human dignity, the achievement of equality and the advancement of human rights and freedoms', and 'non-racialism and non-sexism' (1996: section 1). The Bill of Rights (sections 9.3 and 9.4) unambiguously proclaimed that individuals and 'the state may not unfairly discriminate directly or indirectly against anyone on one or more grounds, including race, gender, sex, pregnancy, marital status, ethnic or social origin, colour, sexual orientation, age, disability, religion, conscience, belief, culture, language and birth' (sections 9.3 and 9.4). The state was enjoined to 'respect, protect, promote and fulfil the rights in the Bill of Rights' (section 7.2). With regard to higher education, the 1997 Higher Education White Paper proclaimed the intention 'to provide a full spectrum of advanced educational opportunities for an expanding range of the population irrespective of race, gender, age, creed or class or other forms of discrimination' (DoE 1997: 1.27).

A politics of equal recognition cannot, however, be blind to the legacies of colonialism and apartheid. Nor can it blithely proceed from a notion that the advent of democracy is in itself a sufficient condition for the erasure of the structural and institutional conditions, policies and practices that have, for decades, grounded and sustained inequalities in all domains of social life. It is precisely this reality that gives salience to the idea of redress and makes it a fundamental and necessary dimension of higher education transformation, and of social transformation in general. Thus, the Constitution states that 'to promote the achievement of equality, legislative and other measures designed to protect or advance persons, or categories of persons, disadvantaged by unfair discrimination may be taken' (section 9.2). It also makes clear that 'conduct inconsistent' with its provisions is invalid and that the 'obligations imposed by it must be fulfilled' (section 2). In similar vein, the Higher Education White Paper enunciates 'equity and redress' as fundamental principles. It states:

> The principle of equity requires fair opportunities both to enter higher education programmes and to succeed in them. (It) implies, on the one hand, a critical identification of existing inequalities which are the product

of policies, structures and practices based on racial, gender, disability and other forms of discrimination or disadvantage, and on the other a programme of transformation with a view to redress. Such transformation involves not only abolishing all existing forms of unjust differentiation, but also measures of empowerment, including financial support to bring about equal opportunity for individuals. (DoE 1997: 1.18)

The goals are to become more socially equitable within higher education, and to promote social equity more generally by providing opportunity for social advancement through equity of access, opportunity and outcomes. The equity and redress imperatives apply not only to the domain of students but also to the arenas of academic and administrative personnel.

In as much as higher education institutions must debate and make choices and decisions on numerous issues, social equity and redress are not so much matters of choice as they are pressing constitutional obligations that 'must be fulfilled', and societal imperatives in terms of which institutions must take 'measures' to 'advance persons, or categories of persons, disadvantaged by unfair discrimination'.

Equity and excellence/quality

In debates on higher education transformation, it has sometimes been contended that the increased participation of historically disadvantaged social groups in higher education and the pursuit of equity and redress must necessarily compromise excellence, and result in the diminution of the quality of provision, qualifications and graduates. While these are certainly risks, such outcomes are not preordained. There may be an intractable tension between the simultaneous pursuit of equity, redress and quality, but there is no inevitable conflict between them. The imperatives of social equity and redress do not require an inevitable reduction of quality or the compromise of appropriately defined standards.

'Quality' and 'standards' are not timeless and invariant. It is unwise and inappropriate to conceive of quality as being attached to a single, ahistorical and universal model of higher education or type of institution. Quality and standards are historically specific and must be related to the objectives of institutions and to broader educational and social purposes.

For good reasons, the higher education systems of many countries evince institutions that are highly differentiated and diverse, in terms of which institutions have different missions, pursue differing social and educational purposes and goals, and necessarily have differing entry requirements and academic standards as appropriate to the objectives and purposes specified. The meaning of a university is not to be found in its admissions policies, the content of its teaching and research or in how these are undertaken. Instead, the core characteristics of a university are four-fold:

- A university produces and disseminates knowledge, which advances understanding of the natural and social worlds and enriches accumulated cultural inheritances and heritage.
- A university cultivates and forms the cognitive character of students so that they: 'can think effectively and critically'; have 'achieved depth in some field of knowledge'; have a 'critical appreciation of the ways in which we gain knowledge and understanding of the universe, of society, and of ourselves'; have 'a broad knowledge of other cultures and other times'; are 'able to make decisions based on reference to the wider world and to the historical forces that have shaped it'; have 'some understanding of and experience in thinking systematically about moral and ethical problems'; and can 'communicate with cogency' (Task Force on Higher Education and Society 2000: 84).
- A university is committed to 'the spirit of truth' (Graham 2005: 163).
- A university possesses the necessary academic freedom and institutional autonomy to produce and disseminate knowledge effectively.

While academic freedom and institutional autonomy are necessary conditions if universities are to advance the public good and be democratically accountable, they must also be understood as values in which both rights *and* duties inhere (Jonathan 2006). In this regard, 'the legacies of intellectual colonisation and racialisation' must be recognised 'as threats to academic freedom' (Du Toit 2000: 103), and it must be acknowledged that 'the powers conferred by academic freedom go hand in hand with substantive duties to deracialise and decolonise intellectual spaces' (Bentley et al. 2006: 23).

In as much as quality and standards are not invariant, the 'educational process in higher education – including curriculum frameworks, the assumptions on which these are based, course design, and approaches to delivery and assessment' (Scott et al. 2007: 73) – is also neither immutable nor a technical or neutral issue. Instead, it is 'historically constructed' and 'constitutes a significant variable affecting performance and determining who gains access and who succeeds'. However, there is frequently opposition to critical engagement on 'the educational process as a variable, at least partly because changing embedded structures and practices is seen as eroding standards' (Scott et al. 2007: 73). Also pertinent to the theme of equity and quality, some have sought to explain the provision of poor quality higher education in terms of providing access and opportunities to historically disadvantaged social groups. This is, of course, a cynical and distorted notion of equity, and does not substantively or meaningfully contribute to eroding the domination of knowledge production or high-level occupations by particular social groups. Without the provision of high-quality learning and research programmes, institutions do not in any significant way contribute to the production of graduates who can contribute to the economic and social development of societies and to the public good. There may be private benefits for individuals but no or little benefit to society.

While the achievement of social equity with quality, and quality with social equity, may be challenging, these are not impossible goals. Without quality, the prospect of meaningful social equity is compromised and rendered meaningless. On the other hand, 'quality' pursued in a manner that is oblivious to the imperatives of equity and redress means that social advancement through equity of opportunity in higher education is precluded, the class, race and gender character of the occupation and social structure of apartheid is reproduced rather than eroded and transformed, and the pursuit of democracy is effectively compromised.

None of the above is to deny that the *simultaneous* pursuit of social equity, redress and quality within higher education may be characterised by intractable tensions that give rise to difficult political and social dilemmas and unenviable choices and decisions. Trade-offs between principles, goals and strategies may be necessary – especially in a context of scarce financial resources. An exclusive concentration on social equity and redress could lead to the privileging of this issue over the question of quality, thus compromising the goal of producing high-quality graduates with the requisite knowledge, competencies and skills. Conversely, an exclusive focus on quality could result in social equity and redress being delayed or retarded, with consequences for social justice.

When confronted with an intractable tension between dearly held goals and values, various 'simplifying manoeuvres' are possible (Morrow 1997). One simplifying manoeuvre is to refuse to accept the existence of a dilemma – a kind of moral blindness. A second manoeuvre is to elevate one value or goal above all others, making this *the* criterion in terms of which all choices and policies are made. A third simplifying manoeuvre is to rank values in advance so that if there is a conflict between them one will take precedence. In the latter two cases, the effect is to privilege one value or goal over another (Morrow 1997).

Under particular political and social conditions, simplifying manoeuvres may, however, not be open to social actors. An alternative path may be to accept that, for good reasons, goals and strategies that may be in tension may have to be pursued simultaneously. Paradoxes have to be creatively addressed, and policies and strategies devised that can satisfy multiple imperatives, can *balance* competing goals, and can enable the pursuit of equally desirable goals. The making of choices and decisions, including conscious trade-offs, are opportunities to forge – through participatory and democratic processes – an institutional democratic consensus on the fundamental values, purposes, orientation and goals of a university. However, consensus on values and goals is no guarantee of success. That is to say, while the goals may not be at issue, the policies, strategies, instruments, pace and timeframes for achieving goals can be sources of conflict and even resistance. Democratic consensus is also not likely to be a one-off activity, but rather one that has to be renewed regularly. The words of C Wright Mills (1959) are especially appropriate here:

> Freedom is not merely the chance to do as one pleases; neither is it merely the opportunity to choose between set alternatives. Freedom is, first of all, the chance to formulate the available choices, to argue over them – and then, the opportunity to choose.

> Beyond this, the problem of freedom is…how decisions about the future of human affairs are to be made and who is to make them. Organisationally, it is the problem of a just machinery of decision. Morally, it is the problem of political responsibility. Intellectually, it is the problem of what are now the possible futures of human affairs. (1959: 174)

Mills wonderfully captures especially significant challenges. In a nutshell, how is a university to 'formulate the available choices' with respect to the advancement of social equity and redress, equity and quality, and how is it 'to argue over them' and innovate the 'just machinery' that provides the 'opportunity to choose' and to make decisions?

Equity of access and opportunity/outcomes

It is necessary to distinguish between equity of access and equity of opportunity and outcomes for historically disadvantaged social groups, such as black and female South Africans, those of working class and rural poor social origins and those with special needs. While access may be secured through various mechanisms, equity of opportunity and outcomes crucially depend on supportive institutional environments and cultures, curriculum innovation, appropriate learning and teaching strategies and techniques, appropriate induction and support, and effective academic mentoring. These are all vital if students are to succeed and graduate with the relevant knowledge, competencies, skills and attributes that are required for any occupation and profession, be lifelong learners and function as critical, culturally enriched and tolerant citizens.

The challenge of opportunity must also be viewed as 'part of a wider project of democratising access to knowledge' (Morrow 1993: 3). This means that, beyond providing students formal access, also ensuring 'epistemological access' is vital (Morrow 1993: 3). This 'epistemological access' 'is central not only to issues such as throughput and graduation rates but also to the very institution of the university itself and to the role it can play in a new democracy such as South Africa'.[5] As a consequence of colonialism and apartheid, knowledge production in South Africa has been predominantly the preserve of a particular social group – essentially white men. The democratisation of knowledge requires inducting previously excluded social groups such as black and female South Africans into the production and dissemination of knowledge. While 'formal access is a *necessary* condition for epistemological access (in respect of the kinds of knowledge distributed by universities) it is... far from being a *sufficient* condition' (Morrow 1993: 3, emphasis in original). The implication for teaching is that 'a reduction of the role of teaching to that of simply "conveying knowledge"...fails...to acknowledge the need to develop a citizenry which can be critical of knowledge which has been produced and which can contribute to processes of knowledge production itself'.[6]

Diversity, equity and quality

The pursuit and achievement of social equity and redress, concomitantly, has great value for diversity within universities as well as for quality.

Diversity and difference, whether social, geographic, national, cultural or linguistic in nature, are powerful wellsprings of institutional vitality and personal, intellectual and institutional development. Diversity in higher education, as former Harvard president Neil Rudenstine argues, is a necessary condition for 'human learning, understanding and wisdom', and a powerful means of 'creating the intellectual energy and robustness that lead to greater knowledge' (cited in Moore 2005: 8). Further, 'diversity enriches the educational experience', in that students 'learn from those whose experiences, beliefs and perspectives are different from' their own, 'and these lessons can be taught best in a richly diverse intellectual and social environment' (Moore 2005: 9). Conversely, the quality of education is diminished by an absence of diversity and 'educational opportunities are drastically limited without diversity, and that compromises an institution's ability to maintain its own missions and goals' (Moore 2005: 9).

Finally, diversity facilitates 'critical examination of oneself and one's traditions', knowledge and understanding of different cultures, 'of differences of gender, race, and sexuality', and democratic citizenship, and 'the cultivation of humanity' (Nussbaum 2006: 5, 6). It is also vital to forging, through higher education, greater social cohesion in deeply fractured societies.

Affirmative action

Two kinds of injustice prevail in South Africa. One kind is rooted in beliefs, prejudice, stereotypes, chauvinism, intolerance and fear of the 'other' – whether the 'other' are people of different 'races', social classes, sex, gender, sexual orientation, cultures, religions, languages, or nationalities, or live in specific geographical areas. Its effects are patterns of unjust social inclusion and exclusion, and domination and subordination of particular social groups. The other kind of injustice is deeply woven into the social and economic structures and relations of South African society, which have ossified so as to be thought of as natural and preordained, even though they are, of course, reproduced through human action and agency. These social and economic structures and relations ensure that great privileges and unbounded economic and social opportunities for a small minority coexist with harsh deprivation and an absence of opportunities for the majority; that the country remains one of the most unequal societies in the world in terms of disparities of wealth and income, living conditions and access to education, health and various social services; and that severe race, class, gender, geographical and other inequalities continue to be reproduced.

In the face of these conditions, pervasive inequities, as Sachs (2006: x) writes, 'cannot be wished away by invoking constitutional idealism', and 'equal opportunity' and 'equality of treatment...is unlikely to reduce disadvantage (but) merely maintain it' (Sikhosana 1993: 10). Moreover, if for good reasons no great reliance should be placed on the 'free market' or 'natural processes' to promote social equity and redress, specific measures and strategies are necessary. One such strategy is affirmative action,[7] which can take different forms, including quotas, targets and preferences (Moore 2005).

Affirmative action seeks to 'take proactive steps to reduce or address the impacts of discrimination with the ultimate goal of eliminating differences between genders, race and ethnicities, under-represented and dominant groups' (Moore 2005: 80). Sikhosana notes other definitions of affirmative action: 'an active process that attempts to reduce (or more optimistically eliminate) the effects of discrimination, namely disadvantage', and 'preference, by way of special measures, for certain groups or members of such groups (typically defined by race, ethnic identity, or sex) for the purpose of securing adequate advancement of such groups or their individual members in order to ensure equal enjoyment of human rights and fundamental freedoms' (1993: 3–4). Sachs defines affirmative action as 'focussed and deliberate governmental intervention that takes account of the reality of race to deal with and overcome the problems associated with race' (2006: x).

An important distinction needs to be made between the use of race to discriminate and exclude social groups and individuals, and the use of race to facilitate redress and enhance social equity as part of the quest to create more inclusive and more educative learning environments and processes. Sachs points, however, to 'two basic tensions inherit in the concept of affirmative action' (2006: ix). One is that certain social groups have to give up certain privileges and advantages; the other is that with respect to racial equity 'it involves conscious use of racial distinctions in order to create a non-racial society' (Sachs 2006: ix). The aim of affirmative action, however, 'is not to establish a form of anachronistic or disjunctive compensation for past injustices. It is to rectify the way in which these injustices continue to permeate the world we live in' (Sachs 2006: ix). Furthermore, the aim is also not to 'replace one form of social inequality with another, that is, to elevate "now-its-our-turnism" into a principle of equitable redress. The objective must be to overcome all forms of structured advantage' (Sachs 2006: ix). He also makes the crucial point that 'we should never lose sight of the fact that the goal is to establish a non-racial society in which social and cultural diversity is celebrated and seen as a source of vitality, and in which race as such ultimately has no political or economic significance. That must always be our goal' (2006: xi).

Sikhosana, however, wonders whether affirmative action can indeed 'overcome all forms of structured advantage', noting that 'most current conceptions of redress are limited to "affirmative action"; in other words, they are confined to the elimination of race- and gender-based inequalities and ignore those inequalities based on class or socio-economic position', and thus fail to lay 'the foundation for effective programmes of redress' (1993: 1). Mahmood Mamdani presents another significant challenge, namely,

> whether a strategy designed to address the grievances of a racially oppressed minority could be adequate to dismantling the apparatus of domination which strangled a racially oppressed majority. In other words,

no matter how open the access to minority white institutions, in the name of 'Affirmative Action', will this not simply alter the racial composition of that minority with little consequence for the oppressed majority except to legitimize their exclusion as based on merit this time round? In the final analysis, will not embracing the language and vision of 'Affirmative Action' obscure the very task that must be central to democratisation in a 'new' South Africa, that of institutional transformation? (cited in Sikhosana 1993: 16)

Sikhosana's conclusion is that affirmative action is a 'very limited and reformist form of redress' in that it 'does not look beyond race or ethnicity and gender', is 'based on efforts to move target groups into the predominantly white male mainstream without questioning that mainstream system itself', and will 'widen class inequalities' (1993: 22, 18–19).

This is to be contrasted with policies and strategies that erode and eliminate the economic and social basis of inequalities and bring about institutional and social transformation. However, Sikhosana unfortunately conflates 'reform' and 'reformist'. Nothing, in principle, precludes the use of affirmative action also to redress class inequalities and transform hegemonic cultures. Moreover, what distinguishes affirmative action as a 'reformist' measure from affirmative action as a 'reform' measure is whether it is viewed as a sufficient condition for redress and educational and social transformation (reformist), or simply as one measure among a package of measures designed to achieve fundamental social change (reform). Indeed, Sikhosana recognises this, for he acknowledges that affirmative action 'can be a necessary step towards transformation' (1993: 19), and argues that it 'is a site of struggle' (1993: 23), and must be located 'within (and not independent of) more comprehensive and transformative strategies of socio-economic restructuring and redress' (1993: 21).

Admissions: policy and practice

A commitment to social equity and diversity of the student body, and affirmative action as a strategy for achieving this, has implications for student recruitment, admissions and support – financial as well as academic, if access to higher education is not to be just formal but also substantive and 'epistemological'.

Moore correctly argues that there is great misunderstanding of the issues of 'eligibility' and 'admission' (2005). As she notes, 'the first step in the admissions process is determining the eligibility of applicants' (2005: 15); that is, the specified requirements that students must meet to be considered for admission to university. Admission, in contrast, has to do with the 'set of criteria the university will employ in making a decision on which students' will be admitted (2005:16) – such criteria can include academic results, school attended, geographic origins, race, gender, income levels, home language/s, civic involvement, special talents and abilities, nationality, hardships overcome and so on.

A restrictive admissions policy confines itself to or privileges academic accomplishments. In contexts where inclusion and exclusion, privilege and disadvantage, and domination and subordination, are structured along class, race, gender and other social lines, a restrictive admissions policy is very likely to reproduce historical and prevailing social inequalities. By contrast, a more open and extensive admissions policy has greater prospects of eroding and contributing to the elimination of existing social inequalities. Here, 'merit' is not defined solely in terms of, or reduced to, academic accomplishments; rather, a wider set of criteria are deliberately employed to establish merit. In as much as academic accomplishment must be highly valued and encouraged and mediocrity disdained, it is arguable whether there should be any automatic right to admission based purely on academic results, that is, unconditioned by constitutional or social imperatives, the vision and mission of a university, the needs of society, development objectives and the realisation of a particular kind of intellectual, learning and educational environment and process.

Equity, redress and admissions under democracy

As was noted, before 1994 higher education institutions were reserved for specific 'race' and ethnic groups. With the advent of democracy, discrimination on racial and other grounds was prohibited by the Constitution. However, the deracialisation of higher education institutions began before 1994, as part of a strategy of repressive reformism, through which the apartheid state sought to crush political opposition and resistance to white minority rule, while concomitantly attempting to create a black middle class that, it was hoped, could be co-opted and galvanised behind a reformist project.

Under democracy, the Higher Education Act (No. 101 of 1997) proclaimed the desirability of redressing 'past discrimination' and ensuring 'representivity and equal access', pursuing 'excellence', promoting 'the full realisation of the potential of every student', the 'tolerance of ideas' and the 'appreciation of diversity'. Section 37 of the Act dealt specifically with admissions policy. It stipulates that the governing body of a higher education institution 'determines the admission policy', the 'entrance requirements in respect of particular higher education programmes' and 'the number of students who may be admitted for a particular higher education programme and the manner of their selection' (sections 1, 4a and 4b). The governing body, however, 'must publish the admission policy and make it available on request'. Furthermore, the admission policy 'must provide appropriate measures for the redress of past inequalities and may not unfairly discriminate in any way' (section 3).

The White Paper proclaimed the need for higher education to be 'transformed to meet the challenges of a new non-racial, non-sexist and democratic society committed to equity, justice and a better life for all' (DoE 1997: 1.6). It also noted that 'there is an inequitable distribution of access and opportunity for students along lines of race, gender, class and geography', and the 'gross discrepancies in the participation rates of students from different population groups' (DoE 1997: 1.4). The vision set out is of a 'non-racial and non-sexist system of higher education that will promote equity of access and fair chances of success to all who are seeking to realise their potential through higher education, while eradicating all forms of unfair discrimination and advancing redress for past inequalities' (DoE 1997: 1.14).

As was noted earlier, the White Paper articulated 'equity and redress' as among its fundamental principles. Sensitive to history, there was an emphasis on the need to eradicate 'all existing forms of unjust differentiation'; looking to the future, there was stress on the need for 'measures of empowerment, including financial support to bring about equal opportunity for individuals and institutions' (DoE 1997: 1.18). It was also argued that 'ensuring equity of access must be complemented by a concern for equity of outcomes. Increased access must not lead to a "revolving door" syndrome for students, with high failure and drop-out rates' (DoE 1997: 2.29).

There was understanding that, 'in order to improve equity of outcomes, the higher education system is required to respond comprehensively to the articulation gap between learners' school attainment and the intellectual demands of higher education programmes' (DoE 1997: 2.32). It was thus suggested that 'systematic changes in higher education programmes (pedagogy, curriculum and the structure of degrees and diplomas)' might be needed. There was also a historical awareness that an

enabling environment must be created throughout the system to uproot deep-seated racist and sexist ideologies and practices that inflame relationships, inflict emotional scars and create barriers to successful participation in learning and campus life. Only a multi-faceted approach can provide a sound foundation of knowledge, concepts, academic, social and personal skills, and create the culture of respect, support and challenge on which self-confidence, real learning and enquiry can thrive. (DoE 1997: 2.32)

At the same time, it was recognised that 'academic development structures and programmes are needed at all higher education institutions' to facilitate effective learning and teaching (DoE 1997: 2.33).

The White Paper expressed the commitment to increasing 'the relative proportion of public funding used to support academically able but disadvantaged students' (DoE 1997: 2.26), and to providing funds for academic development programmes (DoE 1997: 2.24), although a call was also made to institutions to 'mobilise greater private resources' as well as to 'reallocate their operating grants internally' (DoE 1997: 2.27).

In accordance with the Constitution, the mechanism of quotas was not employed to achieve equity and redress. Nor were prescriptive targets or goals set for institutions. Rather, institutions were required 'to develop their own race and gender equity goals and plans for achieving them, using indicative targets for distributing publicly subsidised places rather than firm quotas' (DoE 1997: 2.28). Further, in congruence with the Higher Education Act, and on the basis of the 'principle of institutional autonomy', student admission was placed under the authority of higher education institutions. It was, however, emphasised that there was 'no moral basis for using the principle of institutional autonomy as a pretext for resisting democratic change' and that institutional autonomy was 'inextricably linked to the demands of public accountability' (DoE 1997: 1.24).

The White Paper's emphasis on transformation resulted, albeit unevenly and at different pace and to differing degrees, in institution-level changes to admissions policies, criteria, processes and practices. It must be noted, though, that, notwithstanding the Higher Education Act's injunction that institutions 'must publish the admission policy and make it available on request', many do not have an admissions policy – as opposed to admissions criteria and particular practices. Instead, in many instances the vision and mission statements of institutions set out commitments with respect to admissions.

Thus, Rhodes University's mission statement[8] states its intention 'to acknowledge and be sensitive to the problems created by the legacy of apartheid, to reject all forms of unfair discrimination and to ensure that appropriate corrective measures are employed to redress past imbalances'. The University of the Witwatersrand expresses in its mission statement its commitment to 'continue redressing historical injustices, thereby providing new and fulfilling opportunities for black students', while the University of Pretoria declares its commitment to being 'locally relevant' through its 'promotion of equity, access, equal opportunities, redress, transformation and diversity'. The University of KwaZulu-Natal has an incomplete and draft admissions policy, while its mission statement says that it will be 'demographically representative, redressing the disadvantages, inequities and imbalances of the past', and that the university will 'promote access to learning that will expand educational and employment opportunities for the historically disadvantaged, and support social transformation and redress'.

One institution that has an explicit admissions policy is the University of Cape Town (UCT). The policy states that UCT 'is committed to being flexible on access, active in redress and rigorous on success', and that its policy 'is framed within the values of the Constitution and the requirements of legislation'. It interprets these as 'an obligation to address the legacy of racial discrimination in schools and in the higher education system, and to build a diverse student profile that substantially reflects the demographics of South African society, while also reflecting the University's international profile'.

UCT argues 'that the more diverse the student body, with all students contributing their prior life experiences to the educational process, the better will be students' appreciation of the applicability of what they are learning and the better will be their preparation for work in South Africa after graduation'. The policy signals its awareness of 'the danger of perpetuating the use of race as a criterion for admission to higher education', but regards 'the categorization of applicants by race as a necessary transitional mechanism for giving effect to the requirements of redress and as the best initial broad basis to measure past inequalities and for redress of past discrimination'. It states that, 'in order to move beyond the use of race alone, we shall actively seek ways of differentiating between applicants on the basis of varying degrees of disadvantage flowing from social class and educational experience, or a combination of these'. Finally, UCT indicates that it will 'set overall enrolment and equity targets per programme' – such targets being inspirational targets, not quotas. All faculties will aim to admit specified minimum numbers of eligible black, coloured and Indian[9] students in accordance with these targets'.

A number of mechanisms have been used or developed to support the pursuit of equity and redress in higher education enrolments, again unevenly and to differing degrees at institutions. First, alternative admissions tests have been devised to complement the national final secondary schools examination to determine eligibility for access to institutions. Second, provision has been made for the recognition of prior learning to facilitate access for mature students, in particular. Third, mature-age exemption has been used in cases where students do not fully meet admission requirements. Finally, academic governing bodies have made use of the discretionary powers that they have long had to admit students to postgraduate studies on special grounds.

As a result of the ongoing deficiencies associated with schooling for, especially, historically disadvantaged social groups, considerable numbers of students are underprepared with respect to the cognitive competencies and academic skills that are required for optimal participation and performance in higher education. Moreover, many students are handicapped in that the language-medium of higher education institutions is not their mother tongue and often represents a second, or even third, language. Therefore, considerations related to the effective support of underprepared students to ensure equity of opportunity and outcomes have loomed large at many institutions.

Typically, academic development programmes have been created to address the underpreparedness of students and facilitate the development of the content knowledge and the academic skills and literacy and numeracy required for academic success. Over the years, the approaches of institutions to these development programmes have undergone changes. As Boughey notes, 'the Academic Development movement in South African higher education has gone through a number of theoretical and ideological shifts which have contributed to the complexity of the forms in which student support initiatives now manifest themselves at an institutional level' (Boughey 2005: 1). She identifies three phases, 'broadly termed 'academic support', 'academic development' and 'institutional development', which 'are not distinct from each other and are indicative more of dominant discursive formulations than actual periods of time' (Boughey 2005: 1).

A key characteristic of the 'academic support' approach 'was a deficit assumption about the students they served in the context of an assurance about the "rightness" of the practices which characterized the institutions to which they had been admitted' (Boughey 2005: 2). Support was an 'add-on' to the existing academic programme, which remained unreconstructed.

The 'academic development' model, especially in its more fully developed form, 'had a much more embracing understanding of the notion of support constructing it as occurring through the development of curriculum and appropriate teaching methodologies and, thus, through work in the mainstream' (Boughey 2005: 33). As opposed to the 'add-on' support model, this was an 'infusion' model of the development of students alongside the reconstruction of curriculum, and of learning and teaching strategies and techniques.

The current 'institutional development' model seeks to embed the enhancement of student learning 'across the curriculum' and to locate initiatives 'within a wider understanding of what it means to address student needs framed within the context of a concern for overall quality' (Boughey 2005: 36). Strategies here have included credit or non-credit bearing 'foundation' modules or courses that complement existing modules/courses, 'extended programmes' in which the academic programme is lengthened by up to a year to make space for additional foundation' modules/courses, and 'augmented courses' in which additional tuition is provided and more time is devoted to a course or the course is taken over a longer period (Boughey 2005). Of course, academic development programmes, whatever their form and content, require expertise and finances for both their and student success.

Earlier, the skewed and inequitable participation rate in higher education was noted, with African participation in 1993 being only 9% while that of whites was 70%. Also noted was that, of total student enrolment at 473 000 in 1993, black students constituted 52% of the student body (African students 40%) and white students 48%. Women students made up 43% of total enrolments.

As will be seen, there has been tardy progress in so far as an improvement in the participation rate of Africans in higher education is concerned. With respect to enrolments, however, a significant deracialisation of the student body occurred in the years between the advent of democracy in 1994, and 2007. By 2007, black students comprised 76% (578 433) of the total student body of 761 090; African students made up 62.6% (476 768) of students, and white students 23.7% (CHE 2009: 19). There was also commendable progress in terms of gender equity: women constituted 55.5% (422 535) of the total student body (CHE 2009: 23).

Continuing challenges

Notwithstanding some significant achievements in terms of enabling legislation, national and institutional policies and practices, state and institutional initiatives, and the greater enrolment of black and female South Africans in higher education, a number of key challenges continue to confront the state and higher education institutions.

- Despite the legislative requirement, few institutions have an admissions policy. Of course, 'policy' has a wide variety of meanings, and institutional practices often best represent actual policy. However, the absence of formal admissions policies hinders public scrutiny and critical analysis, and must leave open the question of whether institutions have clearly and rigorously thought through social equity and redress in the light of South Africa's history and inherited and contemporary social structure. At a minimum, an institutional admissions policy would need to reflect the engagement of the institution with the apartheid legacy, the current social structure, constitutional, legislative and other social imperatives, and the institution's interpretation of the concepts of social equity and redress. In addition, it would need to indicate – in the light of its particular history, its vision and mission, academic structure, eligibility and admissions criteria and current student body's social composition – how it proposes to pursue social equity and redress at the undergraduate and postgraduate levels, including through what specific strategies and mechanisms.

- Affirmative action as a strategy for enabling redress and advancing social equity continues to be the object of contestation. Unexceptionally, on the part of sections of the historically privileged and advantaged social classes and groups, charges including 'discrimination' and 'reverse racism' and claims of an inevitable erosion of 'quality' and 'standards' and perpetrating 'psychological damage' on the beneficiaries of affirmative action are levelled against the strategy[10] (Sikhosana 1993). However, those committed to social justice have also raised concerns about affirmative action primarily benefiting a growing black capitalist class and middle class and reinforcing class inequalities, the efficacy of the use of race and gender as proxies of advantage and disadvantage, and the possibility of race categories becoming ossified rather than eroded (Alexander 2007). The debates on affirmative action parallel others on reconciliation and social justice.

Affirmative action is undeniably contentious and, as Kapur and Crowley note, raises 'a number of complex questions' (2008: 59). These include the goals of affirmative action: are they 'redress for past injury to a group, compensation for ongoing disadvantage, or increased diversity in a learning environment?' Furthermore, should affirmative action 'be class-based, rather than identity-based? How are group rights balanced against individual rights?' (Kapur and Crowley 2008: 59). Given that disadvantage takes myriad forms 'how should an institution weigh different forms of disadvantage?' Finally, 'what criteria (or sunset clauses) should be used to phase out affirmative action?' (Kapur and Crowley 2008: 59–60).

There are other crucial issues regarding affirmative action. The question was earlier posed whether affirmative action can eliminate enduring class and socio-economic inequalities as opposed to 'race and gender-based inequalities' (Sikhosana 1993: 1). Mamdani raises yet another fundamental issue, when he asks whether a strategy that has its origins in the United States and sought 'to address the grievances of a racially oppressed minority' can deliver social justice for 'a racially oppressed majority'. As he argues, affirmative action could 'alter the racial composition' of student enrolments and still shut out the majority of students, with 'merit' now the key exclusionary mechanism. The danger, as he points out, is that affirmative action could 'obscure the very task that must be central to democratisation in a "new" South Africa, that of institutional transformation' (cited in Sikhosana 1993: 16).

• Although black student enrolments have increased since 1994, the gross participation rate of black, and especially African and coloured, South Africans continues to be considerably lower than for white South Africans (see Table 5.1).

It should be noted that in 2001 the National Plan for Higher Education estimated the gross participation rate to be 15% and set a target of 20% gross participation rate by 2011/16 (MoE 2001: 18). Clearly, there has been only minimal improvement in the overall gross participation rate, and severe inequities continue to exist in the participation rates of African and coloured South Africans, relative to white and Indian South Africans. Indeed, 'given that the participation is expressed as gross rates and includes appreciable numbers of mature students – well under 12% of the (African) and coloured 20 to 24-year age groups are participating in higher education [it] must be a cause of concern, for political, social and economic reasons, if the sector is not able to accommodate a higher and more equitable proportion' of those social groups that have been historically disadvantaged and under-represented in higher education (Scott et al. 2007: 11).

TABLE 5.1 Participation rates by 'race' (1993–2007)

'Race'	Participation rate (%)	
	1993	2007
African	9	12
Coloured	13	12
Indian	40	43
White	70	54
Overall	17	16

Source: CHE (2009: 19–20).

- Enrolments at a number of historically white institutions continue to reflect lower black representation than their demographic representation. Thus, even though there has been a significant deracialisation of these institutions, white students continue to be concentrated at the historically white institutions. Conversely, there has been little or no entry of white students into the historically black institutions, which means that they remain almost exclusively black.

  There is an important social class factor at play here. Students from the capitalist and middle classes tend to be concentrated at historically white institutions, while those from the working class and the rural poor are concentrated at historically black institutions. One reason for this is that under apartheid the higher education system was differentiated along lines of 'race' and ethnicity, resulting in the advantaging (educational, infrastructural, financial and geographical) of historically white institutions and the disadvantaging of historically black institutions. Despite initiatives to reshape the apartheid institutional landscape through mergers of institutions and other means, the historical patterns of advantage and disadvantage continue to condition the current capacities of historically black institutions to pursue excellence, and to provide high-quality learning experiences and equity of opportunity and outcomes. In short, if equity of opportunity and outcomes were previously strongly affected by race, they are now also conditioned by social class.

- The progress of both black, and especially African, and female students, while significant, masks inequities in their distribution across institutions, qualification levels and academic programmes. Large numbers of African students continue to be concentrated in distance education, and both African and female students continue to be under-represented in science, engineering and technology, and business and commerce programmes. Postgraduate enrolments across most fields are also low.

- Further, judging by dropout, undergraduate success, and graduation rates, a substantial improvement in equity of opportunity and outcomes for black students remains to be achieved. Contact undergraduate success rates should, according to the Department of Education (DoE), have been 80% (in 2006) 'if reasonable graduation rates are to be achieved' (2006a). Instead they ranged from 59% to 87%, with an average of 75%. White student success rates in 2005 were 85%, while African student success rates were 70%. The DoE's target for throughput rates is 'a minimum of 20% which would imply a final age cohort graduation rate of about 65%' (DoE 2006a). Instead, throughput rates for 2000 to 2004 were between

13% and 14%, and the age cohort graduation rate was 45% in 2004, with an overall dropout rate of 45% (DoE 2006a). A 2007 study noted that

> the major racial disparities in completion rates in undergraduate programmes, together with the particularly high attrition rates of black students across the board, have the effect of negating much of the growth in black access that has been achieved. Taking account of the black participation rate, the overall attrition rate of over 50% and the below-average black completion rates, it can be concluded that the sector is catering successfully for under 5% of the black (and coloured) age-group. (Scott et al. 2007: 19)

The conclusions are clear: 'this has central significance for development as well as social inclusion', and 'equity of outcomes is the overarching challenge' (Scott et al. 2007: 19). Clearly, if higher education institutions 'are to contribute to a more equitable South African society, then access and success must be improved for black (and particularly black working class) students who, by virtue of their previous experiences, have not been inducted into dominant ways of constructing knowledge'.[11]

There is, however, a further and important conclusion, namely that the underperformance of black students 'will not change spontaneously. Decisive action needs to be taken in key aspects of the educational process – and at key points of the educational "pipeline" – to facilitate positive change in outcomes'[12] (Scott et al. 2007: 20).

• One reason for the very high rate of dropouts among black students is almost certainly inadequate state funding in the forms of scholarships, bursaries and loans. Although the National Student Financial Aid Scheme (NSFAS), which operates on a means-test basis, has been successfully established and considerable funding has been allocated to effect redress for indigent black students, the overall amounts allocated have fallen far short of providing effective support for all eligible students in need. This highlights the reality of the interconnection of race and class – equity of access for black students from working class and impoverished rural social backgrounds will continue to be severely compromised, unless there is a greater commitment of public funding for financial aid to indigent students.

The colonial and apartheid legacy has meant that there is a strong coincidence between class and race, with black South Africans hailing from predominantly working class and rural poor social backgrounds and white South Africans having their social origins largely in the capitalist and middle class. There are, however, also white South Africans of working class and rural poor origin. If the goal is not only redress for historically disadvantaged social groups but social equity more generally, the needs of all who are of working class and rural poor origin must be addressed.

- However, the extent to which academically supportive cultures exist at all institutions is also a moot point. By 'supportive cultures' I mean those that cater for the varied learning needs of a diverse student body, through well-conceptualised, designed and implemented academic programmes and academic-development initiatives, and that include mechanisms to promote and assure quality higher learning. Scott et al. (2007) argue that 'systemic responses are essential for improving educational outcomes', and that

> necessary conditions for substantial improvement include: the reform of core curriculum frameworks; enhancing the status of teaching and building educational expertise…to enable the development and implementation of teaching approaches that will be effective in catering for student diversity; and clarifying and strengthening accountability for educational outcomes. (Scott et al. 2007: 73)

Until recently, equity of opportunity and outcomes has been constrained by the absence of state funding for academic development initiatives. While the provision of funds is welcome, the amounts, however, remain inadequate for enabling the changes and initiatives that are required to address underpreparedness (conceptual, knowledge, academic literacy and numeracy, linguistic, social) of, especially, indigent students.

Here, it is necessary to emphasise the continued underdeveloped institutional and particularly academic capabilities of historically black institutions. While they provide access to and admit students from rural poor and working class families, the inadequate state support for institutional redress compromises the ability of historically black institutions to ensure equity of opportunity and outcomes.

- Institutional cultures, especially at historically white institutions, could, in differing ways and to varying degrees, compromise equity of opportunity and outcomes. The specific histories of these institutions, lingering racist and sexist conduct, privileges associated with social class, English as the language of tuition and administration, the overwhelming predominance of white academics and administrators and male academics, the concomitant under-representation of black and women academics and role-models,[13] and limited respect for and appreciation of diversity and difference, could all combine to reproduce institutional cultures that are experienced by black, female, and working class and rural poor students as discomfiting, alienating, exclusionary and disempowering. This has possible negative consequences for equity of opportunity and outcome for these students. Even if equity of opportunity and outcome are not unduly compromised, the overall educational and social experience of such students may be diminished. The reproduction and limited erosion of class-based, racialised and gendered institutional cultures also obstruct the forging of greater social cohesion.

• Finally, the pace of social equity and redress in higher education continues to be severely constrained by conditions in South African schooling. Despite almost universal formal participation in schooling, South Africa's schools evince significant problems related to dropouts, retention, progression and successful completion. As has been noted, 'the simple reality is that enrolment is not the same as attendance and attendance does not imply learning' (Sayed 2007: 8). South African school students perform extremely poorly on a range of international assessment tests, in terms of which '65% of school leavers…are functionally illiterate' (Sayed 2007: 6).

There remains a powerful link between the social exclusion of disadvantaged social classes and groups, and equity of access, opportunity and outcomes and achievement in schooling. In 2007, 60% of African children in South Africa came from families that earned less than R800 a month; conversely 60% of white children were from families with an income of more than R6 000 per month. The consequences of this are manifest in differential school performance and achievement. Without appropriate and extensive interventions on the part of the state, significantly to improve the economic and social circumstances of millions of working class and rural poor (and primarily black) South Africans, the experiences of school dropouts, poor retention, restricted educational opportunities and poor outcomes will be principally borne by these social classes.

One measure of the formidable challenge is that, in 2007, 10% of some 7 000 secondary schools – independent schools and public schools previously reserved for white students – produced 60% of all university entrance passes. (Another 10% of mainly historically black schools produce a further 20% of all university entrance passes.)[14] Thus, in 2007, 80% of university entrance passes were generated by 20% of secondary schools, while the remaining 80% of secondary schools produced a paltry 20% of university entrance passes. It is clear that a fundamental challenge is to improve the quality of education in schools.

Conclusion

It is evident that, post-1994, there was a significant expansion in the enrolment of black and female South Africans in higher education, so that by 2010, 80% of students were black and 57% were women (DHET 2012: 37). Yet this development has been characterised by a number of paradoxes.

Even prior to 1994, the trajectory was one of increased enrolment of black and female students, under the impetus of the reformist objectives of the apartheid state. This trend continued after 1994, as part of the social goals of the new democratic state. At issue is whether the significant increase in enrolment of black and female students after 1994 has been specifically a consequence of measures related to advancing social equity and redress, including the strategy of affirmative action, or simply a concomitant of the prohibition of discrimination occasioned by new constitutional and higher education legislation.

A reading of the higher education White Paper makes clear that government cannot be faulted at a policy level in its grasp of the measures that are required to advance social equity and redress. Further, the introduction of a means-tested NSFAS, and funds devoted to supporting academic development initiatives, have been critical in promoting equity and redress for working class and rural poor students. This is true. Yet the inadequacy of funds devoted to NSFAS and academic development, and limited funding for institutional redress, have compromised attempts both to increase access and to expand equity of opportunity and outcomes for disadvantaged social classes and groups. In addition, opportunity and outcomes have been affected by institutional conditions and cultures. Overall, the motive force behind increased enrolment of black and female students was arguably a *combination* of the outlawing of discrimination and the active national and institutional measures of social equity and redress that have been formulated and implemented to varying degrees at individual institutions.

Moreover, although the enrolments of black and female students had increased, by 2007 the increase in the participation rate of African and coloured students was minimal, and the overall participation rate had declined. Measured in terms of participation rates, and given the intersection of race, class, gender and geography and schooling in South Africa, it is clear that a significant advance in social equity and redress for those of working class and rural poor social origins remains to be achieved.

Notes

1   I use the term 'transformation' since this is how government and a wide range of higher education actors describe the nature of change that is being attempted.

2   Unless otherwise specified, the term 'black' in this chapter refers to African, coloured and Indian South Africans.

3   The contemporary popular usage of the terms 'human resources' and 'human capital' is a most peculiar way of speaking about people, but not altogether surprising in a period characterised by the hegemony of the ideology of neo-liberalism.

4   Gross participation refers to the total enrolments in higher education as a proportion of the 20 to 24-year age group within the total population.

5   C Boughey, personal communication, 2008.

6   C Boughey, personal communication, 2008.

7   The words 'affirmative action' do not appear anywhere in the South African Constitution. However, Sachs contends that 'their spirit animates the whole document' (2006: x).

8   For the mission statements of the institutions: Rhodes University – www.ru.ac.za; University of the Witwatersrand – www.wits.ac.za; University of Pretoria – www.up.ac.za; University of KwaZulu-Natal – www.ukzn.ac.za; University of Cape Town – www.uct.ac.za.

9   Note that, while UCT uses the terms 'black', 'coloured' and 'Indian', others, including the state in its Employment Equity Act, use the terms 'African', 'coloured' and 'Indian', with the term 'black' being used to collectively denote 'Africans', 'coloureds' and Indians'.

10   It should be noted that white minority governments made effective use of affirmative action in tackling the problem of 'poor whites'. The 'civilised labour' policy of the 1920s and 1930s is one example (Sikhosana 1993: 13).

11   C Boughey (2008), personal communication.

12   'Such key points occur particularly at the interface between major phases of the system: between general education and FET, for example, as well as between FET and higher education, and, increasingly significantly, between undergraduate and postgraduate studies…[C]ontinuity in the system as a whole is necessary for improving graduate outcomes, without which meeting national developmental needs will continue to be an elusive goal' (Scott et al. 2007: 20).

13   While black South Africans made up 90% of the population, black academics constituted only 41.6% of the total academic staff of 42 446 in 2009, comprising between 12% and 90% of universities. Women academics comprised 28% to 52% of universities, and overall made up 44.2% of academics. Women tend to be concentrated at the lower levels of the academic hierarchy (HESA 2011: 2, 3).

14 Statistics presented at a Development Bank of Southern Africa think tank on education chaired by Dr Mamphela Ramphele. The author is a member of the think tank.

References

Alexander N (2007) 'Affirmative action and the perpetuation of racial identities in post-apartheid South Africa', *Transformation* 63: 92–108.

Badat S (1991) 'Reformist strategies in black tertiary education since 1976', in E Unterhalter, H Wolpe, T Botha, S Badat, T Dlamini and B Khotseng (eds) *Apartheid Education and Popular Struggle in South Africa*. Johannesburg: Ravan Press.

Badat S (1999) *Black Student Politics, Higher Education and Apartheid*. Pretoria: Human Sciences Research Council.

Bentley K, A Habib and S Morrow (2006) *Academic Freedom, Institutional Autonomy, and the Corporatised University in Contemporary South Africa*. Pretoria: Council on Higher Education.

Boughey C (2005) Lessons Learned from the Academic Development Movement in South African Higher Education and their Relevance for Student Support Initiatives in the FET College Sector. Unpublished report commissioned by the Human Sciences Research Council, Pretoria.

CHE (Council on Higher Education) (2004) *Higher Education in the First Decade of Democracy*. Pretoria.

CHE (2009) *Higher Education Monitor No. 8: The State of Higher Education in South Africa*. Pretoria.

DHET (Department of Higher Education and Training) (2012) *Green Paper for Post-school Education and Training*. Pretoria.

DoE (Department of Education) (1997) *Education White Paper 3: A Programme for the Transformation of Higher Education*. Pretoria.

DoE (2006a) 'Aspects of the higher education planning context. 17 July', document made available to the author by DoE, Pretoria.

DoE (2006b) *Education Statistics in South Africa at a Glance in 2005*. Pretoria.

Du Toit A (2000) 'Critic and citizen: The intellectual, transformation and academic freedom', *Pretexts: Literary and Cultural Studies* 9 (1): 91–104.

Graham G (2005) *The Institution of Intellectual Values: Realism and Idealism in Higher Education*. Exeter: Imprint Academic.

HESA (Higher Education South Africa) (2011) *Proposal for a National Programme to Develop the Next Generation of Academics for South African Higher Education*. Pretoria.

Jonathan R (2006) *Academic Freedom, Institutional Autonomy and Public Accountability in Higher Education: A Framework for Analysis of the 'State-sector' Relationship in a Democratic South Africa*. Pretoria: CHE.

Kapur D and M Crowley (2008) *Beyond the ABCs: Higher Education and Developing Countries*. Working Paper No. 139, February, Center for Global Development, Washington, DC.

Kennedy-Dubourdieu E (2006) *Race and Inequality: World Perspectives on Affirmative Action*. Hampshire: Ashgate.

Malherbe EG (1977) *Education in South Africa (Volume 2): 1923–1975*. Johannesburg: Juta and Co.

Ministry in the Office of the President (1994) *White Paper on Reconstruction and Development*, 23 November 1994, Government Gazette, Vol. 353, No. 16085. Cape Town: Office of the President.

MoE (Ministry of Education) (2001) *National Plan for Higher Education*. Pretoria: MoE.

Moore J (2005) *Race and College Admissions: A Case For Affirmative Action*. Jefferson, NC: McFarland & Company.

Morrow W (1993) 'Epistemological access in the university', *AD Issues* 1 (1). Belville: Academic Development Programme, University of the Western Cape.

Morrow W (1997) *'Varieties of Educational Tragedy'*. Paper presented at the Harold Wolpe Memorial Conference, University of the Western Cape, April 1997.

Nussbaum M (2006) *Education for Democratic Citizenship*. Institute of Social Studies Public Lecture Series 2006, No. 1, Institute of Social Studies, The Hague.

Sachs A (2006) 'Foreword', in E Kennedy-Dubourdieu (2006) *Race and Inequality: World Perspectives on Affirmative Action*. Hampshire: Ashgate.

Sayed Y (2007) Education and Poverty Reduction/Eradication: Omissions, Fashions and Promises. Unpublished mimeo.

Scott I, N Yeld and J Hendry (2007) A case for improving teaching and learning in South African higher education, *Higher Education Monitor No. 6*. Pretoria: CHE.

Sikhosana M (1993) *Affirmative Action: Its Possibilities and Limitations*. EPU Working Paper No. 1, May, Education Policy Unit, University of Natal.

Task Force on Higher Education and Society (2000) *Higher Education in Developing Countries: Peril and Promise*. Washington, DC: World Bank.

Wright Mills C (1959) *The Sociological Imagination*. London: Oxford University Press.

PART III: INCLUSION AND EXCLUSION

Chapter 6

The struggle, global challenges and international strategies in the University of Fort Hare's music department

Bernhard Bleibinger

GLOBALISATION HAS NOT REDUCED TRAVEL DISTANCES, but it has opened innumerable possibilities for cultural contact through the media, international exchange programmes, migration and multinational companies. Tertiary institutions worldwide are exposed to global challenges, such as international rankings systems and the international job market. Academics have to be flexible and mobile in furthering their careers, as they may never find employment in their home countries and may have to seek employment abroad. International networks are, thus, indispensable for the career development of individuals in a world that is increasingly 'pluricultural'.[1] In this context, given its history and its rural setting, the University of Fort Hare presents a unique case.

The university of Fort Hare is located in South Africa's Eastern Cape Province. Its main campus is in the small town of Alice, and it has two other campuses, one in Bisho and one in East London. The Music Department is based in Alice and – since 2012 – in the Miriam Makeba House of Performing Arts in East London. Founded in the 1970s by Georg Gruber,[2] a music professor who had previously taught at Rhodes University in Grahamstown, the University of Fort Hare's music department had a promising start, but initially it was not really open to global participation. Indeed, its political circumstances (including being located in one of the apartheid state's bantustans, and the academic boycott by many international academics that took place during the anti-apartheid struggles of the 1970s and 1980s), meant that the campus was relatively isolated.

In the late 1990s, after the demise of apartheid, Dave Dargie introduced a new African syllabus, and shifted the focus of the department away from

'Western' and towards 'South African' music. This brought a sense of balance to the curriculum and increased the relevance of the department to the life of the local community. But, even though the country's political struggle against apartheid was over, the university's struggle for survival has continued. A high percentage of students at the university come from rural areas, and are both socially and economically disadvantaged. In addition, because of its history, the Alice campus attracts predominantly black students and, in a certain sense, it occupies a world of its own, which, when compared with other universities, might appear a bit disconnected. This is unhelpful in an academic world based on international contacts and pluriculturality.

Since 2008, the university has officially stated that it aims to become 'non-racial', more academically rigorous, and to extend its networks and links with international universities. In this chapter, after sketching some background about the university and the music department, I outline three strategies employed by the department to achieve these goals, namely: (i) developing new degree programmes, based on national and international standards, to help us attract new students and obtain higher budget allocations; (ii) establishing links with local schools and communities, in an effort to raise intake standards and improve the preparedness of students to cope with university study; and (iii) enhancing our links with international universities via student exchanges and participating in international conferences, etc., to help prepare our students for the global job market.

The struggle, old and new

The term 'struggle' has a rather specific meaning at the University of Fort Hare, not only because the university is built on one of the battlefields of the frontier war of 1850 and 1851 – one could almost say it is standing on a graveyard – but also because many important and iconic leaders of the liberation movement, including Oliver Tambo and Nelson Mandela, studied here. Through these leaders, the university itself became a sort of symbol of anti-colonial and anti-apartheid struggle. Founded in 1916 as the South African Native College, it was renamed the University College of Fort Hare in the 1950s, and the University of Fort Hare at the beginning of the 1970s. In the 1980s, and in the context of the apartheid state's bantustan policy, the institution was sometimes referred to pejoratively as a 'bush college'. In fact, Fort Hare is an almost mythical place; buildings and roads on the Alice campus are named after anti-apartheid activists, making it seem like a vast memorial. The history of the struggle seems to be everywhere, and the institution holds a special place in the hearts of intellectuals all over Africa.

However, new hi*stories* of struggle are now being lived by some of the younger students who tend to feel lost in the realities of modern global networks where intense competition, innovation and efficiency seem to be the driving forces of daily life. For some of these students, the old struggle continues in a new form. Even though apartheid has been abolished and the new South Africa is a democratic country trying to live up to the vision of being a rainbow nation, many students struggle to obtain access, firstly to a university education, and secondly to the national and international networks that might offer them job opportunities in the future.

The real struggle, as Abdullah Ibrahim explained during a visit to the university's music department in March 2008, is (as I understood him) a mental one.[3] Ibrahim seemed to be referring to a type of struggle related to the circumstances and challenges of modern life. He argued that these challenges can be overcome only through the (above all mental) liberation of the individual, a state that can only be successfully attained through the acquisition of knowledge and self-knowledge. And, to acquire this knowledge, individuals must have or develop a sense of discipline and responsibility. With reference to the students at the University of Fort Hare, the ongoing challenges relate to issues such as their economic situations, the high unemployment levels among their family members, the lack of quality schooling in the areas they live in, and diseases such as HIV and AIDS.

HIV infection rates are high in the Eastern Cape, and were estimated at 29% in 2007,[4] while prevalence levels in the 15 to 49-year age group seem to have increased in the Eastern Cape between 2002 and 2008.[5] According to the South African Institute of Race Relations (SAIRR), the total unemployment rate in South Africa (using the expanded definition) in 2007 was 35.8%. This reflected a tiny improvement on the 2006 unemployment rate of 36.8% (SAIRR 2008). Unemployment in the Eastern Cape Province in 2007 was the third highest in the country (after Limpopo and the North West Province) at 42.9%. In 2006, the Eastern Cape's unemployment rate was 36.9% and, in 2005 it was 43.6% (SAIRR 2008). According to the *Amathole District Municipality Growth and Development Summit Socio-Economic Profile 2007*, the Eastern Cape's unemployment rate was as high as 53.5% in 2005 and 65.2% of households survived on an income of less than R1 500 a month (Amathole District Municipality 2008: 29).[6]

By 2012, the unemployment rate in the Eastern Cape seemed to be declining slightly. Using the narrow definition of unemployment, the rate was estimated at 28.3% in the first quarter of 2012 and 28.6% for the second quarter 2012 (Stats SA 2012: vix and 7). Thus, one might talk of a slight improvement but, according to an economic survey of South Africa carried out in July 2010 and published by the Organisation for Economic Co-operation and Development (OECD), black youth remain particularly badly affected by unemployment:

South Africa has an extreme and persistent low employment problem, which interacts with other economic and social problems such as inadequate education, poor health outcomes and crime. While the unemployment rate fell steadily from 2002 through 2007, helped by the strong cyclical upswing, it never fell below 20% and by the first quarter of 2010 was back above 25%, near the levels of 2004. In addition to high open unemployment, South Africa's very low labour force participation rate in part reflects a large number of discouraged job-seekers, so that on a broader measure, including such individuals, the unemployment rate is above 30%. As in other countries, vulnerable groups are most affected by unemployment, and in South Africa the problem is most extreme for black youth, for whom the unemployment rate exceeds 50%. (Barnard and Lysenko 2010: 9)

A high percentage of the University of Fort Hare's students are drawn from this socio-economically disadvantaged region, and this may partly explain why, between 1991 and 2004, only 12% of them obtained their BA degrees in the minimum time. Another 37% of students finished their studies after two additional years of study, and 42% after three additional years (University of Fort Hare 2008: 20, 23).

Schooling in the Eastern Cape, often hits the news. Headlines such as, 'Chaos! Schools disaster. Damning report: Education on brink of utter collapse', which appeared in the *Weekend Post* on 2 October 2010, were common when school teachers went on strike for over a month. According to the *Weekend Post,* 80% of the schools involved were dysfunctional and 80% of the teachers were either underqualified or not qualified at all (Stander 2010a; see also Solomon 2010). Many schools in the region don't have the facilities necessary for adequate teaching, and the Eastern Cape and Limpopo education departments 'produced matric results that were among the country's worst' in 2010 (Mokone and Davids 2010). The problem of 'ghost schools' even occurred (Stander 2010b).[7] In 2012, Jonathan Jansen, the vice-chancellor of the University of the Free State and president of SAIRR, argued that President Jacob Zuma must admit that South Africa's education system is in crisis. Jansen also noted that taking population growth into account, proportionally fewer pupils were actually finishing school and the number of pupils writing matriculation exams had decreased since 2008 (Kimberly and De Jager 2012).

Students who wish to study music face an additional handicap: music is rarely offered as a subject in secondary schools in the Eastern Cape.[8] Only a few schools in the area (Bulelani High School near Queenstown is one example) offer music as a subject. While the best of our students tend to come from such schools, among the students accepted by the music department in 2006, quite a number could hardly speak English, had no musical knowledge, and little understanding of what the study of music entails. Not surprisingly, a percentage of our intake expressed frustration after their first encounters with music theory and after their first few practical music lessons.

Admittedly, problems such as unemployment and poor schooling will not be solved by universities alone, but tertiary institutions do have to cope with their consequences. In other words, universities must respond to their students' lack of schooling and poor socio-economic backgrounds as well as try to provide an education that meets (or comes close to meeting) international standards and enhances the employability of students in both the national and international job markets.

New challenges

The University of Fort Hare aims to convert itself into an institution of international standing before 2016.[9] Probably the most challenging obstacles it faces in this regard are mentioned in the institution's mission statement:

The mission of the University is to provide high quality education of international standard contributing to the advancement of knowledge that is socially and ethically relevant, and applying that knowledge to the scientific, technological and socio-economic development of our nation and the wider world. (University of Fort Hare 2008: 20)

In other words, the university is tending towards modernisation through academisation and internationalisation; it intends to gain knowledge and apply it in society. 'Scientific, technological and socio-economic development' clearly refers to the sciences and the economic growth they are believed to generate. University departments related to the sciences and technologies have been ordered by the government to expand. Much of our institution's funding goes to these departments and their intake limits are significantly higher. This leaves little space for holistically educated human beings. Indeed, the humanities appear a bit disadvantaged by this mission, in which individuals are less relevant than the development of the nation and the wider world.

Trends in higher education, as outlined by Deane Neubauer and Victor Ordoñez (2008: 53) indicate that the University of Fort Hare's goals are in accordance with global developments:

Inevitably, the globalized world involves the rapid forming, reforming and un-forming of knowledge societies. With knowledge as the dominant currency of future growth and development, universities have little choice but to recognize their ever-changing roles as creators, transmitters and preservers of knowledge at the service of society as a whole.

Thus, as Neubauer and Ordoñez explain: 'The knowledge society is a society based entirely on lifelong learning' (2008: 54) and universities have to engage with this reality. But, beyond their 'function of catering to market-driven demands for professional updating' (2008: 54), universities must also meaningfully contribute to the development of societies. Neubauer and Ordoñez do mention the importance of indigenous knowledge in the 'field of the preservation and enhancement of cultural and national identities and heritages' (2008: 52), yet their primary focus is on knowledge. Skills, attitudes and personalities come a bit short in the approach they propose. 'Knowledge is the currency of future growth', they argue.

However, this kind of knowledge, when linked primarily with economic 'growth', may well be too one sided. Most 'societies' and 'nations' are polyethnic. In the globalising world, with its ever-widening networks, cultural knowledge provides another crucial kind of 'currency'. Cultural knowledge improves and strengthens our ability to understand others, their ways of thinking and their self-perceptions. It also helps one locate one's own position on the map, and thus it has the potential to facilitate interaction across ethnic borders. Music is in a privileged position here, for it deals not only with knowledge, but also with skills and interaction. In other words, music is able to connect the local with the global.

In the next section, I discuss strategies adopted by the music department at the University of Fort Hare since 1995, in its attempt to address this challenge.

Strategies adopted by the music department, 1995 to 2012

As mentioned earlier, the introduction of an African music syllabus by Dave Dargie in 1995 was a response to the end of the political struggle against apartheid.[10] Through this syllabus, African music became an integral part of the courses offered by the department, and the culture of the formerly politically oppressed ethnic groups began to be rehabilitated and recognised by both staff and students.[11] However, the new syllabus was not simply a symbolic step towards liberation. There were practical considerations too. African music is easier for the students to master, because many of them absorb a lot of knowledge through the exposure they have to this music throughout their childhood. It is interesting and affirming for them to experience this music as a recognised university-level subject, being taught in an appropriate way – that is, in a *concretely African* manner by playing and repeating pieces of music (Bleibinger 2008a, 2008b; Dargie 1988, 1996;).[12] Our courses were carefully shaped to build on the students' existing knowledge, and this made obtaining degrees more achievable. Initially, students' financial problems were partly addressed through donations that Dargie was able to organise via individuals and parishes in Germany, such as St Stephan's Parish in Munich.

These solutions were effective in the late 1990s, but struggles define themselves through the circumstances in which they are embedded, and circumstances have since changed. As noted, South Africa's transition – particularly with reference to its education system – is far from over. On the one hand, the universities are expected to meet global standards and prepare their students to participate in an increasingly globalised world after they complete their studies. On the other hand, as in the case of Fort Hare university, the majority of students come from rural areas, and tend to be unaware of what it means to live in a global community. The struggle now is partly a result of the tension that occurs when tradition is seen as a counterpoint to innovation. In this situation, polarising positions ('us' versus 'them') tend to be constructed. In fact, tradition and innovation are not contradictory at all. As illustrated in the three development strategies adopted by the music department and outlined below, innovation can take place within existing traditions or even establish new traditions.

New staff

In 2007, the music department had four 'active' teachers (three full-time, one part-time). As a first strategy to meet new national and global challenges, and to provide sufficient and high-quality teaching, three more part-time lecturers were appointed in 2008 for choral studies, singing, piano and music theory. Our aim was to improve choral singing among our students and to improve academic standards. From then onwards, all modules were taught more intensely and solo lessons for singers were included. As a result of the new teachers, we not only obtained excellent singers, but the university choir won several awards,[13] and one of our students won the 2011 Grahamstown Music Competition. The engagement of the part-time lecturers meant that our courses became more oriented towards practice. For example, students are encouraged to participate in choral adjudication,[14] and these opportunities are highly appreciated by students.

New degree programmes
The music department's role within the university had long been limited by the fact that it was able to offer students only a plain Bachelor of Arts (BA) degree. The music department forms part of the social sciences and humanities faculty and, like other departments in the faculty, the department is allocated an annual intake limit for first-year students by faculty management.[15] At the same time, we often had to accept students who had been unable to secure a space in other faculties and we were given no say in the enrolment process. In other words, the majority of the students enrolled through the faculty's regular application and registration processes, which meant that no musical requirements and no auditions were expected of them. And, in exceptional cases only, were we able to take any steps to get students accepted who met the academic intake requirements and had some musical background. In some cases, this meant that students who specifically wished to study music were excluded.

To address this situation, we began developing new degrees, namely, the BA in Music, for the Alice campus, and a BMus degree with specialisations in performance, musicology and ethnomusicology for the East London campus.[16] The BA in Music and the BMus degrees were both accredited by the South African Council of Higher Education's Higher Education Quality Committee in 2011 and were implemented from 2012. Both of these degree programmes aim to improve the knowledge and performance standards as well as the international connectedness and the employability of our students. We also applied for and received funding from the National Arts Council to cover the fees of students in need, thus improving the financial situation of our students.[17]

The development of the new degree programmes occurred partly in response to the strategic considerations mentioned, but we also consulted with our own staff and students and engaged with teachers at secondary schools. Both groups informed us that there was need for practice-oriented studies and programmes that are more centred in music. In October 2009, after we had developed our first outline of the new BMus degree, we asked our students for their opinions. We received some comments orally and two written submissions. The written submissions reflected the opinion of several students for, as is common at this university, students talk about departmental issues and one of them writes down the outcome of their discussions. One submission proposed that courses suited to the needs of the music industry, including music marketing and management be developed, and requested that classes in Western instruments be offered to establish more 'balance'.[18] Thus, to a certain extent, the students addressed global issues. Some former students who had gone on to study to become teachers indicated that it would be useful for us to re-introduce piano and recorder as instruments as these are useful for teaching music in secondary schools. They also recommended that the theory components relating to piano and secondary instruments should be strengthened.[19] Overall, our attempts to improve standards were perceived positively and we were told that we should aim even higher.

The BMus programme has a stream for performers (focused on solo voice and instruments), and one for future academics and teachers (focused on musicology and ethnomusicology).[20] Originally, we considered including music education as well, but were told by a member of the Teaching and Learning Centre that this might lead to complications with the education faculty.

The music department extended beyond the confines of the Alice campus in 2012, when we began operating from the Miriam Makeba Centre for Performing Arts in East London as well. First-year students began enrolling in the BMus programme from May 2012. Strategic considerations and global developments mean that we encourage our students to specialise early in order to make them competitive on the national and (even global) market. In approving the degree, the Council on Higher Education stipulated that we have to ensure that our students can read and write music. Thus, for the first time, we *have* to be involved in the intake process and we therefore introduced – as in European conservatories or *Musikhochschulen* – auditions and entrance requirements. But, being mindful of the circumstances of our students, we aim to include, rather than exclude, students from learning opportunities, and have thus ensured that entry requirements take the country's educational situation into consideration. As soon as the BMus is fully functional and viable, we will continue to develop new streams, including music production, as well as courses in marketing and management related to the music industry.

Addressing intake standards and extending community outreach

The music department is in touch with people in rural villages in the Eastern Cape, and we support various schools by offering music training for possible future students. For example, our lecturers give recorder lessons, form marimba bands and give workshops to HIV-related community projects.[21] Concerts and recitals, to which we invite school pupils, also form part of our community outreach programme.[22]

We also got involved when a local school, which has the potential to become a feeder school for the music department, decided to develop a fully accredited music programme. The proposed programme is pitched at Levels 2 and 3 of South Africa's National Qualifications Framework, and draws on materials used in our first year. Students from this school should, thus, be equipped with sufficient musical knowledge to embark on music studies at tertiary level, if they choose to do so. If extended to other schools and colleges in future, this project has the potential to create jobs, raise the standards and produce school leavers who are better prepared for university study.

Community outreach is also an integral part of the Indigenous Music and Oral History Project at the University of Fort Hare. The project is led by the music department and has an academic component. The project involves collecting indigenous music through field research. We then preserve and promote the use of collected indigenous music knowledge in classes, workshops and concerts. For example, the Ngqoko Cultural Group were invited by the department to make recordings and give a concert. Since then, members of the group have assisted us as interpreters and consultants. Thus, its original bearers bring indigenous knowledge to us and we then use the material in classes on campus or during workshops held in communities, and, in this way, we take indigenous culture and knowledge back to communities. 'Outreach', as ethnomusicologists would call it in the classical sense, then becomes 'inreach'.[23]

International exchanges

Indigenous musicial knowledge has also been spread through publications and lectures given in Munich and Barcelona.[24] Visiting lecturers and researchers are encouraged to give lectures – preferably on topics related to African music.[25] However, these lectures are only the beginning of an internationalisation process, which we plan to intensify. Our postgraduate students already participate almost regularly in national and international conferences and colloquiums, and in March 2009 a group of our students performed in a musical programme in Munich and Kempten in Germany. Our primary aim is to establish a student-exchange programme. An agreement between Fort Hare and the Ludwig-Maximilians University (LMU) in Munich was signed at faculty level in March 2008 and two other bridges between ourselves and Europe and the USA are under discussion. In 2012 the first two exchange students from the LMU visited our department for a semester.

To sum up

As reflected in its mission statement, the University of Fort Hare aims to contribute to South Africa's intellectual, social and economic growth. However, the attitude of students, their socio-economic background and the financial situation of the university demands a unique approach to this project – especially if the institution wants to include, rather than exclude, students from the surrounding communities.

As discussed, the music department has developed a specialisation in music within the existing BA degree programme and established a new BMus degree; it has established direct links with local communities through teaching in schools and offering workshops to NGOs; it was also involved in the development of an accredited music programme for a potential feeder school. Through these initiatives, the department aims to improve student preparedness and access to music studies, as well as to offer courses of a standard that enhances the international employability of graduates.

Music occupies a special space in the nexus between global and local; it deals with skills and blurs boundaries. It has the potential to bring people from different ethnic backgrounds into contact and thus contribute to the cultural development of individuals in a global community.

As explained, we try to give students real options. However, the often-desperate socio-economic backgrounds of students and the poor state of education in the Eastern Cape have the potential to hamper real progress. The former problem can be partly solved through sourcing additional funding. Unfortunately, the latter problem is largely outside of our control, and will not be solved until students, parents and teachers develop a stronger sense of the value of education and of their own responsibilities in this regard. Without this, many South African children will have few real opportunities. Our new degrees and international linkages offer students a doorway to a wider world; it is the students who must decide whether or not to pass through.

Notes

1　To avoid any ideological implications I – like my colleague Josep Martí – use the term 'pluricultural' instead of 'multicultural'.

2　Gruber dedicated a book on notation to the music department (see Gruber 1974). The history of the department is briefly described in Bleibinger (2008b). For further background on the general situation of music and musicology in South Africa until the 1980s, see Paxinos (1986).

3   Ibrahim lived not far from my hometown in Germany while he was in exile. I discovered this during a conversation with him on 4 March 2008 when I expressed surprise at his detailed knowledge of the Chiemgau area, and he then explained that he had lived in Aschau for some years.

4   See, for instance, data from Dr Norma Van Niekerk, cited in Bleibinger (2008a: 42).

5   With reference to the HIV prevalence in 2008, there is some uncertainty. The decline of HIV prevalence in South Africa for 2008 was questioned because the use of anti-retroviral therapies, and the longer lifespan connected with these, seems to have led to an increase in the number of HIV-positive people. Thus, Rehle and Shisana (2009: 634, Table 1) indicated an increase in the HIV prevalence in the Eastern Cape, in the 15 to 49-year age group, but see also Dorrington (2009a, 2009b).

6   R1 500 was equal to approximately US$210, in 2007.

7   I experienced the disaster of rural education in the Eastern Cape, when some colleagues and I visited schools during a fieldtrip around Hobeni in the Transkei area, in 2008. At one school, facilities were in bad shape, yet the teachers were motivated, while another brand new school was closed, because the teachers had 'gone to collect their salaries' that day. We were told by a chief in one of the villages that children often miss school because they 'prefer to take care of the cattle', following the 'tradition of their fathers'. Thus, even if facilities and teachers are provided, children will have few real opportunities until parents and teachers take responsibility for ensuring that children receive the best education possible.

8   In fact, in many rural and urban areas, music is taught only superficially as part of a subject called 'Arts and Culture'. In some urban settings, however, some of the better-resourced schools have their own bands, choirs and even stage opera and other musical productions. Students from these schools generally experience a higher standard of education and are better prepared for music studies at university level. Unfortunately, these elite schools are not accessible to all – competition for places means that such schools tend to accept only the better performing students, and an inability to afford the school fees excludes the majority of others.

9   In meetings concerning the academic restructuring process that will be ongoing until 2016, one topic has been standards. Yet published output is seen as almost more important, as this generates income for the institution – each academic staff member at the university is expected to have at least 1.25 articles published in accredited journals each year.

10 Literature on Xhosa music was rare in the mid-1990s and Dargie had to research and write all the material for his lectures. See, for instance, Dargie (1988, 1993, and 1995).

11 For additional information on Dargie's work, see Hawn (2002).

12 In his (1996) article, 'African methods of music education: Some reflections' Dargie describes his own negative experiences of learning piano in a Western way, and explains that he had to learn how people teach each other indigenous music skills in the villages and how he later applied these methods while teaching at Fort Hare university. We now use several ways of teaching and we try to encourage students to participate, as much as possible. In some honours courses, for example, the student-teacher role is partially blurred in musical-instrument-making workshops, where the students contribute knowledge learned in villages. The workshops are highly successful and popular with students.

13 Some of our students play a leading role in this choir and it is, to a great extent, their work that led to the awards.

14 As was done in 2009 by Mr Mkululi Milisi; the students appreciated this practical extra work very much, as their expertise as music students was acknowledged.

15 The social sciences and humanities faculty consists of two schools, namely the School of Social Sciences and the School of Humanities. The official intake limit in 2008, 2009 and 2010 was forty students per year for the whole School of Humanities (that is, students accepted by the departments of music, philosophy, history, African languages, English, etc.). Since 2010, the intake limits allocated to all departments in this school have been decreasing, leading to an unviable staff-student ratio. Some departments were under threat of being closed and were told that one way out of this would be to introduce a new degree, in addition to the general BA offered by the School of Humanities.

16 Further specialisations were under discussion as this chapter was being written (in late 2012).

17 I want to express my sincere thanks to the National Arts Council, especially Lindi Ngcobo. Many students would not have been able to study without financial support from this institution.

18 Comments on the proposed BMus degree, 6 October 2009 (copy in my possession).

19 African music remains a central part of our syllabus. The reintroduction of piano and – to a certain extent – recorder simply means that we again teach instruments were on the syllabus, but that had been neglected for some years. Thus, both 'local' and 'global' music are taught in a more holistic way.

20 Both streams contain compulsory African components.

21 I have run drum-making workshops with NGOs such as the HIV Hope Project in Hogsback. Members of the project subsequently made their own drums and sold them, partly to finance their anti-retroviral medication and food.

22 Recitals are organised by lecturers who have set up or lead ensembles, such as our piano teacher, Mariel Ilusorio from Grahamstown, and our voice teacher, Gwyneth Lloyd from Hogsback.

23 The term 'inreach' is used in applied ethnomusicology; for more background information see, for instance, Pettan (2008) and Sheehy (1992).

24 Dargie gave guest lectures in Munich and I have given lectures in Barcelona. But it is important to note that the music department's research is closely linked to its relationships with the local communities. Thus, while Ordorika (2008: 15) laments the general state of research at universities as follows: 'Research productivity is fundamental in establishing a university as a prominent institution at international and local levels. The networking and global interacting potential of institutions is strengthened if they adhere to the dominant productivity model. They therefore constantly reproduce it, purposefully or not. Their national prominence and influence on public policy have also become increasingly dependent on their research productivity. This often hampers the institution's ability to commit to local problems and constituencies'; the music department at the University of Fort Hare is in little danger of losing its contacts with, or commitment to, local communities.

25 For example, in March and April 2009, Nepomuk Nitschke from Germany visited the department and gave lectures on tonic sol-fa and his research in Cameroon, and in September 2010, Dr Joseph Matare from Switzerland gave two lectures on improvisation and African-drum notation.

References

Amathole District Municipality (2008) *Amathole District Municipality Growth and Development Summit Socio-Economic Profile 2007*. HTML version available online.

Barnard G and T Lysenko (2010) *OECD Economic Surveys, South Africa, July 2010: Overview*. Available online.

Bleibinger B (2008a) 'La oralidad, la conservación de tradiciones y la batalla contra el SIDA: Observaciones y orientaciones en el Departamento de Música de la Universidad de Fort Hare, Sudáfrica', *Oráfrica* 4: 29–48.

Bleibinger B (2008b) 'Rural backgrounds and academic strategies: Higher education, the Music Department and the Indigenous Music and Oral History Project at the University of Fort Hare', *Proceedings of the Fourth International Barcelona Conference on Higher Education: Vol. 4, Higher Education, Arts and Creativity*. Barcelona: GUNI.

Bleibinger B (2010) 'Solving conflicts: Applied ethnomusicology at the music department of the University of Fort Hare, South Africa, in the context of IMOHP', in K Harrison, E Mckinlay and S Pettan (eds) *Applied Ethnomusicology: Historical and Contemporary Approaches*. Newcastle: Cambridge Scholars.

Dargie D (1988) *Xhosa Music, its Techniques and Instruments: With a Collection of Songs.* Cape Town: David Philip.

Dargie D (1993) Thembu Xhosa *umngqokolo* overtone singing: The use of the human voice as a type of 'musical bow', paper presented at the conference of the International Council for Traditional Music, Berlin. (Available from Dave Dargie as booklet with cassette titled 'Umngqokolo'.)

Dargie D (1995) *Make and Play Your Own Musical Bow: A First Guide to Making and Playing the* Umqangi *Mouth Bow and the* Uhadi *Calabash Bow of the Xhosa of South Africa, the People of Nelson Mandela.* Hogsback and Munich: Self published.

Dargie D (1996) 'African methods of music education: Some reflections', *African Music* 7 (3): 30–43.

Dorrington R (2009a) 'Does the 2008 HSRC survey indicate a turning tide of HIV prevalence in children, teenagers and the youth?' *South African Medical Journal* 99 (9): 631–633.

Dorrington R (2009b) 'Professor Dorrington's response', *South African Medical Journal* 99 (9): 636–637.

Gruber G (1974) *From Tonic Solfa to Staff Notation: A Manual for African Composers, Music Teachers and Choir-masters.* Cape Town: Nasou.

Hawn M (2002) *Gather into One: Praying and Singing Globally.* Michigan and Cambridge: William B Eardmans.

Kimberley M and S De Jager (2012) 'Zuma must admit crisis', *The Herald* (Port Elizabeth), 16 October 2012: 1–2.

Mokone T and N Davids (2010) 'South Africa: R 44bn disappears', *Times Live,* 13 October 2010. Available online.

Neubauer D and V Ordoñez (2008) 'The new role of globalized education in a globalized world', in Global University Network for Innovation, *Higher Education in the World 3: Higher Education, New Challenges and Emerging Roles for Human and Social Development.* New York: Palgrave Macmillan.

Ordorika I (2008) 'Contemporary challenges for public research universities', in Global University Network for Innovation, *Higher Education in the World 3: Higher Education, New Challenges and Emerging Roles for Human and Social Development.* New York: Palgrave Macmillan.

Paxinos S (1986) 'Musicology in South Africa', *Acta Musicologica* 58 (1): 9–24.

Pettan S (2008) 'Applied ethnomusicology and empowerment strategies: Views from across the Atlantic', *Muzikološki Zbornik/Musicological Annual* 44 (1): 85–99.

Rehle T and Shisana O (2009) 'National population-based HIV surveys: The method of choice for measuring the HIV epidemic', *South African Medical Journal* 99 (9): 633–636.

SAIRR (South African Institute for Race Relations) (2008) 'Unemployment still high across all provinces', press release, 24 April 2008.

Sheehy D (1992) 'A few notions about philosophy and strategy in applied ethnomusicology', *Ethnomusicology* 36 (3): 323–336.

Solomon M (2010) 'Education: DA slams department for 'gross' failures', *Daily Dispatch*, 4 October.

Stander Y (2010a) 'Chaos! Schools disaster. Damning report: Education on brink of utter collapse', *Weekend Post*, 2 October.

Stander Y (2010b) 'Ghost schools debacle', *The Herald*, 24 August.

Stats SA (Statistics South Africa) (2012) *Labour Force Survey: Quarter 2*. Pretoria. Available online.

University of Fort Hare (2008) Institutional Quality Audit 2008: Living Our Mission. Unpublished report distributed internally to heads of department in February 2008.

Chapter 7

The migration of African students to South Africa: motivations, integration and prospects for return

Gabriel Tati

IN THIS CHAPTER MY FOCUS is on the migration of young people from West and Central Africa to South Africa, with particular emphasis on migration driven by the desire to access higher education and on migrants who self-finance their studies with a view to improving their prospects for future employment. Throughout the chapter the term 'young' (or 'youth') refers to any person between the ages of 18 and 30 years. This is in line with the definition conventionally adopted, including by the United Nations. Therefore, such terms as 'young migrant', 'young-age migrant' and 'youth migration' are used interchangeably to refer to migrants who are, technically and in terms of the definition, between the ages stated. At the same time, this terminology appreciates that actual experiences of 'youth age' vary across space and time, and that being of 'young age' does not necessarily mean that the young people concerned are regarded as 'young' in particular contexts and situations, or see themselves as young, for that matter. On the subject of definitions, the term 'francophone Africa' refers to countries in sub-Saharan Africa that use French as an official language; that is, countries in West and Central Africa that were colonised by France and Belgium.

Why study educational migration among youth from West and Central Africa? For one thing, in recent years considerable numbers of young people have migrated from francophone sub-Saharan Africa in search of better quality higher education in South Africa. Further, student migration is an increasingly important phenomenon worldwide, although this has received scant attention from either policy-makers or researchers (Anthias 2006; Baas 2007; Balaz and Williams 2004; Castles and Miller 2003). South Africa, along with many other comparatively 'rich' countries, is among the most popular and highly regarded study destinations, and this form of migration is likely to increase, given the deterioration or collapse of educational systems in many parts of francophone Africa and the restriction of traditional migratory gateways into Europe.

Students come to South Africa from different geographical regions, social trajectories and educational backgrounds. This chapter provides a critical assessment of some of the challenges of adaptation and adjustment that face students in South Africa in general, and in the country's higher education system in particular. The chapter is based on a combination of primary and secondary sources. The literature on student migration was used to build up a theoretical framework and a broader context for understanding student migration from francophone Africa to South Africa. A range of secondary statistical sources was used to probe patterns of foreign-student migration to South Africa as well as the most sought after academic institutions, fields, courses and provinces. The primary data source was a 2009 survey of 207 students from francophone Africa who had migrated to South Africa and were based in the Western Cape province (Tati 2010). Respondents completed the questionnaire via face-to-face interviews or in writing.

Some intersecting issues emerged. While some respondents expressed satisfaction with their experiences of study in South Africa, others expressed the opposite. On the positive side, many students found that the educational programmes offered were suitable for improving their prospects for future employment, and many considered it much easier to study successfully in South Africa than in their countries of origin. Yet, for some, there were hurdles on the path to success. Besides frequently mentioned problems related to language barriers and official documentation, some students considered the level of responsiveness to their specific problems from university authorities to be inadequate. Further, many academic institutions provide little space for foreign students to contribute to the transformation process or to become integral agents of change in the post-apartheid higher education system. Meanwhile, most of the students interviewed had to find ways of sponsoring their studies – usually through self-employment or taking jobs in exploitative working conditions. The research found that migrant students employ various strategies to avoid interrupting their studies or staying in the country illegally. Such strategies range from, for example, working casually to pay tuition fees, to trying to obtain refugee status, or even marrying someone who has citizenship or a residence permit.

The research went beyond student experiences, to gauge the extent to which their return to the home country was planned, after their studies were completed. It transpired that migration for study to South Africa often forms part of a project of staying longer for employment purposes. In this sense, migration might be seen as contributing to brain gain from the South African perspective, and to brain drain from that of the sending country. Skeldon (2005) states that, in most cases, students who migrate to developed countries stay and work in those countries as skilled professionals. However, other analysts challenge the ideas of brain gain and brain drain, arguing that student migration does not necessarily constitute a loss for the sending country. Asian countries, for example, provide telling examples of migrant students who have returned to their countries with skills and contributed significantly to the region's continued economic development.

Young people as migrant students have emerged as a 'newly' discovered social constituency in intra-African migration. But a similar trend is being observed around the globe (see, for example, Baas 2007; Balaz and Williams 2004; Shen 2007). From the perspective of the host country, specific forms of youth and educational migration tend to be discussed in terms that are disconnected from migrants' rights to education. In other words, these migrants tend to be referred to as 'international students', 'young asylum seekers' and 'foreign students', which blurs the actual *labour migration* element. This disconnection 'others' forms of youth migration, with some problematic consequences. For example, isolating the migration of young people from other forms of migration risks losing sight of the structural relations, and the ways in which migrant students as social actors engage with, resist or negotiate the structural relations embedded in the societal contexts where they live and interact with the locals – yet from an often-vulnerable position. While studying abroad may be seen as relatively positive and something to be encouraged, meeting the costs of study through self-employment or casual work in a host country may entail considerations and experiences for migrant students that are less benign.

As I argue in this chapter, these two forms of migration – educational and labour – are often connected. This is of interest because this issue has thus far received no explicit attention in the context of reduced levels of international assistance to African countries in the training of young people. In the past, African students were sent to Europe, especially to the former Soviet Union and other socialist republics, to obtain advanced tertiary education or specialised training. Since the end of the Cold War, however, this practice has almost disappeared. Rather, the migration of young people to South Africa takes place in the context of drastic cuts in public spending on bursaries to study at home or abroad, and students involved in educational migration generally receive little or no support from their governments and instead cover most of their own costs.

The higher education system is now part of a global education industry. Issues of educational and labour migration, and brain drain versus brain gain, resonate at continental level, too, in the sense that the New Partnership for Africa's Development (NEPAD), as an enabling continental institution, has as one of its main underlying principles the free movement of academia and related individuals. For these reasons, this particular form of migration is likely to increase, rather than decrease in years to come.[1]

A theoretical framework on youth migration

From a theoretical point of view, migration has traditionally been associated with younger age sets. The propensity to move from one administrative unit to another is believed to decline as age increases. An analysis of age patterns reveals that migrants are generally in the early years of their adult lives and research on migration generally corroborates the proposition that persons in their late teens, twenties, and early thirties are more migratory than their older counterparts. The interpretation is that the young are able to adapt more easily to new situations. Also, as the young are close to the beginning of their working lives they are envisaged as being more readily inclined to take advantage of new opportunities involving migration, while older people are apt to be constrained by a host of more permanent social and economic ties at their places of residence.

On the educational front, a considerable number of studies, while controlling for a wide range of socio-economic factors, support the proposition that migration correlates quite highly with education levels (see, for example, Shaw 1975). The rationale is simply that the higher an individual's level of educational attainment, the more likely it is that they will be aware of differential opportunities, amenities, and so on, to be had in other places. Further, migration to more *distant* destinations is highly correlated with *higher* levels of education, particularly university training. However, generalisation about the impact of various levels of educational attainment on migration behaviour is a different matter.

A microanalysis of the more subjective elements in the migration process and of individuals' motives for migration illuminates the link between educational aspiration and migration. Factors such as social status or family attachment have a direct bearing on an individual's receptivity to various migration stimuli. In this regard there may be some theoretical justification for relating youth migration to the concept of an individual's subjective perception and evaluation of place of residence, and to broadly conceived motivations that may trigger the move (Simmons 1982; Waters 2006). The so-called 'push' and 'pull' factors that impact on decisions to migrate have been well documented in the literature (see, for example, UIS 2009). The frustrations of under-resourced universities at home and aspirations to pursue particular fields of study fit into the 'push' category. In the 'pull' category, choices of destination for students can be determined by reputable academic institutions and affordability of tuition (UIS 2009). South Africa as a major students' destination is likely to be in this category.

Three elements are worth considering in this regard. The first is an attitude of aspiration; a young person perceives and evaluates migration as an opportunity for realising ambitions and aspirations. Such an individual is typically already somewhat dislocated from primary and secondary groups in their area of residence. (The 'primary group' refers in most cases to the parental node or nuclei – biological or extended family at large – while the 'secondary group' includes the community or networks of persons with whom the individual is acquainted.) The second element to consider is that, in a state of dislocation, the youth may view migration as a solution to some of the limitations experienced at the place of origin. As a result, migration may be perceived and evaluated as the best alternative to factors such as unemployment or as a means to realise specific and limited objectives such as educational attainment. Therefore, and this is the third element, young people view migration as a means to contend with unique personal factors such as educational challenges.

As Taylor (cited in Shaw 1975) proposes, a motivational approach to migration among the youth suggests a conceptualisation of this event in relation to the degree of structural strain at the place of origin, and how the concerned individual perceives and evaluates elements of stress. Thus, we may assume that, at the level of the individual, there are stimuli for both short-term (education) and long-term (employment) aspirations, there is a feeling of dislocation (failure to achieve autonomy), there is the belief that conditions are better elsewhere, that migration is a feasible option, and that trigger factors spur the decision to migrate.

The move to a place outside one's country of origin may be prompted by considerations that, in migration studies, are generally associated with the concept of *place utility*. Young people may be prompted to move as a result of feeling deprived of educational facilities, employment opportunities and so on. Once again, this comes as a result of subjective evaluations of utilities available at the individual's place of origin versus utilities available in alternative places of residence. At the same time, it cannot be assumed that individuals will automatically relocate to a place of higher utility. Rather, this depends on an individual's ability to adjust to the utility profile offered at the new place of residence, and their ability to cope with stress – or what is termed the 'strain threshold' (Simmons 1982).

Relocation to a place of higher utility also depends on the information available (and its perceived accuracy) regarding utilities to be had elsewhere. Therefore, an important aspect of place utility as a concept central to research on youth migration is the way in which young people *perceive* their existing environment versus the utilities to be had in distant environments other than their own. This aspect is, to a certain extent, tied up with individuals' needs, drives and abilities, which may be constrained within the space occupied at the time the move is being initiated. This space varies in accordance with the person's characteristics and developments in their environment.

To put this in the context of the research reported in this chapter, living conditions in many African countries create environments of considerable stress, and are thus as capable as other factors of generating motives for mobility. (From a research standpoint, it would be interesting to attempt to identify the actual strain threshold – the point at which a young person decides to relocate.) Research indicates that the decision to relocate will be a function not only of the availability of alternative options, but also of the individual's strain threshold (especially associated with actual job searches or the prospect of finding future employment) (Simmons 1982). Balac (2010), in his study of young Moroccans' emigration to Spain, shows that unemployment and vulnerability are dominant causes. It can be inferred that educational migration to distant locations among young people takes place when stresses in the place of origin, as experienced by the individual, cause the individual's strain threshold to be surpassed. At that point, what the existing social and physical environment can provide in relation to a person's wants is insufficient to restrain them from relocating. Most of the frustrations come from the failure of a state to fulfil its mandate of providing inclusive access to education of good quality (UIS 2009). Students increasingly face difficulties accessing tertiary education due to dysfunctional states – this problem affects most of the tertiary institutions on the continent (CODESRIA 2008). This is not, however, a situation confined to the present day. In fact, the collapse of the higher education system is an enduring trend, which started in the 1970s and deepened in the 1980s and 1990s with the implementation of structural adjustment programmes, supported by the Bretton Woods institutions (Burja 1994; CODESRIA 2008). These programmes advocated, among other things, drastic cuts in public spending and commercialisation of higher education (Barro 2012; Chachage 2001; Sawyerr 1998).

An approach to youth migration using stress factors relates well to the concept of place utility, based upon both the characteristics of young migrants and their places of residence. Variables such as family status, employment prospects, political instability and insecurity, the capacity (or lack thereof) of the higher education system in the home country to absorb students, and the perceived quality of the higher education institutions in the host country account to a great extent for increases in migration. Place utility evaluations as factors in migration are likely to occur in areas that are deprived, when compared to other, similar areas.

However, there is a problem in any generalisation of this concept of place utility. It is deemed a function of aspirations of the individual concerning residential environment. In turn, the aspirations of any young person are likely to be a function of education, family status, stage in lifecycle development and so on. In other words, the orientation to family, which is a component of the cultural system, also plays a critical role in the decision to migrate. Regardless of the age factor, the role of the extended family or family cohesion – as either stimulus to or constraint on migration – has been extensively identified with regard to the receptivity of individuals to migrate. More specifically, young people with close family attachments and a tertiary education attainment level are more likely to receive financial support for migration, as the degree of persuasion and valuation tends to be strong. Such young people are seen as migrating for better opportunities and as having greater chances of success and of sending remittances home once employment has been secured (Stahl 1989; Suksomboon 2007).

Data and analytical methods

As mentioned, this chapter is based on a combination of primary- and secondary-source information. The primary data was collected via a survey of 207 students from francophone Africa who migrated to South Africa and were based in various departments at the University of the Western Cape. A few students from the nearby Peninsula Technikon[2] campus were also interviewed. The survey took place from March to April 2009. The survey was of a cross-sectional design, with respondents selected using a purposive method and the snowball sampling technique. Respondents in the sample were therefore selected subjectively because I did not have a list of students from which a representative sample could be drawn. The snowball sampling involved contacting a member of the student population of interest and asking whether they knew anyone else with the required characteristics. The two interviewers I worked with (postgraduate students under my supervision) were very helpful with regard to arranging contacts with respondents. The approach targeted students from francophone countries in West and Central Africa only, including Gabon, Cameroon, Rwanda, Congo, Democratic Republic of Congo, Burundi and Côte d'Ivoire. A questionnaire was drawn up which aimed to provide insights into respondents' educational patterns and trajectories. Both structured and unstructured questions were included in the questionnaire, and information was gathered on students' current personal details, pre-migratory social situations, migration decision-taking, post-migration experiences, and intention to re-migrate. Informed consent was obtained from all respondents and respondent's details were kept confidential. The two interviewers conducted face-to-face interviews and some respondents completed the questionnaire in writing themselves as the questions were self-explanatory.

As is often the case during any data-collection operation, some problems were encountered. These were mainly to do with respondents' susceptibility, refusal, tracking take-home questionnaires, and not showing up for appointments. Despite these minor problems, there was general enthusiasm for participating and respondents said they were happy to be given a space to express their views.

Using the information gathered, the analytical challenge was to organise the responses into a narrative that captured differing individual experiences of migrant status, location, housing, study and livelihoods. A systematic approach was adopted to turn the material into a consistent narrative on selected migrants' individual experiences relative to their conditions of departure, accommodation arrangements, work, study, social capital and networks at different places. Understanding young migrants' trajectories necessitated a *tuning* of the primary material, blending events and experiences into a coherent whole, and considering various activities that migrant students have been involved in since arriving in South Africa. The intention here was not to sketch a precise typology of youth mobility with regard to the migration process. At most, from the interview data gathered, a series of insights – limited but factual – could be derived, and assumptions or hypotheses proposed for possible testing in an objective model. (Such a testing exercise is described in the following section.) It is also worth noting that such hypotheses could be first assessed as assumptions to be approved or rejected through a rigorous reading of the spectrum of responses. For example, the assumption that some young people migrating to South Africa would be more involved than local students in trading activities as street vendors could be tested. Similarly, the related assumption that these young migrants might have some predisposition to these activities, due to survival skills they had learned while living under stressful social conditions in their home countries, or because of the networks they establish with other migrants before or after arriving in South Africa, could be put to the test.

From an analytical point of view, the experiences of migrant students can be used to make connections between different pieces of 'objective' information and to obtain insights into certain elements of the ideology of the subject. Three significant types of discourse may be derived from the narratives. The first is an exposé of the reasons for departure from the country of origin. The second focuses on the links (of diverse nature) maintained between the place of origin and the place of current stay, while the third focuses on projects for betterment or wellness in relation to educational and (possibly) professional achievements.

The continental context

South Africa is a new destination for young migrants looking for higher education facilities and, as has already been stated, this is particularly the case with migration of young people from francophone Africa. Most of these migrants started to arrive around 2005, although it remains difficult to date or quantify in an exact manner the magnitude of different waves. Massey (2006) argues that the end of apartheid in 1994 seems to have contributed to the formation of a migratory sub-system centred on this country. Up to the collapse of apartheid, immigrants were predominantly non-Africans, while the entry of Africans was controlled and limited (Crush 2000). Soon after apartheid was abolished, an intense movement of traders took place between these countries and South Africa, with Johannesburg being the main supply centre for goods (Akokpari 2002; Legoko 2006). This trade-related mobility may have contributed to South Africa's image as a viable destination country for income-generating and educational opportunities. With its modern infrastructure and relatively developed economy, the country is seen as an alternative to traditional destinations such as France, Belgium, the United Kingdom and some North African countries. South Africa has gained significance as those countries have implemented increasingly selective admissions policies with regard to foreign students. The statistics compiled from the Department of Higher Education and the Council on Higher Education (CHE 2009) show consolidated growth in the number of students from different geographical origins. In spite of the language barrier and the costs involved in relocation, significant numbers of young people from francophone Africa choose to migrate to South Africa for study-related purposes.

Figures compiled from national educational bodies indicate a consistent increase from 1994 to 2010 in foreign student numbers coming to South Africa (see Table 7.1). These foreign students originated predominantly from sub-Saharan Africa (UIS 2008 cited in CHE 2009). South Africa is the only country in sub-Saharan Africa to attract substantial numbers of foreign students. The potential for benefits to be gained from foreign students has motivated the authorities in charge of the higher education system to increase recruitment of students from within the Southern African Development Community (SADC). The benefits are particularly directed at the postgraduate level, where low numbers of South African candidates are a matter of concern, both from an academic and a research capacity point of view. It is, thus, no surprise that the majority of foreign students in South Africa enrol in postgraduate programmes. Overall, South African students still represent more than 92 per cent of the total enrolments, but they are proportionally in decline. Although statistics are hard to come by, Table 7.1 displays the evolution of enrolments from 1994 to 2010.

TABLE 7.1   Student enrolment at public universities by region of origin, South Africa 1994–2010

Year	South Africa	SADC countries	Other African countries	Rest of the world	Unknown	Total
1994	–	6 209	1 521	4 827	–	–
1997	–	7 822	2 079	5 268	–	–
2000	545 184	21 318	4 263	5 568	14 228	591 561
2003	666 367	36 207	6 664	7 108	1 447	717 793
2004	691 910	36 302	6 874	7 836	1 564	744 486
2005	683 473	35 074	7 196	7 839	1 491	735 073
2006	687 642	35 922	8 569	7 673	1 574	741 380
2007	701 853	41 713	8 682	7 136	1 706	761 090
2008	735 538	45 851	9 554	6 619	1 928	799 490
2009	876 923	41 906	10 663	7 011	1 276	937 779
2010	826 887	46 496	10 986	7 302	1 353	893 024

Sources: Data from 2004–2007 derived from CHE (2009). Data for 1994–2003 and 2008–2010 (excluding South African nationals) derived from the DHET (2011, cited by IEASA 2011).

As shown in Table 7.1, the population of foreign students from other African countries has grown substantially, overtaking students from the rest of the world in the period under consideration. This growth is considerable when one considers that in 2000, for example, South African universities had only 4 263 students from other parts of Africa (*excluding* the SADC region) against 5 568 students from the rest of the world (outside Africa). Students from the 'rest of the world' category come mainly from Europe, Asia and to a lesser extent North America (USA and Canada), and mostly via student exchange programmes. For the same year, 2000, the SADC region was represented by 21 318 students enrolled at South African universities. Thus the country draws its foreign student population mainly from its geographical zone of traditional economic influence, as it did for foreign labour recruited on mines during the apartheid era. The migrational relations are geographically maintained, despite some change in the composition of the migrants' demographics and motives. Zimbabwe is a major source of foreign students. A country once well endowed with good quality educational facilities, the economic and social crisis of the past years has seriously undermined the higher education system and resulted in massive influxes of students to South Africa. No doubt the substantial decline in the number of students from SADC countries in 2009, as evident in Table 7.1, is a reflection of the violent xenophobic attacks, which took place in 2008 and 2009 and mainly targeted African migrants. These attacks probably deterred some of the potential candidates from neighbouring countries from migrating to South Africa and may have prompted others to leave the country. An increase is evident in 2010, when new migratory measures between South Africa and Zimbabwe were implemented such as short-term work permits and the regularisation of cross-border migrants in irregular situations.

The precise number of these migrants in South Africa is not known because some of them enrol in private education institutions. The private higher education sector has undoubtedly also experienced a considerable increase in the number of students from African countries who have enrolled since 1994. In 2011, the South African education department released a list that indicated that there were 114 private tertiary institutions authorised to operate in the country, although only 84 were fully registered (IEASA 2011). Quite a few of these institutions are linked to international universities and give preference to vocational programmes, tapping into market-oriented skills (IEASA 2011). Notwithstanding the growing importance of the private sector, it is reasonable to assume that each year hundreds, if not thousands, of young people attempt to enrol in South African public higher education institutions.

From the literature on this subject (Bunting 2003; IEASA 2011; Jooste 2011; Marko 2009; UIS 2009, 2012;), some unanimity regarding motives for migration emerges. As already noted, most of these migrants are pushed out of their countries of origin by lack of appropriate higher education institutions, highly competitive entry requirements at their home institutions, as well as by poor career and income-generation prospects. Supplementary push factors are the poor quality of education that tends to be offered at the home higher education institutions, and considerations of the fitness (or lack thereof) of qualifications to specific jobs. Many sub-Saharan African countries, especially those in the central region, are affected by the complete breakdown of social and economic systems – markets, services and security. Young people therefore rely less and less on their 'localities of belonging' to meet their aspirations in terms of education and employment. Moving to richer countries on the continent has increasingly become a first-choice strategy among young people looking for quality education or better employment opportunities.

So, the desire to pursue studies in South Africa (or one of the other richer African countries such as Morocco or Côte d'Ivoire) is one of the major drivers of migration among the more educated youth. This is clearly related to personal aspirations and ambitions of obtaining an education that will enable them to gain access to meaningful employment at some level in the global economy. The educational migration of young people can be viewed as part and parcel of a 'lifecycle development', in that it combines with a search for employment in the place of destination. In most cases, as stated earlier, migration to South Africa occurs after failed attempts to reach Europe.

The motivations behind the choice of destination, the trajectories migration can take, and the modes of educational and labour market insertion are highly complex. In their places of origin, young people are pushed to move as they feel deprived with respect to educational facilities, employment opportunities and other factors. For these migrant students, social capital and social networks provide the channels through which costs (anticipated and actual) associated with migration are minimised. At the place of destination, getting a better education is not incompatible with participating in the labour market, albeit informally, to cover their tuition costs. Some make it that way to legitimise their stay in the country as students while others choose alternative options, one of which is to seek refugee status. The research on which this chapter is based found that it is common practice among young migrants to be simultaneously involved in the lower-paid segments of the labour market and in studying at a higher education institution. For some young people migration and insertion in the host society may be facilitated through the support received from home; for others that may not be the case.

South Africa is a preferred destination because of its developed educational infrastructure. This does not come as a surprise. Globally, South Africa was rated in 2009 among the top ten destinations for foreign students wanting to pursue a university education away from home (UIS 2009). With international students forming just over 8 per cent of South Africa's total university population (761 000 students at the time), the country was ranked as the world's eighth most popular study destination. According to the 2009 *Global Education Digest* published by UNESCO's Institute for Statistics (UIS), one in five foreign students from Africa was studying at a South African university. Table 7.2 provides figures on foreign students enrolled at 12 South African universities in 2009, while Table 7.3 shows the distribution of students in South African higher education institutions, by geographical origin, in 2006 and 2007.

TABLE 7.2 Foreign enrolments at South Africa's public universities, plus foreign student numbers in the world's top ten study destinations, 2009

University	No. of foreign students	Foreign student numbers in the world's top 10 study destinations
University of Cape Town	4 423	US 595 900
University of Pretoria	3 008	UK 351 500
Stellenbosch University	2 731	France 246 600
University of KwaZulu-Natal	2 229	Australia 211 500
University of the Witwatersrand	2 189	Germany 206 900
University of Johannesburg	2 112	Japan 125 900
University of the Free State	1 945	Canada 68 500
Nelson Mandela Metropolitan University	1 891	South Africa 60 600
University of the Western Cape	1 357	Russia 60 300
Walter Sisulu University	341	Italy 57 300
University of Zululand	250	
University of Limpopo	182	

Source: Compiled from UIS data cited in Govender (2009: 6).

Institution	Year	South African citizens	SADC citizens	Other
Cape Peninsula University of Technology	2007	27 103	1 267	582
Central University of Technology	2007	9 902	532	44
Durban University of Technology	2007	22 381	243	78
Tshwane University of Technology	2006	49 401	1 495	550
Mangosuthu University of Technology	2006	9 978	115	3
Vaal University of Technology	2007	14 834	871	441
Nelson Mandela Metropolitan University	2006	22 321	1 095	829
University of Johannesburg	2007	40 000	1 084	527
University of South Africa	2006	208 720	13 375	4 676
Rhodes University	2006	4 490	1 151	273
Walter Sisulu University	2007	23 884	157	79
North West University	2006	34 828	3 536	345
University of Cape Town	2006	16 498	2 299	2 159
University of Fort Hare	2006	7 425	1 012	89
University of the Free State	2007	22 802	1 533	183
University of Kwazulu-Natal	2007	35 516	1 386	948
University of Limpopo	2007	16 905	331	233
University of Pretoria	2007	36 045	1 515	1 073
University of the Western Cape	2006	13 522	598	382
University of the Witwatersrand	2007	23 272	1 010	819

Source: SARUA (2009).

Note: The University of Stellenbosch, the University of Zululand and the University of Venda provided no breakdown in student numbers by citizenship and are excluded from this data.

Although Tables 7.1 and 7.2 do not provide a breakdown of the geographical origin of foreign students in South Africa, it is likely that a considerable number have come from Africa in recent years. As shown in Table 7.3, students from the SADC region outnumber those from outside that region. The number of SADC versus non-SADC students varies across the institutions, but the attractiveness of well-ranked national universities is clear; the higher the ranking, the larger the number of non-SADC foreign students. The only detailed data I managed to gather on the geographical origin of students dates back to 2000 (see Table 7.4).

University	SADC	Rest of Africa	Asia	Australia and Oceania	Europe	USA/ Canada	South America	Total
University of Cape Town	860	148	136	14	437	249	9	1 853
University of Durban-Westville	127	57	11	2	3	3	24	227
University of Fort Hare	112	12	0	0	0	0	0	124
Medical University of South Africa	182	143	42	1	10	2	1	381
University of the North	3	3	0	0	2	0	0	8
University of the Free State	363	91	14	0	26	23	2	519
University of Port Elizabeth	3 783	1 591	13	5	21	12	2	5 427
University of Potchefstroom	1 961	51	30	1	40	5	3	2 091
University of Pretoria	498	188	120	37	292	49	17	1 201
Rand Afrikaans University	248	43	28	1	51	6	2	379
Rhodes University	843	96	30	1	166	26	0	1 162
University of South Africa	6 539	658	628	59	1 542	112	64	9 602
University of the Western Cape	192	78	5	0	28	3	0	306
University of the Witwatersrand	597	314	293	9	326	78	12	1 629
University of Zululand	40	71	1	1	1	0	0	114
Vista University	739	2	3	0	0	1	0	745
University of Venda	2	0	0	0	0	0	0	2
Total	17 109	3 546	1 354	131	2 945	569	136	25 770

Source: Adapted from CHE (2009).

Note: Many of the names of higher education institutions have changed since the mergers that took place as part of the transformation of the South African higher education landscape between 2000 and 2010.

It is important to note that students from the Democratic Republic of Congo (DRC) are included in the SADC figures since, for geopolitical reasons (mainly serving the interests of South Africa), the DRC is a SADC member. In the SADC category, Zimbabwe sends the highest number of students to South Africa, and this is undoubtedly related to the under-resourcing of universities in that country, as already mentioned. Other SADC countries that had high numbers of students in South Africa in 2000 were Namibia

(10 169 students), Botswana (4 963 students), Swaziland (2 825 students) and Mauritius (1 213 students). The presence of Mauritius is quite surprising when one considers its level of development in comparison to much of continental Africa. The reason seems to relate to specific courses offered in South Africa. (This also seems to be the case for some students from Europe who have enrolled at institutions such as Rhodes University, the University of Cape Town and Stellenbosch University.)

The data in Tables 7.1 to 7.4 suggest that South Africa is a destination for an increasingly diverse flow of international students, and students from elsewhere in Africa are strongly represented among these young migrants, even if their exact number is difficult to determine.

Thus, there is little doubt that South Africa's educational services are probably among its major growth sectors in terms of export earnings. International students from non-SADC countries pay higher fees than their South African counterparts. The financial contribution of foreign students to the South African economy, and to the higher education sector in particular, is, therefore, considerable and nearly all foreign students are self-financed from their first to their last year of study.

The South African higher education system has not yet reached the stage of being a *major* export industry, as is the case in the United Kingdom (Shen 2007) or Australia (Baas 2007) in attracting Asian students, for example. Yet the expectation is that the educational sector in South Africa will grow considerably in that direction, given the increased deterioration of tertiary institutions in other parts of Africa. It is perhaps in view of this that the policy towards facilitating students' entry into the country has become more flexible. From what was previously a very restrictive student-permit, South Africa has gradually introduced a more progressive policy regarding the issuing of visas to students from elsewhere in Africa. Thus, while refugees and asylum seekers are exempted from obtaining study permits, other students are allowed to enrol, provided they can cover their costs. Yet, despite the implementation of faster and more efficient processing procedures, visa or entry clearance remains the main obstacle for students from other African countries entering South Africa. Obtaining a visa in the country of origin requires the possession of sufficient resources, proof of admission to a South African higher education institution, and medical insurance. Nevertheless, the number of students from other African countries flocking to South Africa appears to be constantly on the rise.

Another pull factor is that, unlike universities in Western Europe, South African higher education institutions do not systematically require proof of English proficiency such as the Test of English as a Foreign Language (TOEFL) score. South Africa's policy in this regard really facilitates the admission of students from francophone Africa, some of whom have limited or no English language skills. It must be noted that the economic imperative to increase the intake of students played in favour of these students (Bunting 2003).

Having examined the patterns of foreign students' mobility at the macro and institutional levels, it is important to look at this migration from the perspective of students themselves. These are the main decision-takers in this mobility, and listening to their voices is as important as looking at enrolment figures. In the sections to come, I make use, where appropriate, of the in-depth interviews conducted with foreign students enrolled at the University of the Western Cape. This institution serves as my case study. While it is important to recognise the uniqueness of this institution's experience with foreign students, it may have traits in common with other, similar institutions in the country. From the interviews conducted, I gained some insights into patterns regarding the motives behind the choice of a particular institution, as well as the reasons behind the choice of South Africa as a study destination. All the tables displayed in the sections to come were generated from Tati (2010).

Patterns in the socio-spatial trajectories of migrant students

Without exception, the young people surveyed clearly suggested that they chose to migrate for personal reasons and were quite positive about their experiences of relocation. Migration had allowed most respondents to develop skills in educational fields that are either not available or are difficult to gain entrance to in their own countries. As one of the respondents put it, 'Here [in South Africa] you can study in such prestigious disciplines as engineering, computer science, medical and pharmaceutical studies or business, with no problem, as long as you have the minimum requirements and a bit of money to pay registration fees'. Others emphasised the possibility of earning income while studying, to pay for their higher education. The disciplines chosen by respondents were diverse, with science subjects such as physiotherapy, nursing, microbiology, science, chemistry and medical technology tending to predominate.

Motives, educational access and prospects for employment

The interviews conducted revealed that dysfunctional tertiary education systems in the countries of origin played a critical role in generating migration. Many students had struggled to find work or educational opportunities at home; although in lower numbers compared to undergraduate foreign students in the *overall* statistics, students at the postgraduate level are the ones who seemed to have encountered that situation most. Destinations such as South Africa become particularly attractive for those entering the postgraduate cycle and looking to settle down on their own. Confronted with increased competition for admission at postgraduate level – vocational training or higher education – in the countries of origin and the prospect of long-term unemployment, many see migrating to South Africa as a viable alternative. This explains why the pursuit of formal postgraduate education (honours and master's degrees) emerged as a major reason for migration by most of the young people interviewed.

Some respondents said that they covered their costs either by earning income or by working for a relative or someone known to them in return for financial support. Others acknowledged that migration came with hardships associated with being away from one's family and cultural environment. For most, these disadvantages and potential dangers were considered to be more than offset by the potential benefits, tangible or otherwise. It was very clear that the choice of South Africa was strongly associated with the respondents' desire to improve their marketability through better education.

The language factor was seen as quite critical in shaping prospects for employment. When asked if studying in English was not an impediment to success, those with no prior fluency in the language stated this was not the case. On the contrary, they pointed out, improving their skills in English was part of their strategy to boost their prospects of finding a job, either in South Africa or elsewhere. In fact, many had already considered the possibility of English being an obstacle when they were considering migration and they had attended English courses before migrating. All of the interviewed students indicated that they had not been required to take a fluency test in English when applying for admission to South African higher education institutions.

It is important to point out that several students' decisions to move were strongly motivated by offers of financial assistance of whatever type from the institutions to which they had applied. As South Africa's higher education system comes to function increasingly like an industry, universities' recruitment strategies tend to advertise these sorts of offers, raising the expectations of financial support among potential migrant students. Upon arrival, though, several students had been disappointed by not getting what they thought they had been promised prior to migrating. As explained by a female student (EJ, holder of a DEA in mathematics[3]) from Cameroon:

I was admitted at UCT for doctoral studies in mathematics. At the time of admission, my supervisor agreed to support me financially with a studentship. When I arrived in South Africa, he instead told me that I should apply for a doctoral scholarship within a special NRF [National Research Foundation] programme for African students. I did it, but failed to get a scholarship. I decided to look for another institution with the hope of getting some financial aid. I ended up by joining the African Institute for Mathematical Sciences.

The above student has since left the country to relocate to Florida in the United States, after being offered a doctoral scholarship there.

South African law allows foreign students with a 'study permit' to obtain paid employment on or off campus for a maximum of twenty hours per week. Most students interviewed had a number of compelling reasons for wanting to work while studying. Having come to South Africa with a limited amount of money, they had usually spent this on books, rent and transport within a couple of months of their arrival. After that, as they often pointed out, they were on their own. Finding employment was thus necessary to cover their living expenses. In addition, some respondents were expected to send money home. As they explained, paying back what they owe was often part of the bargain from the beginning – their families helped to provide the necessary initial funds but hoped that one day soon a return on their investment would be made in the form of remittances. This situation meant that many respondents admitted to working more than twenty hours per week, and also seemed to find this quite normal. Due to the temporary and informal nature of such work, there tends to be significant under-reporting for tax payment purposes. Respondents reported a case of a female student from Mauritius routinely working forty hours a week in a consultancy firm without being registered with the South African Revenue Services. One hears of many similar cases. On the one hand, the respondents were perfectly aware that twenty hours was the legal maximum number of work hours, but, on the other hand, they argued that they simply had to earn more, and that 'everybody else' was doing this too. In my view, their sense of this being normal related not only to the financial pressures they were under but also to what they saw as being normal for a migrant as temporary migration for work-related reasons is the most common form of young-age student migration.

Besides, not all students take every step in a fair or legal manner and various tactics seem to be quite commonly be used in order to circumvent the formal procedures. It was gathered from indirect sources that some foreign students attempt to gain access to higher education in South Africa using fake certificates, unsupported applications for refugee status, bribes to South African Department of Home Affairs officials, and arranged marriages, to name but a few. Such unlawful strategies tend to be justified by those using them with reference to the fact that the legal framework around residential permits is constraining and procedures are overly bureaucratic.

In other southern African countries, it seems that finding temporary employment with a study permit is virtually impossible. Drawing on a study I conducted in Swaziland (Tati 2006), for example, young Congolese students (from DRC) pursuing their studies reported finding it difficult to cover their costs with the money they received from their impoverished families back home. Swaziland's immigration regulations also require foreign students to pay their tuition fees in full before allowing them to register. This rule also applies in the case of senior students who may require more than one year to obtain a degree. The relocation of the office of the United Nations High Commissioner for Refugees from Mbabane (capital city of Swaziland) to Pretoria in South Africa also apparently made it difficult for students to obtain funding for study because the processing of applications became increasingly time consuming and difficult because of the long distances involved. Many undergraduate Congolese students had to give up their studies in Swaziland (Tati 2006).

Choosing South Africa in a globalising higher education system

In the world of today, the international system of higher education operates like a market in which there is both supply (the universities with their programmes) and demand (the student population). This market is of course influenced by factors such as prices, migration policies, and university policies, to name but a few – in other words, so-called market forces apply. However, in the 'real world', subjective or personal considerations matter too, and they add to the domain of market-driven considerations.

In the survey conducted at the University of the Western Cape (Tati 2010), student respondents were asked to compare South Africa with universities in other countries to which they had intended or contemplated migrating for study. Respondents were thus asked to call upon the knowledge they had gleaned from different sources (the internet, leaflets, friends, among others) about the quality of education and life in those countries. Because of the purposive character of the sample of respondents, the data collected should be regarded as mere indications. Nevertheless, Table 7.5 summarises the ways in which respondents perceived South African tertiary education institutions to compare favourably and unfavourably with similar institutions in the North.

TABLE 7.5   Respondents' perceptions of South African universities and those in the North

South Africa compares favourably	Agree	South Africa compares unfavourably	Agree
Offers almost the same quality of education	11	The standard is higher in the North	9
Study costs are low	9	Crime and xenophobia are less in the North	7
Unemployment is high in South Africa and locals get jobs first	2	The North offers more job opportunities and it is easier to obtain residence status	7
Offers a 'more African' (relatively familiar) environment	6	The North is more welcoming/accommodating	2
Offers an appropriate social environment for study (respect for human rights)	1	Students in the North receive more financial and other support	1

Source: Tati (2010).

Note: The categories of responses shown here were compiled to collate responses to the questionnaire that were closely related. The numbers shown are low as they reflect responses only from those respondents who attempted to apply (or contemplated applying) for admission to universities outside South Africa.

As shown, South Africa is perceived to provide an appropriate social environment for study in terms of respect for human rights. This finds resonance in the popular recognition that South Africa has one of the most protective constitutions in the world when it comes to individual rights. Its tertiary education is also considered affordable. In real terms, it can cost an African student five to six times more to study in the United Kingdom. Interestingly, the area that attracted the highest score is the recognition among the respondents that the quality of education is almost the same. When probed during the interviews, students indicated that they were referring to programme content and access to learning material. The programmes offered generally met their expectations. South Africa is also viewed favourably because of its location within the continent; indeed the country has a locational advantage for students from the SADC region, and especially those from the Southern African Customs Union and Zimbabwe. These students do not have to travel as far as Europe or further to study, and can also to avoid the hassles associated with visa requirements.

Most respondents also thought that the culture shock was probably less dramatic in South Africa than they might experience in the North.

Conversely, based on feedback from the same respondents, universities in the North were valued more highly in terms of the support they provide to students. Bursaries and other forms of financial aid were frequently mentioned in this regard. Northern institutions were also seen as places where levels of crime and xenophobia are low, compared to the situation in South Africa (in this regard it is likely that respondents were referring to events that happened in South Africa in 2008 and 2009). Standards of education were presumed to be higher in the North, although, as mentioned, quite a number of respondents viewed the quality of higher education in South Africa as being on a par with the universities in the North. To a few respondents, the universities in the North are more accommodating than their counterparts in South Africa. When this statement was probed, it came out that this had to do with the way students are integrated into the structures of the university and how they become more socially integrated in the host country through the university. Although not mentioned by many respondents, a few did strongly state that foreign students from Africa are somewhat isolated from South African society. They do not interact or mingle socially with South African nationals, even on campus and they learn little about the society in which they are living. It goes without saying that widespread perceptions of rampant crime and xenophobia mentioned do not improve this situation and it comes as no surprise that students viewed the universities in the North as offering more opportunities than those in South Africa. Job opportunities during and after study were the most cited in this regard, in addition to the ease with which residential status can be changed.

Looking at Table 7.5, it is important to remember that many factors play in favour of the universities in the North. The major one is their well-established reputation built over several years (extending, in some cases, over centuries). Universities in the North remain attractive to many young Africans and the countries to which they intended to go for study revealed a strong preference for traditional destinations. Countries mentioned most by respondents were the United States, the United Kingdom, Australia and Canada. South Africa is still seen as 'a new kid on the block' in the higher education industry. While relatively competitive, when it comes to costs, quality and the advantages of proximity and culture, the social climate that seems to count against South Africa; crime and xenophobia are the major contributory elements to this perception. An additional 'negative' factor is that South Africa is an African country – the stereotypes surrounding the image of the continent are often

TABLE 7.6   Respondents' preferred place of study outside South Africa

Country	No. of respondents this applied to
America (US)	13
United Kingdom	9
Home country	8
Africa	6
Australia	6
Canada	5
Anywhere in Europe Germany	4
Scandinavia	3
Anyplace	3
France	2
Netherlands	2
Anywhere outside Africa	2
Belgium	1

Source: Tati (2010).

Note: The numbers shown reflect responses only from those respondents who attempted to apply (or contemplated applying) for admission to universities outside South Africa.

reinforced in the media; and among young Africans the view that life in Western Europe or North America is much better than in Africa remains strongly entrenched.

It is important to consider the distribution of countries where respondents indicated that they would like to go and study. As shown in Table 7.6, North America, Western Europe and Australia were the preferred choices. Interestingly, quite a few opted for institutions based in southern and East Africa. The universities of Botswana, Zimbabwe and Uganda were each mentioned by one or two respondents. This suggests that South Africa may have been a second choice for some students, and had they been given a chance to go and study in Europe, they probably would have taken it.

Failing to make it to the North

Translating one's intention to migrate abroad into a reality is not always an easy process. Even after being offered admission by an institution of choice, there is no guarantee that migration will take place as planned. For most students aspiring to migrate to Western countries, the biggest obstacle they are likely to face is securing funds to cover the costs of study. State-sponsored bursaries or personal resources are not always available, especially in this time of drastic cuts in the financing of higher education. As indicated in the previous section, relatively lower costs work in South Africa's favour.

Given the direct link between financial eligibility and the granting of visas to enter the desired country, a lack of financial resources was the main reason why respondents had failed to migrate to the North as is shown in Table 7.7.

Looking at the responses listed in Table 7.7, lack of financial resources was indicated by about 62 per cent of the respondents as the reason why they failed to migrate to the North. Far below, in second place, respondents indicated that they had experienced problems related to obtaining the required visa (although these two reasons would probably have been linked). Putting these negative outcomes aside, some respondents noted with hindsight that studying in South Africa had worked out better for them than they had expected.

As indicated in Table 7.7, some students opted for South Africa because of its proximity to their home countries, the ease of migrating and the financial support available. Obtaining refugee status and social commitment were two other reasons given by respondents. Since the major factors mentioned by respondents were the relative affordability of study in South Africa and the quality of education offered here, the country's higher education institutions should capitalise on these issues if they wish to attract additional African students to their universities.

TABLE 7.7   Reasons for not migrating to the North

Reason	No. of respondents this applied to
Financial problems	85
Visa problems	13
Found better opportunities in South Africa	7
Insecurity	5
South Africa was my first choice	5
South Africa is closer to home	4
No connections	3
Had bursary a bursary to study in South	3
Africa	3
Social commitment to Africa	2
Not stated	1
Application submitted late	1
Easier to come to South Africa	1
'Free' education in South Africa	1
No admission	1
Refugee status	

Source: Tati (2010)

Choosing a university in South Africa: things that matter

As in any other part of the world, African students applying for admission to South African universities face various considerations. Securing admission is, of course the most important one. With this come expectations around the quality of education, the availability of a study programme that is suited to one's needs, the institutional environment and the sense of social belonging, to name but a few. Obviously these considerations can overlap, compete or gain prominence sequentially when one is choosing where to study. Table 7.8 lists the issues that motivated respondents to choose the University of the Western Cape as a learning institution.

As shown, the cost of study was the *prime* consideration for respondents and this was followed by the reputation of the institution. Thus, once the quality of education at a particular institution is perceived as being good, the students are likely to flock there in numbers. This is not merely a perception; it can be ascertained by examining the ranking of the South African universities in relation to the number of foreign students registered as shown in Tables 7.2 and 7.3.

TABLE 7.8   Respondents' reasons for choosing the University of the Western Cape

Reasons	No. of respondents this applied to
Affordability and flexibility in payment	36
Good reputation and quality	25
Friends studying here	23
Specific programme of study	15
Convenient and supportive	13
Any place to study further will do	9
Easy admission	8
Family members in the area	6
No knowledge of any other places to study further	6
Accessible and flexible mode of payment	4
Historically black university	3
Financial support secured	3
Second choice	3
Availability of supervision	2

Source: Tati (2010).

To what extent are these young student migrants relying on social networks to accomplish their educational objectives upon arrival in South Africa? The data gathered suggest a choice of destination guided by the presence of social capital, but also a search for a place that can offer economic, educational and cultural possibilities. Again, as shown in Tables 7.2 and 7.3, the major cities offering prestigious universities seem to be first choice for young migrants from francophone Africa. The major urban centres offer certain other advantages linked to concentrations of migrants from the same country. Not only does this have the potential to reduce isolation, it also provides migrants with a valuable network for finding employment and accommodation. Associations based on country citizenship are generally used as a channel through which assistance, information and moral support are obtained in times of hardship and in the search for opportunities. Specific strategies are also worked out within these associations to deal with possible constraints encountered in relation to local administrative structures. Most respondents stated that they were able to secure admission to university prior to moving to South Africa, with the assistance of persons related to them (often siblings) or friends. For others, admission was accomplished through university websites, which they accessed via the many internet cafés in their countries of origin.

Although all major cities offer similar advantages, the choice of a particular city is greatly influenced by the stock of information communicated to potential migrants by those who have already migrated about the quality of life in the area. For example, some respondents mentioned that they preferred Cape Town to Johannesburg because foreigners reportedly encounter less harassment from police officers on the streets. Others stated that it is more difficult to find a casual job or to run a business in Johannesburg than it is in Cape Town even if one is suitably qualified. Respondents who had previously stayed in Johannesburg confirmed that living in Johannesburg comes with a lot of police harassment and the city has a reputation for placing administrative hurdles in the way of foreigners who apply for residence or work-related documents at the offices of the Department of Home Affairs. Thus considerations related to what were seen as 'friendly' urban environments were of major importance and they informed the choices made by young migrants as to where to relocate within South Africa.

Staying or leaving after graduation

An analysis of responses regarding intentions to leave or stay in South Africa upon completion of study shows an interesting pattern, which contrasts somewhat with the generally accepted view that student migrants are predominantly candidates for *departure*: of 207 respondents, 111 (54 per cent) had positive attitudes towards leaving South Africa, 88 (42 per cent) were willing to stay, and only eight (4 per cent) were uncertain about whether to stay or leave. For those planning to leave, the timing tended to fall within a one to three years of completing their studies, and naturally this was conditional on actual completion of study. Thus, for the majority of survey respondents, returning to their home country was part of their plans for the near future, and it seemed likely that migration would not translate into a permanent residential relocation for them.

Among the group who said they would opt to stay in South Africa, the major reasons cited were related to pursuing further studies and finding employment. This intention was well expressed, with strong optimism, among those with refugee status. This is understandable, as South Africa's refugee policy makes provision for individuals who have no place to go to remain in the country. The respondents had not, however, reckoned on the difficulty involved in finding the much-desired job. One computer science student put it succinctly:

If I get an excellent job, I can continue my career in IT without change of place. I will need to get a job first to be able to apply, and when I apply for a job they ask for resident permit. Well, that's funny, don't you think?

For some students, the reason for staying is marital, and their migration may have been induced in the first place by family regrouping. As a country of relocation, South Africa is not always hostile to foreign students and new family attachments are a significant reason for graduates not leaving the country. As one medical science student (from Rwanda) put it, 'My family stay here; South Africa feels like home for me'.

However, among those opting to leave South Africa (54 per cent), some opposite sentiments emerge. A considerable number stated that they wanted to return home for family-related reasons. Other reasons included xenophobia, insecurity, bureaucracy, discrimination, and better job prospects elsewhere. While the home country was frequently mentioned, other major destinations cited included Canada, the United Kingdom, Australia and the United States. Excluding the United Kingdom, the fact that none of the respondents mentioned European countries in the Schengen Zone is an indication of the extent to which these countries are increasingly seen as hostile to immigration from Africa. France, for instance, no longer represents a preferred destination for francophone students who possess a good command of professional English. Table 7.9 presents selected views collected from respondents regarding the reasons for planning to leave South Africa.

TABLE 7.9   Selected statements from respondents on their motives for leaving

(The question posed to survey respondents was: What is the motive for your departure from South Africa?)

1. To develop my country with skills I have acquired in my field of study.

2. Discrimination for foreign people. I don't trust this country and this people. What happened in 2008 [in reference to xenophobic attacks] can happen again.

3. To earn a bigger salary. My home country, higher wages, and meet friends and relatives. African international students often regarded as a threat in the job market, and I would not like to be part of the threat.

4. South African people are xenophobic…am tired of them!

5. Do not like the place, because of discrimination. They do not want foreigners.

6. Settle at home.

7. To go and apply the knowledge I have acquired for the development of my country (charity starts at home).

8. I wanna develop my country when there is still a possibility of making a change.

9. To develop my country and be close to family.

10. I am not happy here and peoples are not that friendly. This is really a not safe country to live in.

11. Discrimination, violence, crime, xenophobia and development in my field of study. Home Affairs officials especially don't like Nigerians, same as South Africans. South Africans believe all Nigerians are drug dealers or in shady deals. I do not think the stereotype can easily be dealt with. A colleague once told me she grew up hating foreigners due to what her mother told her. The xenophobia (Negrophobia) incidents of last year [2008] attest to this.

12. Find a job in a secure country. I feel insecure here with xenophobia. Being accepted as someone who can help in the system. Here they are thinking that giving a job to a foreigner is a great favour.

Note: Student responses are quoted verbatim.

Viewed from the perspective of South Africa and the country of origin, the considerable numbers of students returning home is an indication of the element of brain gain. For the sending country, it brings the benefits related to developmental impact. As most of the respondents indicated, migrant students intend to use the skills acquired in the South African education system to help develop their respective countries.

Students who do not return home after completing their studies risk becoming undocumented, irregular or illegal migrants, thus being excluded from any kind of official support (such as welfare benefits or social security) in the host country. For young migrants who decide not to return home, prospects in the home country tend to be even more tenuous and employment conditions even more insecure than in the host country. According to UNESCO statistics, the number of foreign African students applying for work permits after graduation is high (UIS 2009). For these students, South Africa does not just offer an interesting study-abroad option with the possibility of becoming a resident; it also offers, quite simply, an opportunity to obtain employment.

Interestingly, most of the students interviewed mentioned the issue of parental approval for staying abroad, as it brings families a strong promise of remittances in future. This is an indication of inter-generational contract, where interdependence and autonomy coexist, albeit that the relationship is unequally balanced in favour of the parents. However, as argued by Hashim (2006), such a contract benefits both the young person involved in the migration, and his or her relatives, and thus some degree of equilibrium in the relationship is reached.

A degree of unanimity emerged from respondents' in terms of not being forced by parents or other relatives to migrate for study. This is not to say that there were no apprehensions of any kind from the parents' side. It seems that in most cases the decision to migrate, however, had been negotiated – either with parents or other relatives – in order to secure the necessary material support, or simply to get the parental blessing for the venture. As one respondent put it:

My parents had to act as mediators in persuading my cousin in South Africa to facilitate my migration. In the first place he was opposed to it, saying he had no money to cover the costs. In fact, it's the problem of accommodation. He was sharing a two-bedroom flat with five other persons and could not therefore provide for accommodation. I had many problems finding accommodation upon arrival, until I got one in the students' hostels.

The situation of this respondent is not uncommon. At destination, young people experience, to varying degrees, specific problems, including overworking, wages below the statutory minimum, illegal residential status, xenophobia, inappropriate accommodation and so on. Yet, against the backdrop of all these challenges, almost all the young people interviewed stated they preferred the South African environment to their countries of origin. Some viewed life at home as being much more difficult than the problems faced in the host environment. Such a view suggests a positive evaluation of the real and potential opportunities that migration might offer.

Insertion into the labour market after graduation

As noted, migration to South Africa for study purposes is associated with the objective of finding or taking up a better job after graduation, either back home or in the current location. Prior to the migration, this objective was not automatically achievable in the students' countries of origin. Many respondents mentioned numerous acquaintances at home who had failed to find employment, despite having obtained tertiary qualifications in their home country. Others stated that their decision to migrate to South Africa was strongly motivated by friends or relatives – also migrants – who had gained access to local employment after studying in South Africa. It was clear that the relationships they had with such people not only helped them to obtain information about higher education institutions, but was expected to be equally helpful when it came to searching for employment after they graduated. Such statements tend to lend credibility to the operation of social capital or social networks among prior migrants to the destination. This social capital is especially evident among young migrants originating from regions with a strong culture of migration, for example, young migrants from the western regions of Cameroon. From the interviews, most Cameroonians, for instance, indicated that prior to their arrival in South Africa they had some knowledge of how to find employment in specific segments of the labour market. Some were aware of the relative ease with which they could find formal employment and of the possibility of working as casual workers or street traders. As reported in numerous studies on migration, home-visiting migrants represent an important source of information for prospective migrants. These visitors consolidate the perception among young people that life elsewhere can be much better.

This prospect of future employment is reinforced by the experiences of fellow migrants or other foreigners who have managed to find regular employment. Yet the transition from study to employment is not barrier-free, as already mentioned. Securing employment is subject to obtaining proper documentation, namely a valid work permit. Immigration policy makes provision for changing one's residential status from a study permit to a work permit, but this is highly regulated and restricted and is only possible under specific circumstances. Obtaining a South African qualification does provide such a possibility, especially at master's or PhD level, or in areas classified as 'scarce skills'. This is one of the reasons why foreign African students see postgraduate programmes, beyond the bachelor degree level (*licence*), as holding greater promise of eventual employment than staying at home.

Discussion and some concluding comments

The findings presented in this chapter on the patterns of departure and relocation among young educational migrants confirm that they have strong incentives to migrate. This is so because, for many, migration offers the most viable alternative to long-term deprivation. Taking responsibility for expenditure, such as educational costs, forms part of the migrational decision to pursue a personal desire to be independent and escape from a difficult environment. Migration is also seen as a channel through which migrants may fulfil the expectations of their parents, both materially and socially, through remittances and other transactions. At the migrants' destination, university attendance, in most cases, does not preclude engagement in paid work. University teaching timetables are generally flexible enough to allow the students to undertake employment, be it casual or formal. Moreover, such employment is often seasonal or night-economy work that is dependent on student labour. Under the guise of learning or studying, the clear evidence of a work component can, in fact, be said to blur the distinction between migration for work and migration for study purposes.

What theoretical insights can be drawn from this synopsis of trajectories? The patterns examined suggest that the meaning of an individual's migration or relocation decision develops over an extended period in their home environment. When asked about their reasons for moving, young migrants' responses provided some unambiguous, though limited, statements of their motivations, which revealed that the relocation or migration decision was embedded in the feelings of dislocation developed over a certain (if not the entire) period of the life course, rather than being linked only to circumstances in the period immediately prior to departure.

Equally reflected in the trajectories is, on the one hand, the developing meaning of migration to the individuals involved and, on the other, the multiple social influences shaping their perceptions of place. The personal objective of being independent of parents tends to be juxtaposed with the perception of a happier life elsewhere. This juxtaposition in the end makes migration an option worth considering. The trajectories and biographical accounts also reveal a complex web of cultural values and sources of social influence nested in the individual's general socio-economic milieu that favour and shape migration. In other words, family environment, educational attainment, kinship ties and country fellows contribute, in varying degrees, to the construction of the desirability of relocating.

Within the limitations of the study reported in this chapter, and by approaching the issues from different angles, it has been possible to begin to trace the taken-for-granted values that shape migrants' mobility decisions. In conclusion, though, it must be cautioned that a comprehensive analysis of the practical consciousness of these young migrants requires a more detailed documentation of their temporal–social interactions, and additional analysis of the actions and conversations in which they are involved.

Starting such a process is urgently needed, given the uneven development among African states in a time of declining aid and global financial crisis (African Development Bank 2009). The higher education sector seems likely to reflect this uneven development. Only a handful of countries, including South Africa, seem set to benefit from what some analysts call the 'export education industry' (Baas 2007). In such a socially diverse educational landscape there is an urgent need to go beyond globalised normative understandings of 'a responsive educational system' at the national level and instead gain a greater understanding of how young people of different genders and backgrounds perceive, experience and engage with the images, challenges, opportunities and vulnerabilities of an expanding and 'Africanising'[4] educational system.

Moreover, migration cannot be viewed in isolation from underlying processes. Yet, little is known about the institutional dimensions of youth migration in the fast-changing socio-economic contexts exemplified by the NEPAD and African Union member states. For example, how are NEPAD's regional frameworks – its projects of 'mobility of scientists or academics', and the roles it presents for youth organisations – perceived and experienced by young people looking for further and higher education? Thus far, very few studies accurately depict what it means to grow up in an African state with a dysfunctional education system and a non-responsive government, or probe how young people see their lives in relation to the risks and opportunities that a (not necessarily) regionally integrated Africa presents. These questions and many others, that are not explicitly raised in this chapter, merit careful attention by researchers dealing with youth-related issues.

Notes

1 It is important to note though that little empirical evidence has been produced to substantiate the intensification of migratory movements of young people from the central part of Africa to distant education institutions in francophone Africa, North Africa and southern Africa. South Africa is the main destination country examined in this chapter.

2 This institution has since merged with Cape Technikon to become the Cape Peninsula University of Technology.

3 DEA, which stands for *Diplôme D'études Approfondies*, is a degree delivered by French universities and is equivalent to a master's degree.

4 This word is coined in preference to the term 'globalising'.

References

African Development Bank (2009) *African Development Report 2009*. Tunis.

Akokpari JK (2002) 'International migration, xenophobia and the dilemma of the South African State', in S Buthelezi and E Leroux (eds) *South Africa Since 1994: Lessons and Prospects*. Pretoria: Africa Institute of South Africa.

Anthias P (2006) *Student Migration from Bangladesh to the UK*, RMMRU Occasional Paper No. 15, Refugee and Migratory Movements Research Unit, University of Dhaka, Bangladesh.

Baas M (2007) 'Learning how to work in the grey zone: The case of Indian overseas students in Melbourne, Australia', paper presented at ISS conference, International Migration, Multi-local Livelihoods and Human Security: Perspectives from Europe, Asia and Africa, Institute of Social Studies, The Hague, The Netherlands, 30–31 August 2007.

Balac R (2010) 'Les mobilités internationales des étudiants marocains', *Espace Population Sociétés* 2 (3): 395–411.

Balaz V and AM Williams (2004) '"Been there, done that": International student migration and human capital transfers from the UK to Slovakia', *Population, Space and Place* 10 (3): 217–237.

Barro M (2012) 'Development aid and higher education in Africa', *CODESRIA Bulletin 1 & 2*: 20–29.

Bunting I (2003) 'Foreign students and academic staff in public higher education in South Africa', in P Pillay, P Maassen and N Cloete (eds) *General Agreement on Trade and Services and Higher Education in SADC*. Rondebosch: Centre for Higher Education Transformation.

Burja SA (1994) 'Whither social science institutions in Africa: A prognosis', *Africa Development* 21 (1): 119–166.

Castles S and MJ Miller (2003) *The Age of Migration: International Population Movements in the Modern World* (third edition). New York: Guilford Press.

Chachage CLS (2001) 'Les transformations de l'enseignement supérieur et l'extrèmisme académique', *CODESRIA Bulletin* 1 & 2: 4–12.

CHE (Council on Higher Education (2009) *Higher Education Monitor No. 8: The state of higher education in South Africa.* Pretoria.

CODESRIA (Council for the Development of Social Science Research in Africa) (2008) *Strategic Plan 2007–2011: Consolidation and Renewal of African Social Science Research.* Dakar: CODESRIA.

Crush J (2000) 'Migrations past: An historical overview of cross-border movement in Southern Africa', in DA McDonald (ed.) *On Borders: Perspectives on International Migration in Southern Africa.* New York: St. Martin's Press.

Govender P (2009) 'Foreigners flock to SA universities', *Sunday Times,* South African edition, 26 July, p. 6.

Hashim I (2006) *The Positives and Negatives of Children's Independent Migration: Assessing the Evidence and the Debates,* Working Paper T16, Development Research Centre on Migration, Globalisation and Poverty, Brighton.

IEASA (International Education Association of South Africa) (2011) (ed.) *Higher Education in Context.* Pretoria.

Legoko R (2006) 'The reasons behind francophone African migration to Cape Town', in S Gallo-Mosala (ed.) *Migration to South Africa Within International Migration Trends.* Cape Town: Scalibrini Centre of Cape Town.

Marko K (2009) 'Internationalisation of higher education in Southern Africa with South Africa as the major exporter', a paper submitted to the University of Mauritius within the framework 'Services sector development in SADC and ESA region'.

Massey DS (2006) 'Patterns and processes of international migration in the twenty-first century: Lessons for South Africa', in M Tienda, S Findley, S Tollman and E Preston-Whyte (eds) *African Migration and Urbanisation in Comparative Perspective.* Johannesburg: Wits University Press.

Jooste N (2011) 'IEASA: Marketing a brand, a higher education system and a country', in International Education Association of South Africa (IEASA) (ed.) *Higher education in context.* Pretoria: IEASA.

Sawyerr A (1998) 'Does Africa really need her universities?' *CODESRIA Bulletin* 3 & 4: 20–25.

SARUA (Southern Africa Regional Universities Association) (2009) *SARUA Handbook 2009: A Guide to the Public Universities of Southern Africa* (available online). Johannesburg.

Simmons BA (1982) 'Hypotheses and analytical approaches for the study of demographic and socio-economic consequences of migration', in United Nations Economic and Social Commission for Asia and the Pacific (ed.) *National Migration Surveys: X Guidelines for Analyses*. New York: United Nations.

Shaw RP (1975) *Migration Theory and Fact: A Review and Bibliography of Current Literature*. Tokyo: Regional Science Research Institute, United Nations Publications.

Stahl WC (1989) 'Overview: Economic perspectives [on international migration]', in A Reginald (ed.) *The Impact of International Migration on Developing Countries*. Paris: OECD

Shen W (2007) 'Chinese student migration in the globalising world', paper presented at the ISS Conference on International Migration, Multi-local Households and Human Security Perspectives from Europe, Asia and Africa, Institute of Social Studies, The Hague, The Netherlands, 30–31 August 2007.

Skeldon R (2005) *Globalization, Skilled Migration and Poverty Alleviation: Brain Drain in Context*, Working Paper T15, Sussex Centre for Migration Research, University of Sussex, Brighton, United Kingdom.

Suksomboon P (2007) 'Remittances and "social remittances": Their impact on lived experiences of Thai women in The Netherlands and non-migrants in Thailand', paper presented at the ISS Conference on International Migration, Multi-local Livelihoods and Human Security: Perspectives from Europe, Asia and Africa, Institute of Social Studies, The Hague, The Netherlands, 30–31 August 2007.

Tati G (2006) From involuntary to voluntary re-migration in the SADC region. Analytical report prepared for the Migration and Urbanisation Node 'Stimulating Research on Migration and Urbanisation in Southern Africa and Africa'. Johannesburg: University of the Witwatersrand, Health Population Division.

Tati G (2010) Research on the educational migration of students from Central and West Africa into the South African higher education system. Unpublished data from a survey carried out at the University of the Western Cape (2009–10), Bellville.

UIS (UNESCO Institute for Statistics) (2009) *Global Education Digest 2009: Comparing Education Staistics Across the World*. Montreal: UIS.

UIS (2012) *New Patterns in Student Mobility in the Southern African Development Community*, UIS Information Bulletin No. 7, Montreal, Canada.

Waters J (2006) 'Geographies of cultural capital: Education, international migration and family strategies between Hong Kong and Canada', *Transactions of the Institute of British Geographers*, 31: 179–192.

Chapter 8

The experiences of Deaf students at a South African university

Lucas Magongwa

THE NUMBER OF DEAF[1] STUDENTS entering South African higher-education institutions grew tremendously after the country's new constitution was adopted in 1996. The increase occurred in response to demands made on the state in the context of its constitutional obligation to increase access to the education system. To accommodate the diversity of learning needs and address barriers to learning, the state, in turn, required education institutions to provide educational support services to students (Department of Education 1997). Higher-education institutions, such as the University of the Witwatersrand, have since begun to offer services such as South African Sign Language (SASL) interpreters and academic support to deaf students. Despite such services and opportunities, deaf students in South Africa, like their counterparts in most other countries around the world, continue to encounter many difficulties and challenges when they attempt to obtain a university qualification (Liversidge 2003).

The philosophy of inclusive education holds that to create equal opportunities for all, an education system must be responsive to the diverse needs and aims of all its students. Inclusive education is being implemented in many countries, notably, the United Kingdom, the United States, Australia and South Africa. According to the World Federation of the Deaf, many policy-makers strongly support the 'full-scale mainstreaming of all disabled students with all students in regular schools near to their homes' (WFD 2007: 3). However, deaf students require particular support services, including Sign Language interpreters and academic support, and when determining the effectiveness of these services in terms of equal access to learning, the social and academic experiences of Deaf students are seldom explored. To begin to counter this trend, I researched the experiences of a group of deaf students registered at the University of the Witwatersrand in Johannesburg, South Africa. This particular university was chosen for two reasons. Firstly, the participants and I and were all students there at the time. Secondly, the university Disability Unit has run a structured student-support service for deaf students since 1986, and the university is open to students from diverse backgrounds, including different linguistic backgrounds such as SASL. This chapter reports on the study in some detail, discusses its findings and draws some conclusions about the need for further research and investigation.

Theoretical framework

The theoretical perspective that underpins this study is that deafness is not merely a physical disability but also a cultural and linguistic phenomenon (Thompson 2004). The European Union of the Deaf (EUD) put it succinctly when it said; 'Deaf people view themselves as a cultural and linguistic minority. But they encounter barriers put up by society, suffer from lack of access and are therefore also "disabled"' (EUD 1997: 10). To clarify: there are two main paradigms related to deafness, the pathological view and the cultural and linguistic view.

The *pathological perspective* on deafness classifies deaf people as a disability group (Peel 2004). According to this view, deaf people have a deficiency that needs to be corrected. To address this deficiency, medical professionals have developed cochlea implants and other hearing devices.

The *cultural and linguistic perspective* acknowledges that Deaf people, who communicate in Sign Language and share certain values and beliefs, identify themselves as members of a cultural and linguistic group, regardless of race or ethnic background. Members of the Deaf community who are protagonists of this view do not regard deafness as a special need or a deficit but as a linguistic and cultural phenomenon, and they propose that Deaf people be recognised as a distinct cultural group (Peel 2004). A Deaf participant in Komesaroff's study (2000: 1) put it succinctly when she said:

I don't consider myself disabled, but I understand the meaning of the word 'disability'. I understand that…and I understand the community's perception of that word and I accept that I have a disability in hearing but I am not physically disabled.

There are, however, some deaf people who, for political reasons, view themselves as disabled because of the difficulties they experience with communication in our hearing-dominated society. Moores (2001) confirmed that many of the societal and educational problems experienced by Deaf people relate to issue of communication. From a socio-cultural perspective, it is therefore appropriate to examine the communication needs of the Deaf community alongside those of other minority language groups, rather than to compare them with those experienced by people with disabilities.

According to Butow (1994), the shift in focus away from the provision of welfare and towards ensuring human rights for all made people realise that viewing deafness solely as pathology can be inappropriate, and tends to contradict the way that Deaf people see themselves. I agree with the Deaf community's approach, and regard Deaf students not as disabled but as able to succeed in higher-education institutions, provided they have access to appropriate services, such as Sign Language interpreters, note-takers and other academic support programmes.

As noted, research reveals that the problems faced by deaf students are primarily related to issues of communication, academic language and literacy, relationships with teachers and other students in the learning environment, and community support (Thompson 2004). Crottey (1998: 8) points out that it is through social interactions that people 'enter into the perceptions, attitudes and values of a community'. How Deaf and hard-of-hearing students see themselves and others, and how they think hearing people see them, impacts on their experiences at educational institutions.

Deaf people in South Africa are a community within a wider community. The Deaf Federation of South Africa (DeafSA 1998) points out that 90 per cent of deaf children are born to hearing parents and 10 per cent are born to deaf parents. A Deaf community is a group of deaf and possibly hearing people, 'who, based on shared experiences among each other and identification with one another, participate together in a variety of activities' (Higgins 1987: 153). Sign Language also distinguishes members of the Deaf community as a separate linguistic group. Penn (1993: 11) states that:

> Sign Language is the language of the eyes and hands, of movement and space. Sign Language is the natural language of the Deaf. One of the most important determinants of acceptance into the Deaf cultural group lies in the proficiency of Sign Language.

Problems experienced by deaf university students

While higher-education institutions have adopted policies stating their commitment to inclusive education, any assumption that equal rights, opportunities and access to education are actually afforded to all would be false. In fact, deaf students encounter a range of barriers when they attempt to enrol at universities (DeafSA 2006). Firstly, SASL is not recognised as being equal to other languages. This is despite the support offered to the language by protective legislation including the South African Constitution of 1996, the South African Schools Act of 1997, and state policies such as the Integrated National Disability Strategy (Department of Social Development 1997).

For example, higher-education candidates, particularly when registering for a degree in the humanities, are required to have obtained a pass in two of South Africa's 11 official languages at secondary-school level (Department of Education 2005). One of these languages must be their home or first language, and the other must be on the Department of Education's (2005) list of recognised additional languages. This requirement constitutes a barrier for Deaf students because SASL is their first language, yet it is not included among the country's 11 official languages, nor is it among the list of recognised additional languages mentioned in the Revised National Curriculum Statement. Secondly, when deaf students do access higher education, they encounter additional academic and social barriers. Reduced levels of communication and social integration, imposed by the lack of a signing environment at most institutions of higher learning, can lead to misunderstandings and the isolation of deaf students.

Aims and rationale of the study

The rationale for the study was threefold. Firstly, I was motivated by my experiences as a Deaf teacher in two schools for deaf learners in South Africa's North West Province. I wanted to find out how best to prepare deaf learners for higher education, and to do so I decided to explore the experiences of deaf students who were already at university. Secondly, I aimed to assess the implementation of an inclusive education policy and the support services provided for Deaf students at one higher-education institution in South Africa with the hope that other institutions might be able to reflect on their own policies and practices. Finally, I aimed to contribute to the body of literature on deaf education, which in relation to the academic and social experiences of deaf students in mainstream higher education, is particularly sparse.

A review of the literature on deaf people and higher education in South Africa shows that DeafSA conducted a pilot study in 1998 on the situation of Deaf students in tertiary institutions. Although this study was a good one, it does not describe the experiences of Deaf students or present a Deaf person's point of view. Other studies, such as that by Howell (2004) on 'Disabled students and higher education in South Africa', do not focus specifically on Deaf students but on disability in general.

Internationally, research has shown that the majority of deaf university graduates were hard of hearing or developed deafness post-lingually (see, for example, Brelje 1999 and Komesaroff 2000). This can be attributed to the scarcity of Sign Language interpreting services at universities. Brelje points out that opportunities for higher education are far greater for hard-of-hearing students in many countries than they are for Deaf students because the communication needs of the latter are not always met. Komesaroff (2000: 1) firmly states that Deaf students are 'grossly under-represented in higher education' worldwide.

The educational transformation that has swept through South Africa since 1994 means that opportunities for deaf people to access higher education have increased, and this is, in turn, making it possible research the experiences of Deaf persons. Education support services are the 'key to equal participation in the learning process' (Department of Education 1997: 12) and their availability to Deaf students in the context of equal participation in the learning process is worth exploring.

As noted, the experience of deaf students with regard to support services in higher education is a complex phenomenon and little research has been conducted in this regard (Liversidge 2003). Furthermore, very little of the research done so far has been conducted by Deaf researchers (Thompson 2004). Therefore, this study aimed to fill a significant gap in the research, contribute to the development of new theory, and identify issues for future research initiatives.

In examining the implementation of inclusive-education policies, it was hoped that the study would have significance for other institutions including, for example, the national and provincial departments of education, which wish to promote equal access and success, particularly with reference to Deaf students. It was also hoped that the study would lead to the identification of factors (such as additional communication options) that help to facilitate positive university experiences for Deaf students, and that this would assist university management, academic and administrative staff in widening access to higher education for Deaf students. It is hoped that the findings of the study will also be useful to Deaf students who plan to access higher education via a mainstream university.

To sum up, the research described in this chapter aimed to explore the experiences of Deaf students from a Deaf perspective, and to inform various stakeholders (Deaf students, institutions of higher learning and the state) about the academic and social experiences of Deaf university students.

Services for Deaf students at the University of the Witwatersrand

According to university archives, the University of the Witwatersrand was founded as an open university and until apartheid legislation forced it to do otherwise from the 1960s to the 1990s, the institution welcomed all students, regardless of race, gender and disability.[2] In the early 1990s, the university's human resources department established a Transformation and Equity Office to address access and employment-equity matters generally, and specifically in relation to people with disabilities, including deaf students and staff. The office has since assumed responsibility for developing, implementing and monitoring the university's disability policy. Essentially, the Transformation and Equity Office focuses on policy implementation, while the Disability Unit, which was established on the campus in 1986, deals with service delivery to students with disabilities, including the Deaf.

The Disability Unit provides academic support, guidance and support to students with disabilities, including the Deaf, and aims to facilitate their adjustment to university life. The service includes the provision of SASL interpreters, note-takers, mathematics tutors, invigilators, adaptive devices, computer training, Braille services, interventions related to physical access to buildings, assistance with bursary and loan applications, as well as applications for extra time for essays and examinations. The establishment of the Disability Unit enabled the institution to lead the way in making university degrees accessible to students with disabilities and Deaf students, thus aligning itself with the principles of South African and international policies on inclusive education.[3]

The Disability Unit has strong links with the education faculty's Advanced Certificate in Education, which is the programme that accommodates the largest number of Deaf and hard-of-hearing students on campus. This certificate was introduced when the Further Diploma in Education that the university had offered since 1996 was phased out. According to Steinberg et al. (2004), the Further Diploma started by providing specialised courses in mathematics, science and English with the aim of upgrading the qualifications of teachers who were underqualified.[4] In 2000, a specialisation related to teaching learners with special educational needs was introduced, and this was followed by the introduction of specialisation in Deaf education in 2001. Thus, Deaf students in the Advanced Certificate in Education programme frequently make use of the support services provided by the Disability Unit.

The institutional and environmental support services for Deaf and hard-of-hearing students offered by the university attracts students from all over the country and from neighbouring countries, such as Botswana, Lesotho and Swaziland. In addition, it is important to note that the university is located within the city of Johannesburg, which has a thriving Deaf community. This offers the students opportunities to socialise and a base from which to receive moral support.

Limitations of the study

The study was limited by several factors, one of which was outside of my control. Firstly, a national strike of civil servants occurred during the time set aside for data collection, that is, May and June 2007. Since many teachers are civil servants, the strike meant that we could not access the participants because they were either participating in the strike action or had to stay away from their usual places of work for safety reasons.[5]

Secondly, the perspectives of hearing students and lecturers were not included. Thus, there was no direct investigation of peer attitudes or lecturers' collaboration and support. Thirdly, the study focused on 12 Deaf students in an academic support programme at one university. The research therefore cannot be generalised to apply to the wider Deaf and hard-of-hearing student population at the university concerned or at other South African higher-education institutions.

Research methodology

Criteria for the selection of Deaf participants were that they were either currently registered at or recently certificated by the University of the Witwatersrand, and that they were both Deaf or hard of hearing *and* fluent in SASL. All students who participated in the study indicated their availability and gave consent for the research. Eight of the students had just completed their Advanced Certificate in Education and four were still studying towards their certificate. In addition, the manager of the university's Disability Unit was asked to complete a questionnaire because, in her capacity as co-ordinator of the Disability Unit, she was the primary facilitator of students' support services on campus. Her responses helped to clarify the range of services offered, how they were made possible, as well as how the Unit envisaged them being used and how they were actually used.

As far as the students were concerned, two data-collection techniques were used, namely interviews and written narratives. A schedule of questions was drawn up and used to guide the interviews with the Deaf participants, and Deaf participants were asked to submit a written description of their experiences as students at the university.

After drawing up the interview schedule, which contained a mix of structured and unstructured questions, I carried out a pilot study in February 2007 to determine the efficiency of the questions in collecting information from Deaf participants. Three Deaf students registered for the Advanced Certificate in Education were interviewed in the pilot study. They were asked to give feedback on the design and content of the interview, discussing any challenges they had experienced in responding and making suggestions regarding the signing, meaning and order of the questions. Minor amendments were then made to the interview schedule.

Interviews with Deaf students were conducted in SASL and recorded on video to ensure that concrete and precise data was captured for analysis. I used the interview schedule as a guide but it was constructed so as to allow me to elicit additional information when, for instance, a question was only partially answered.

Data analysis

I applied an ethnographic approach to analyse the data. I began by studying the transcripts from the interviews and identified common themes that emerged. This was one of the most challenging stages of the study; as Stewart and Shamdasani (1990: 116) have noted, the coding exercise requires 'several passes through the transcript as categories of topics evolve and the analyst gains greater insight into the content of the group discussion'.

This research entailed a social study, therefore it may not correctly generate issues of validity. There is a possibility that the participants in the study presented experiences that were time specific. What they experienced at the University of the Witwatersrand between 2003 and 2007 may have changed as support services became more or less available. In order to enhance validity of the data in this study, the following efforts were made: I compared the findings that emerged from the interviews with the participants' written narrative (documents) of their experiences as students; I then compared the findings with existing literature on the experiences of Deaf students in other integrated education settings; the accounts of participants' perspectives given are based on their own signs or words as recorded on the videotape; and a university colleague reviewed both the data and the conclusions.

About the participants

This section provides brief biographical information about each participant in the study. I changed the names of participants to protect their privacy and preserve confidentiality. The description of the participants provides contextual information about their experiences and assisted in interpreting the findings of the study. The following categories were used to characterise the degrees of the participants' hearing levels (see Table 8.1):

TABLE 8.1   Degrees of hearing

Hearing ability	Decibels (dB)
Normal	–10–15 dB
Slight loss	16–25 dB
Mild loss	26–40 dB
Moderate loss	41–55 dB
Moderately severe loss	56–70 dB
Severe loss	71–90 dB
Profound loss	91+ dB

Source Adapted from WFD (2007).

Celia is a black Deaf woman who is 35 years old. Her hearing level is 26–40 dB. Although Celia wears hearing aids and considers herself hard of hearing, she is fluent in SASL and campaigns for the educational rights of Deaf people. She was the first Deaf student to enrol and graduate from the Further Certificate in Education programme in 2003. At the time of her interview, Celia had returned to the university and was enrolled for an honours degree in adult education. Although she was the only Deaf student in her class and used a SASL interpreter, she was an active learner who participated in all classroom discussions and debates. During our interview, she expressed gratitude to the university for the provision of SASL interpreters but pointed out that Deaf students should be able to decide who interprets for them rather than the Disability Unit.

Paula is a 30-year-old black Deaf woman. Her parents are hearing, but she and a nephew and a niece were all born deaf. Her degree of hearing is 80–110 dB and she does not use a hearing aid. Paula is fluent in SASL and expresses herself much better in this language than in writing. She was repeating her final education module at the time of the interview. She attributed her previous failure in the module to the academic language used at university level and her frustration with the SASL interpreting service. Her interpreter frequently arrived late and sometimes did not show up at all.

Themba is a 29-year-old black Deaf man, who became profoundly deaf at the age of ten, through meningitis. His hearing level is 80–110 dB. He is attracted to the Deaf culture and describes himself as a Deaf person. Unlike other Deaf students in his class, Themba enjoys writing and his assignment marks are always high. He was satisfied with the SASL interpreter service. Themba does not like it when hearing students feel sorry for him because of his deafness. He believes that deafness should not make him a symbol of pity, but that it is a challenge he has had to overcome.

Rosemary is a 35-year-old Black woman who describes herself as hard of hearing and wears hearing aids. Her hearing level is 40–90 dB and she also has a physical disability. Rosemary communicates via SASL and speech (IsiZulu and English). At the time of our interview, she had completed her Advanced Certificate in Education and was in the process of applying for an honours degree in education. She says she interprets voluntarily for other students in the absence of a SASL interpreter.

Razina, a 34-year-old black Deaf woman, is profoundly deaf with a hearing level of 91–110 dB. She describes herself as Deaf and her main language of communication is SASL. Her desire to excel as a teacher of the Deaf had motivated her to enrol at university. At the time of the interview in 2006, she had not been successful in passing her first modules, and planned to take a two-year break before returning to her studies. She cited family commitments as the reason for suspending her studies. Despite the availability of SASL interpreters, she expressed frustration that she had received no academic support.

Misha is an Indian woman aged 32 who has a hearing level of 91–110 dB. She describes herself as Deaf and communicates mostly in SASL. She has a Deaf older sister, who acts as her role model. She was motivated to enter the teaching profession after receiving a scholarship to study at Gallaudet University in Washington DC and because of the many professional Deaf people she met while in the USA. Misha complained about the allocation and co-ordination of SASL interpreters at the University of the Witwatersrand, noting that, at times, a single SASL interpreter was allocated to her for a whole day at a time. This meant that the interpreter became fatigued and Misha felt that she then missed out on important discussions in class.

Siyabonga is a 35-year old black woman who describes herself as hard of hearing and sees herself as part of both hearing and Deaf cultures. Her hearing level is 56–90 dB, and although she became deaf when she was just two years old, she prefers to communicate in a combination of speech and signing. In 2007 she was in her first year of study in the ACE programme. She was the only student who wrote to the Disability Unit requesting an interpreter who could both sign and speak at the same time. She noted that she had not had access to a SASL interpreter service when she completed her initial teacher training at college.

Nandi is a 29-year-old black woman. Like Siyabonga, she describes herself as hard of hearing and communicates in both speech and signs. She is not sure when she became deaf but thinks it was around 10 years of age. Her hearing level is 41–70 dB. Her motivation to enrol for the Advanced Certificate in Education is because during her initial teacher training she had not been trained in deaf pedagogy. She was dissatisfied with the curriculum studies aspect of the certificate course noting that the SASL interpreters did not interpret everything in the class and that the Deaf students therefore did not have equal access to the information given to the hearing students.

Claude, who is 31, is a black man who identifies himself as Deaf. His hearing level is 91–110 dB. There is no other trace of deafness in his family. He prefers to communicate in SASL. He indicated that he was happy with the SASL interpreter service. He was in his final year of study at the time of our interview, and noted that, during his time at the university, he had constructively engaged hearing students who had misconceptions about Deaf and hard-of-hearing people.

Dumisani is a 33-year-old black woman who became deaf at the age of 11. She describes herself as hard of hearing, though her hearing impairment is severe (71–90 dB). Dumisani communicates with hearing people and Deaf people using speech and SASL respectively. She attended a mainstream school where she had no access to SASL interpreters or Deaf classmates. At the time of our interview, she was in her final year of the certificate programme. Dumisani expressed dissatisfaction with the fact that when the students are off campus, the university communicates with Deaf and hard of hearing students mainly by telephone. She also felt disappointed that, at the graduation ceremony, students in the certificate programme they are not capped like students who obtain the same qualification from other universities.

Emmaarah, a 29-year-old Indian woman, is profoundly deaf. Her hearing level is 91–110 dB. She is fluent in SASL and is married to a hearing man. SASL is her main mode of communication. She is not willing to simplify SASL for students who don't know the language well, and prefers to write down her words, albeit reluctantly. Like Paula, she struggled with academic English literacy but, due to hard work and commitment, she succeeded. She noted that she socialises mostly with other Deaf students, and that when they are not around, she doesn't communicate.

Valli is an Indian woman who is 30 years old. She describes herself as hard of hearing. Her hearing level is mild to moderately severe (41–70 dB). She communicates well in both speech and SASL. She can talk on a mobile phone, but only to close friends and family who are able to understand her voice. Valli was the only hard-of-hearing participant who said that she did not depend on SASL interpreters in the lecture halls. As seems to be the case with most Deaf and hard of hearing students, she attributed her struggles with her studies to ill health rather than to communication problems. She had applied for entry into the an honours programme for 2008.

In summary, the group of study participants was made up of Deaf and hard-of-hearing teachers who had been or were students at the University of the Witwatersrand between 2003 and 2008. They had all registered for or completed the two-year Advanced Certificate in Education. All but two participants had been successful in their academic studies at the time of the interviews. The group consisted of mostly women, which is a common trend in schools for the Deaf in South Africa. Seven participants identified themselves as Deaf and five as hard of hearing. Nine participants were Black and three were Indian. Their ages ranged from 29 to 35. The majority of participants (11) had been exposed to SASL interpreter services prior to their enrolment on the certificate programme. One study participant, Siyabonga, had not, and her expectations of the interpreter services offered were also different: she wanted an interpreter who both mouthed and signed every word spoken in the lectures.

In terms of commonalities, however, all the participants had used the SASL interpreter services offered by the university, regardless of their hearing levels. In addition, all had become deaf in their early childhood, between birth and 11 years of age. They all had hearing parents, which means SASL was not their mother tongue, but for most it was their preferred language. Just two participants, Paula and Misha, had Deaf family members.

The hearing levels of the study participants ranged from moderate to profound. It appeared that the levels of hearing did not influence participants' decisions to describe themselves as Deaf of hard of hearing but rather a categorical allegiance. For example, Siyabonga's audiogram showed that she had a hearing level of 80-120 dB, yet she described herself as hard of hearing.

Despite the varieties in the levels of hearing loss, all the participants registered with the Disability Unit for support services. The most frequent service used is the South African Sign Language interpreting. Services such as note-taking were not used because they were not available. The Disability Unit manager indicated that, due to the growing number of students with disabilities enrolling at the university and the need to balance the types of support service provided, there was a limit on the services that could be provided. Interestingly, none of the participants had requested other services such as computerised note-taking or assistance with extra-time applications from the Disability Unit. Although Siyabonga mentioned that she needed an oral communicator, whether she took this up with the Disability Unit is unknown.

Findings

The themes that emerged from the data can be categorised as follows: motivation to study, individual participant's perspective, academic experiences, challenges faced, the university climate and pre-university experiences. Table 8.2 on the next page outlines the categories and themes identified.

What emerged from the data was that two main factors motivated these Deaf and hard-of-hearing students to enrol at the University of the Witwatersrand. The first was their personal commitment to contributing to the improvement of Deaf education. The second was the availability of institutional and environmental support services at the university.

The participants, all stakeholders in Deaf education by virtue of being teachers, felt that their previous training had not adequately prepared them for teaching Deaf learners. They noted that they had entered schools for the Deaf unaware of appropriate teaching methodologies, Deaf culture, the role of SASL and the psychosocial development of Deaf learners. Programmes in Deaf education offered by the university were seen by participants as an opportunity to empower themselves to contribute to the improvement of the education of Deaf learners.

The study confirmed that provision of the support service has a significant impact on deaf students in terms of equitable access and success in learning institutions. It also confirmed the need for reliable support services for Deaf and hard-of-hearing students if they are to succeed at the university level. Some students complained about the quality and inconsistency of the SASL interpreting service, an issue that is indicative of a larger problem in South Africa.

TABLE 8.2   Categories and themes that emerged from the interviews and written submissions

Pre-university experiences	Part of all-Deaf classes Using interpreters Early inclusion Role of interpreters
University climate	Accessibility Awareness 'Club' membership Classroom situation
Motivation to study	Wanting to contribute to Deaf education Following the example of role models Campus recruitment strategy is effective Socialisation Self-empowerment Keen to upgrade existing qualifications
Challenges faced	Peer attitudes Lack of Deaf peers Lecturer attitudes English literacy Learning methods Note-taking Social isolation Environmental constraints Interpreter shortages Fear of failure Multiple visual tasks Dependence on third parties for access to information
Academic experiences	Communication issues Language access Coping strategies Study skills Limiting factors Studies Academic discourses
Institutional factors shaping students' perspectives	Social integration Support services First lecture Assessment processes Administrative issues Campus amenities

In relation to the access and success of these Deaf and hard-of-hearing students, factors such as their own motivations and coping skills, as well as the availability of support services were significant. The data showed that all the participants had coped remarkably well, considering the communication obstacles they had faced. Some participants noted that they experienced tutorial activities that included group work as problematic because of the fast-paced and often overlapping nature of spoken exchanges (see also Foster 1998). Some found these spoken exchanges impossible to follow through speech reading and often felt excluded from discussions. With skilled SASL interpreters and a change of attitudes by students, both Deaf and hearing, group work could be made more accessible and inclusive.

The study confirmed the findings of the existing literature about the need to obtain feedback about inclusive education directly from Deaf and hard-of-hearing people. Traditionally, research in the area of Deaf education has reflected the voice of hearing people. Little attention has been given to the perceptions of Deaf people themselves. In addition, hearing people, who often have had only basic or little knowledge of Deaf culture and related issues, have conducted the research. This meant that the 'Deaf voice' was often disregarded (Komesaroff 1998). Yet, changes made as a result of listening to Deaf voices are more likely to make the university more accessible for Deaf and hard-of-hearing people.

Another key theme that emerged from the study was that Deaf students prefer to relate to other Deaf students. According to Foster (1998), groups of Deaf and hard-of-hearing students 'often find in a community of Deaf peers the real conversation, family, information and friendships which they do not get from interactions with hearing people' (Foster 1998: 130). Furthermore, communication barriers seem to hinder the development of relationships between Deaf and hearing students, although the lack of interaction may also be linked to previous bad experiences that Deaf students do not wish to repeat.

Despite communication barriers in the classrooms, Deaf participants in the study appreciated the positive attitudes of the lecturers in the Advanced Certificate programme. For example, one lecturer secured SASL interpreters from the Disability Unit by continually supplying the Unit with schedules indicating when the interpreters would be required.

Discussion

The availability of support services such as SASL interpreters and the presence of other Deaf students at the institution clearly helped to motivate these Deaf and hard-of-hearing students to enter the higher-education arena.

The presence of other Deaf students offered opportunities for peer interaction and friendship. However, if Deaf and hard-of-hearing students are to have a positive experience of social and academic integration, issues such as the politics of educational practices and research epistemology need to be exposed and challenged.

Deaf students view themselves as culturally and linguistically different but not as disabled. However, the university's policy and practice positions Deaf and hard-of-hearing students as disabled. This 'denial of linguistic and cultural difference, in preference for a disability construction, ignores the situation in which Deaf people find themselves' (Komesaroff 2000: 10). It must be noted that the 'denial' may be unintentional in some cases as, historically, Deaf people have been viewed by society within a pathological paradigm. However, the cultural and linguistic view of deafness cannot go unchallenged. Clearly, Deaf people share some characteristics with other cultural minority groups, but they also share characteristics with the disability sector. Thus Deaf people can be defined as a cultural and linguistic group with a difference (Thompson 2004). Their challenge in a social and academic environment is exacerbated by the fact that they cannot access spoken languages, such as English, in the same ways that other minority groups can. A possible solution would be for society to shift from regarding deafness as a welfare issue to a human rights issue – within a welfare framework, deaf students are viewed as unequal to others but deaf students view equality, as offered by a human-rights perspective, as a cornerstone of their acceptance and happiness.

In terms of academic experience, a number of participants such as Themba, Dumisani and Valli, to name a few, demonstrated high levels of competence in English literacy. However, several expressed the view that English literacy took up most of their energy and time. The low level of English literacy was one of the main barriers that some Deaf and hard-of-hearing students had to overcome. The problem is exacerbated by the poor quality of education in schools for the Deaf, where a lack of role models, low expectations of schoolteachers, and teachers not being fluent in SASL, combine to discourage learning. However, it seemed that participants could have taken more advantage of the academic-support services to improve their English literacy. Limited time on campus was cited as a problem because, as part-time block-release students, they came to campus for just one week per term and their sessions ran from 8 a.m. to 4 p.m. Support services such as the writing centre close soon after 4 p.m. However, as Lang (2002: 277) has noted: Deaf and hard-of-hearing students in higher education must 'become more involved in redirecting their own destinies'.

While Deaf and hard-of-hearing students face particular challenges, there seems to be a lack of awareness about Deaf people's needs as a minority group. Raising and promoting awareness of Deaf and hard-of-hearing students and their needs would encourage their further inclusion in the life of the university. A wider and deeper awareness of deafness would assist Deaf and hard-of-hearing students to feel that they can compete on an equal level with hearing students on campus.

In discussions about the general climate on campus, participants indicated that the university seemed generally aware of Deaf and hard-of-hearing students; however, their social and academic experiences showed that they were not integrated fully in university life. This is due to factors such as poor communication, inadequate support services and students' lack of assertiveness.

My investigation of participants' pre-university experiences revealed that prior educational experiences acted either as a barrier or as an advantage throughout their higher-education studies. Schools thus play a vital role in preparing Deaf and hard-of-hearing students for higher education. However, there is no guarantee that Deaf and hard-of-hearing students will have positive academic and social experiences in either secondary or tertiary education institutions.

Implications for policy and practice

As early as 2000, the University of the Witwatersrand's policy on disability had identified the diversification of the institution's staff and students as a strategic imperative, and proclaimed that 'the university community will reflect and respect diversity' (University of the Witwatersrand 2000: 1). It is necessary, therefore, to assess the impact of the policy on the institutional community. This evaluation should consist of more than annual reports from heads of department. Instead, the perceptions of 'insiders', that is, those most directly affected by such polices such as the participants in this study, need to be sought out and made public. The university could then use an analysis of the experience of Deaf and hard-of-hearing students to identify possible gaps between the goals of the policies and the actual experiences of students.

In addition, activities that raise awareness around the issue of deafness throughout the university community need to be encouraged and promoted. With the presence of the Centre for Deaf Studies, the Disability Unit and the SASL department on campus, the university already has a support structure that could further raise and highlight the issue of Deaf awareness. For example, recently graduated Deaf and hard-of-hearing students could be asked to share their experiences with all new and prospective students. This would give new students an idea of what to expect and an awareness of the support services available to them, and may help to promote Deaf awareness among hearing students and staff.

Deaf and hard-of-hearing students face many unique communication challenges in fulfilling their academic goals in mainstream tertiary institutions. Linguistic competence in SASL is a distinct advantage for educators of Deaf learners. It would be beneficial for the Department of Education to encourage more school teachers and university lecturers to learn SASL by providing resources and funding an investigation on how best to accommodate Deaf students in the context of inclusive education. One of the key stakeholders in such a study would be university-based services such as the University of the Witwatersrand's Disability Unit. Deaf people should also be involved in this investigation and asked to provide suggestions as to how they would like to be accommodated. Further studies of how inclusion policies are being implemented in other educational contexts would contribute to a better understanding of how to make policies more effective, particularly with regard to Deaf learners. As Powers (2002: 230) has confirmed:

> There is an urgent need for teachers to develop a shared language and understanding of what inclusion means at school and at classroom level... beyond vague notions of greater participation in mainstream settings. I contend that educators of Deaf children, and indeed all educators, need to be aware of the oversimplification and confusion that exists and to work towards a clearer definition of inclusion that can help drive the practice.

Research on inclusive education and deaf schoolchildren needs to be done in collaboration with Deaf and hard-of-hearing people so that such studies have an 'insiders' perspective as revealed in this article.

The study on which this chapter is based aimed to create a foundation for future research. Deaf and hard-of-hearing students still face many obstacles to achieving their academic objectives within a university setting. The need to improve support services for Deaf and hard-of-hearing students cannot be emphasised enough, and the need to include Deaf 'voices' in the use and assessment of such services is equally critical.

Although the study explored the experiences of Deaf and hard-of-hearing students who have managed to reach higher education, it is vital to keep in mind that they are a tiny minority within the Deaf community. Far too many Deaf students fail to complete their secondary education, and never have the opportunity to realise their potential via mainstream universities.

Notes

1   Deaf people identify themselves differently; broadly speaking, some spell 'Deaf' with an upper-case 'D', and identify strongly with the Deaf community. They exhibit attitudinal (linguistic, political and social) cohesion with other Deaf people and tend to use Sign Language as their primary means of communication (Baker and Cokely 1980). The other group spell 'deaf' with a lower-case 'd', and tend to have developed deafness post-lingually. They tend to identify more with people who use speech and are more likely to use lip-reading and hearing aids to help them communicate. In this chapter, 'Deaf' is used to refer to the cultural community and 'deaf' refers to the audiological phenomenon of not being able to hear.

2   See also the section on 'The Liberal Tradition' in History of Wits on the university's website.

3   The Unit was established early in the 1985 as the disabled students program. I know no other university that provided such service before that time.

4   The upgrading of teacher qualifications forms part of the transformation of South Africa's education system, a process that has been ongoing since the abolition of apartheid in 1994.

5   Although participants were attending the University of the Witwatersrand where I was studying, they were part-time, 'block-release' students who came to campus for just one week per term, so I had planned to interview them at their workplaces.

References

Baker C and D Cokely (1980) *American Sign Language: A Teacher's Resource Text on Grammar and Culture.* Silver Spring, MD: TJ Publishers.

Brelje HW (1999) 'Postsecondary opportunities for the Deaf', in HW Brelje (ed.) *Global Perspectives on the Education of the Deaf in Selected Countries.* Hillsboro OR: Butte.

Butow H (1994) 'Concepts of impairments, disability and handicap', *Interaction* 7: 12–14.

Crottey N (1998) *The Foundations of Social Research.* London: Sage.

DeafSA (Deaf Federation of South Africa) (1998) *A Pilot Study into the Current Situation of the Deaf in Tertiary Institutions in South Africa* (A report commissioned by the Pan South African Language Board). Johannesburg.

DeafSA (2006) Education Position Paper. Johannesburg.

Department of Education (1997) *Quality Education For All: Overcoming Barriers to Learning and Development* (Report of the National Commission on Special Needs in Education and Training and the National Committee on Education Support Services). Pretoria.

Department of Education (2005) Minimum Admission Requirements for Higher Certificate, Diploma and Bachelor's Degree Programmes Requiring a Further Education and Training Certificate. Pretoria.

Department of Social Development (1997) *Integrated National Disability Strategy*. Pretoria.

EUD (European Union of the Deaf) (1997) *Full Citizenship through Sign Languages* (Conference report). Brussels.

Foster SB (1998) 'Communication experiences of Deaf people: An ethnographic account', in I Parasnis (ed.) *Cultural and Language Diversity and the Deaf Experience*. Cambridge: Cambridge University Press.

Higgins PC (1987) 'The Deaf Community', in PC Higgins and E Nash (eds) *Understanding Deafness Socially*. Springfield: Charles Thomas.

Howell C (2004) 'Disabled students and higher education in South Africa', in B Watermeyer, L Swartz, T Lorenzo, M Schneider and M Priestly (eds) *Disability and Social Change: A South African Agenda*. Cape Town: HSRC Press.

Komesaroff L (1998) 'Deaf education and the politics of language practices', paper presented at the Deaf Studies Research Symposium, Sydney, 22–23 August.

Komesaroff L (2000) 'Diversity and justice: Being different in universities and schools', paper presented at the Association for Active Educational Researchers (ARRE) Conference, Sydney, December.

Lang HG (2002) 'Higher education for deaf students: Research priorities in the new millennium', *Journal of Deaf Studies and Deaf Education* 7: 267–280.

Liversidge AG (2003) Academic and Social Integration of Deaf and Hard of Hearing Students in a Carnegie Research University. PhD thesis, University of Maryland, New York.

Moores D (ed.) (2001) *Educating the Deaf: Psychology, Principles and Practices*. Boston: Houghton Mifflin.

Peel EL (2004) Inclusive Practice in South Africa: A Deaf Perspective. Master's thesis, University of the Witwatersrand, Johannesburg.

Penn C (1993) 'Signs of the times: Deaf language and culture in South Africa', *South African Journal of Communication Disorders* 40: 11–23.

Powers S (2002) 'From concepts to practice in deaf education: A United Kingdom perspective on inclusion', *Journal of Deaf Studies and Deaf Education* 7: 230–243.

Steinberg C, Magongwa L, Barclay H, Inglis, J, Mayisela S, Nakedi M and Snell D. (2004) 'Accommodating diversity: Supporting learning in an in-service teacher education programme offered by the University of the Witwatersrand', in T Welch and Y Reed (eds) *Designing and Delivering Distance Education: Quality Criteria and Case Studies from South Africa*. Johannesburg: NADEOSA.

Stewart DW and Shamdasani PN (1990) *Focus groups: Theory and practice*. London: Sage.

Thompson J (2004) Teaching English Literacy to Members of the Deaf Community: Insights for Bilingual Programming. Master's thesis, Auckland University of Technology.

University of the Witwatersrand (2000) Policy on Disability. Johannesburg. Available online.

WFD (World Federation of the Deaf) (2007) Education Rights for Deaf Children: A Policy Statement of the World Federation of the Deaf. Helsinki.

Chapter 9

Tradition and modernity: the inclusion and exclusion of traditional voices and other local actors in archaeological heritage management in Mozambique and Zimbabwe

Albino Jopela, Ancila Nhamo and Seke Katsamudanga

THE ISSUE OF COMMUNITY PARTICIPATION has taken centre stage in the management of cultural heritage since the early 2000s. All over the world, efforts are being made to involve local stakeholders in maintaining and conserving aspects of cultural heritage. Local stakeholders include traditional custodians, such as chiefs and spirit mediums, as well as other community members who may have a variety of interests in preserving an area's cultural heritage. Similarly, there have been calls to reintroduce traditional management systems, that is, methods of looking after heritage sites that were employed before the advent of colonialism (Chirikure and Pwiti 2008; Chirikure et al. 2010; Maradze 2003; Ndoro 2003; Pwiti 1996; Sullivan 2003). These methods were previously excluded in favour of what were seen as 'scientific' or formal methods of managing and conserving heritage. There is a growing awareness that these more modern methods have not led to the effective management of heritage sites, and that many communities maintain traditional custodianship systems which have worked effectively to ensure respect for and the survival of sites of cultural heritage (Joffroy 2005; Ndoro 2001b; Pwiti and Ndoro 1999).

In Africa, especially, traditional management systems have preserved sites of cultural significance since time immemorial. Cultural, religious and traditional belief systems (and traditional leaders) have ensured the survival of many archaeological sites (Mumma 2005; Ndoro 2006). Many of these sites, for example mountains, caves and crevices, are still used for rain-control ceremonies, or are spiritual areas where ancestors are buried. Taboos that regulate and restrict access to such sites are strictly enforced by traditional, political and religious authorities. The active engagement of communities living with archaeological sites is evident in southern Africa at places such as Domboshava and Silozwane in Zimbabwe (Pwiti and Mvenge 1996), Tsodilo Hills in Botswana (Thebe 2006), Kondoa-Irangi in Tanzania (Bwasiri 2011; Kessey 1995), Chongoni in Malawi (Ndoro 2006) as well as Chinhamapere in Mozambique (Jopela 2006; Nhamo et al. 2007; Sætersdal 2004).

The formal management of heritage sites imbued with sacred significance has led to conflicts between local communities and heritage-management institutions across the region (Taruvinga and Ndoro 2003). The dilemmas associated with managing such sites have been discussed from different perspectives by a number of scholars since the mid-1990s (see Katsamudanga 2003; Maradze 2003; Ndoro 2001b, 2003; Pwiti and Mvenge 1996; Pwiti et al. 2007). Despite growing awareness of the important role of local communities in the active management and use of sites, formally trained heritage managers often criticise the traditional use of heritage resources as potentially having a negative impact on such sites. Several scholars have argued that this view stems mainly from the rigid heritage policies inherited from the colonial period, which did not allow for inclusion of people other than heritage professionals in the conservation of heritage sites (see Pwiti and Ndoro 1999; Ndoro and Pwiti 2005; Ndlovu 2009).

As a result, heritage professionals have faced incessant opposition from local communities who live with heritage sites. These professionals have been accused of:

• protecting only those aspects of heritage sites that heritage managers consider important and, in most cases, excluding the intangible aspects of heritage, that is, their spiritual or cultural significance;
• presenting heritage resources in a lingo that is familiar (and thus only accessible) to those within the profession;
• dwelling on issues that may not be of interest to the wider public;
• involving local communities in very limited ways if at all; and
• failing to address development issues that are, at times, more important and more relevant to the concerned communities.
• It has been acknowledged that, at times, the aspirations of heritage managers and archaeologists, as well as some of the research and management practices of the past, have been at variance with community interests (Chirikure et al. 2010; Marshall 2002; Smith 2004). On the other hand, the limited resources and capacities of formal heritage organisations, and the failure of their strategies to conserve cultural heritage, has led

scholars and heritage practitioners to recognise that state-based or formal heritage management systems are incapable of ensuring the effective and sustainable management of archaeological heritage on their own (Mumma 2003).

Since numerous communities throughout Africa still use traditional mechanisms to ensure that culturally significant places are respected (Jopela 2006; Ndoro 2003; Sheridan and Nyamweru 2008), the inclusion of traditional systems is increasingly considered a solution to many of the problems facing heritage managers across the continent, especially in relation to the prevention of vandalism and the resolution of conflicts with local communities (Macamo 1996; Maradze 2003; Ndoro and Pwiti 2001; Nhamo 2009). However, as in Chirikure and Pwiti's (2008) discussion of community archaeology, most advocates of this approach do not look critically at the problems such approaches might introduce into the management of cultural sites. Although we do not contest the potential for traditional approaches to function effectively as community-based management systems, we question whether traditional systems *alone* can effectively protect archaeological sites in Africa today. Using archaeological sites in western Mozambique and Zimbabwe, this chapter interrogates some examples of the inclusion of traditional management systems in managing archaeological sites

Traditional systems and heritage management in Mozambique and Zimbabwe

The emergence of colonialism in Africa brought with it new and foreign political, social and economic systems that led to the transformation of indigenous cultures (Mamdani 1996). In the political arena, the colonialists brought the concept of a nation, where all people within a defined geographical boundary identify themselves as part of a nation, regardless of their totems, clans, religions or traditional polities. In both western Mozambique and Zimbabwe, this was quite contrary to the traditional political systems, where different areas fell under different hierarchical leaders. Each area had its own paramount chief (*Mambo*), headmen (*Sadunhu*) and village headmen (*Sabhuku*). Initially, the colonial rulers had little use for these structures but invoked them when they became useful (in enforcing tax collection, for example). Most colonial systems involved well-structured central governments with ministers of local government, as well as provincial and district administrators, to oversee local political processes. Although the offices of the traditional leaders were maintained, the individual leaders had to be endorsed by the colonial district, provincial and national administration, or they would not be recognised.

In Mozambique, the Portuguese, like other colonising powers, attempted to co-opt and employ the traditional authorities to administer on their behalf. The traditional authorities were framed as indigenous authorities (*autoridade gentílica*) and centred on *régulos* (chiefs or village headmen). To some extent, these chiefs functioned as auxiliaries to colonial rule and as intermediaries between the colonial government and rural communities (Kyed 2007; Lundin and Machava 1995). Traditional authorities thus effectively became integrated into colonial political systems as government employees with very limited powers of attorney – a situation that has remained largely unchanged ever since (Bourdillon 1991). Thus, while some traditional leaders were integrated into the colonial administrations, traditional systems of governance were not recognised or included as part of formal civil-management frameworks. However, in the case of heritage management, it should be noted that traditional systems were not always entirely suppressed either (Jopela 2011).

Colonial institutions and legislation

In relation to the protection and management of cultural heritage sites, new institutions – such as Zimbabwe's (then Rhodesia's) Monuments Commission of 1936 and Historical Monuments Commission of 1958 – were constituted and mandated to look after the country's cultural heritage and the Monuments and Relics Act of 1936 was used to govern various aspects of conservation. In Mozambique, the earliest attempt of the Portuguese colonial authority to protect cultural heritage was through the adoption of Legislative Diploma 825 of 1943, which established a legal framework for the establishment of the National Commission for Monuments and Historic Relics in 1947. The Commission centred its efforts on the conservation of immovable heritage, and in this case, mostly Portuguese colonial monuments, such as churches and fortresses (Macamo 2006).

Thus, formal institutions and legislation took over the work that had previously been performed by traditional leaders, such as chiefs and spirit mediums. The institutions defined standards of acceptable conduct at cultural heritage sites and colonial legislation was used to enforce these standards. The laws prohibited the performance of certain cultural activities at these places, especially those that were proclaimed national monuments (a designation that protects sites of particular importance to a nation). All these structures and laws still exist today, albeit under new names; the Monuments Commission of Rhodesia was renamed National Museums and Monuments of Rhodesia under Chapter 313 of the National Museums and Monuments Act of 1972. When Zimbabwe achieved independence, this institution became the National Museums and Monuments of Zimbabwe, a mere replacement of the name Rhodesia with Zimbabwe. The legislation followed a similar trend in name changing with the most recent adjustment being a change in 1998 of the coding of the legislation from Chapter 313 to Act 25/11. However, in terms of defining and regulating the management of cultural heritage, the content of the legislation has remained unchanged since 1972.

Obviously, heritage legislation was preceded and succeeded by other laws on land ownership that appropriated land and alienated local populations from their land, as well as from sites of cultural heritage to which where they were attached. In Zimbabwe, laws such as the Land Apportionment Act of 1930 and the Land Tenure Act of 1959 were responsible for alienating indigenous people from their lands of origin and moving them to more marginal areas with poorer soils and lower rainfall. As Pwiti and Ndoro (1999) have pointed out, land alienation created both physical and spiritual distance between the local people and their cultural sites. This led to a gradual loss of knowledge about traditional activities and rituals associated with the sites. For many years these legal instruments also effectively suppressed traditional management systems at most cultural heritage sites. Although at some places, traditional custodians managed to sneak in to perform ceremonies and rituals (Pwiti and Mvenge 1996; Sinamai 2006), traditional systems were severely weakened.

The post-colonial period: revised legislation and a reversion to traditional practices

Most African countries inherited the hegemonic colonial systems of heritage management after the attainment of independence and these are still very much in control today (see Ndoro et al. 2008). Many of the restrictions that were put in place by colonial governments were adopted by the new nations. Mozambique did try to break with the colonial legal framework, however. In 1988, the Law for the Protection of the Cultural Heritage (10/88 of 1988) was adopted, and in 1994 the Bill on the Rules for the Protection of Archaeological Heritage (Decree 27/94) set out the principles and norms for carrying out archaeological work and for the conservation of archaeological objects, sites and monuments on national territory (Macamo and Sætersdal 2004). Unfortunately, this Bill largely overlooked issues concerning traditional or community-based management of cultural sites and did not go far enough in integrating these into the post-colonial heritage framework in Mozambique (Jopela 2011).

However, it is important to acknowledge that although community participation has not yet been legislated, actual heritage-management practices have changed in many African countries. For example, since the later 1970s, heritage-management strategy in Mozambique has been broadened to include raising public awareness via community participation in the conservation of certain archaeological sites (Macamo 2003). For instance, by 1978, some four hundred people from local communities had participated in archaeological research and heritage-management projects at the Great Zimbabwe-type site of Manyikeni in south-central Mozambique. The following year a museum was opened at the site in an effort to make the archaeological remains more accessible to these communities, (Ndoro 2001a; Sinclair 2004).

Heritage management since the 1990s

In more recent years, both Mozambican and Zimbabwean governments have tried to restore the powers of the traditional authorities. Mozambique's first multiparty elections in 1994 symbolised the introduction of a new political order purporting to promote the decentralisation of power to the local level (Abrahamsson and Nilsson 1995; Lundin and Machava 1995). A broad study of decentralisation and traditional authority resulted in Mozambique's Decree 15/2000 of 2000 officially recognising traditional authorities – or as they have since been designated, community authorities (*autoridades comunitárias*) – as legitimate representatives of the rural communities. These community authorities can be traditional chiefs, religious leaders, civil-society leaders, village/ward secretaries (*bairro*), or other leaders recognised by the local community according to local traditions (Buur and Kyed 2006). The Decree provides for the extension of state apparatuses to these authorities by delegating to them state functions such as taxation, census/registration duties, law enforcement and policing, land allocation, road maintenance, health, education, as well as the implementation of local development plans including those related to environmental sustainability, employment and food security. The Decree and associated *regulamento* also obligate community authorities to uphold local customs and cultural values, and to participate in investigating and reviving forms of local traditional culture such as dances, cuisine, songs, music and ritual ceremonies (Buur and Kyed 2005).

Similarly, in Zimbabwe the government returned some powers to local chiefs and other traditional leaders with the enactment of the Traditional

Leaders Act 29/17 of 1998 and via amendments made to the Act in 1999, 2001 and 2003. The Act governs the conduct and duties of traditional leaders mandated with the task of reviving traditional value systems. The reinstatement of traditional systems in the management of cultural heritage coincided with the land redistribution programme in the late 1990s and early 2000s whereby the government promised to redress the distortions created by colonialism and to return ancestral lands to their traditional owners. This ushered in a new era in which local communities invaded commercial farms and other areas previously owned by white people in order to reclaim their ancestral lands. This was accompanied by a major drive to revive traditional ceremonies such as rainmaking rituals and rites to appease the ancestors. Some of these ceremonies were even funded by the government (Nhamo 2009).

However, this all took place after almost a hundred years of these traditions being subject to repression and suffocation through the alienation of land rights, the imposition of Western-style education and Christianity, and more recently the impact of urbanisation, globalisation and new technologies (Katsamudanga 2003). Looking critically at the upsurge of tradition, one has to pose a number of questions. For example, what is tradition? Who and what is really traditional? Can tradition transcend modern needs? These questions all have a bearing on how the management and use of cultural heritage should proceed in the new 'traditional' age, and the answers to these questions will help us to evaluate the appropriateness of calls for traditional management systems at cultural heritage sites.

Chinhamapere Hill in Mozambique

One example of the inclusion of communities in the management of a cultural heritage site in Mozambique comes from Chinhamapere Hill, a very prominent hill in the foothills of the Vumba Mountains, in the province of Manica on the border between Mozambique and Zimbabwe. The main site at Chinhamapere Hill relevant to this chapter is Chinhamapere I: a large rock-art panel situated just below the top of the hill (Nhamo et al. 2007; Sætersdal 2004). Surrounding all the archaeological sites on Chinhamapere Hill is a fairly dense savannah woodland that the local community see as an integral part of the sacred landscape, and value as a scarce resource for traditional ceremonies (Jopela 2006). As demonstrated elsewhere (Jopela 2010), the cosmology of the Shona-speaking communities in Manica is very supportive of environmental ethics. In other words, humans are seen as part of an interacting set of living elements in the landscape, and cultural values (such as respect for humans, nature, and above all, for the ancestral spirits) enhance and promote the conservation of cultural and natural resources (see also Berkes et al. 2000; Nyathi and Ndiwini 2005).

The local traditional authority controls and effectively manages Chinhamapere and related places of cultural significance for the community. The political-traditional structures – led by a *Mambo* who is assisted by other leaders such as *Sabhuku* and *Svikiro* (a spirit medium) – are responsible for monitoring activities and behaviour at sacred sites and for making sure that local residents abide by the rules. For example, Mbuya Gondo, the spirit medium and traditional healer (*currandeira*) is responsible for conducting traditional ceremonies around Chinhamapere Hill. All visitors to Chinhamapere are directed to her and she performs rituals to obtain permission from the ancestral spirits for the visitors to enter the site. Furthermore, individuals and groups are not allowed to visit Chinhamapere or its environs without an official custodian or her appointee. Thus, when the octogenarian Gondo is unavailable to guide visitors herself, she empowers another member from the community to do so. This ensures strict adherence to the local cultural norms. The spirit medium has also contributed to the maintenance of the sacred forest by sensitising the community to the deforestation of the hill. This set-up testifies, to a certain extent, that traditional custodianship systems can be used effectively for ensuring the survival of cultural heritage (Jopela 2010).

Nharira Hills: a case from Zimbabwe

In Zimbabwe the trek towards the incorporation of local stakeholders began in the 1980s when community traditions were integrated into interpretations of archaeological sites such as Domboshava and Great Zimbabwe. By the end of the last millennium, local communities were allowed to sell souvenirs and conduct other businesses at most archaeological sites that are open to the public in order to benefit economically from these resources. By 2010, community participation was considered part of good archaeological management, and some sites, such as Nharira Hills (a landscape sacred to the Nyamweda people) and Gomba valley (the headquarters of Charwe, the spirit medium of Nehanda), were left largely to the traditional authorities to manage (Chakanyuka 2007; Mataga 2003). These two sites have since been proclaimed national monuments on the basis of their intangible heritage. They are both under the strict control of spiritual leaders who strictly regulate access even for employees of the National Museums and Monuments of Zimbabwe (Mataga 2003).

Concerns about community involvement in heritage management

Most people agree that traditional authorities and their management systems are important in the effective management of archaeological sites such as Chinhamapere. However, it is also true that such systems can lose their effectiveness in modern contexts. For instance, while Shona cosmology generally stresses the need to respect sacred sites and their surrounding areas, this belief system did not prevent the partial deforestation of the area around the Hill in the 1990s (DNPC 2003). In fact, in the immediate post-war period, the pressures on natural resources increased in many parts of Manica Province in Mozambique. Although local chiefs argued that damage to sacred forests would anger the spirits, bringing suffering to the culprits or to the entire community, this threat was not enough to deter desperate and destitute individuals who cut down trees to make charcoal and for other domestic uses, and whether the culprits and/or the community have really suffered as a result of tempering with sacred places has not been clearly proven. Thus, in scenarios of rapid demographic and economic change, traditional institutions may not necessarily be powerful enough to enforce traditional systems of conservation (Jopela 2011).

As already shown, it is undeniable that traditional management systems in many parts of Africa were suffocated by: the disruption caused by colonialism; the hegemony of rigid post-independence, state-based heritage polices and management systems; changes in the wider economic, social and cultural circumstances; and specific historical developments, such as land-reform measures, migrations, tourism, and globalisation (Cunningham 2001; Katsamudanga 2003; Milton 1996; Mumma 2003; Ndoro and Pwiti 2001). Although most people converted to Christianity, they also held on to some traditional beliefs, and traditional ways of life did not disappear entirely (Sheridan 2008). However, the contents of the traditions and the identities of traditional leaders are often contested. Even some of the chiefs and traditional leaders have only a vague idea of traditional systems. For example, during the reconstruction of Old Bulawayo (the first capital of King Lobengula) in Zimbabwe, traditional leaders argued that it would have been taboo to locate the entrances to traditional huts on the side alluded to by the archaeological evidence but they had to repudiate this later when it was discovered that the archaeological evidence was correct (Chirikure and Pwiti 2008).

Another example is Sekuru Mushore, a spirit medium who claims that his ancestors made the rock paintings found in the Nharira Hills. In academic circles, the paintings are generally regarded as products of the hunter-gatherer societies that populated the whole of the southern African sub-region from the Zambezi River to the coastal areas of South Africa (Garlake 1987), that is, before the area was occupied by the Bantu ancestors of the Shona population to which Mushore belongs. The truth of Mushore's claims is thus open to debate. However, he also claimed spiritual knowledge of the painting technique and threatened to redo the fading paintings. Indeed, the works have since been repainted using very distinct oil paint,[1] probably by him but nobody knows for sure. This repainting is certainly contrary to the modern ethos of art conservation, and whether it could be considered traditional is also open to question. Thus, it is important to critically define the role of traditional spiritual leaders if we are to return the management and use of cultural heritage sites to them.

Tradition and modernity

Many traditional leaders today are influenced by modern ideals and aspirations. In Zimbabwe for example, Chakanyuka (2007) noted that, once traditional custodians take control of cultural heritage sites, they do not abide by traditional ways of life. At Domboshava, for example, the chief of the area permitted the destruction of the Rambakurimwa sacred forest, to pave the way for the building of a gazebo (Chirikure and Pwiti 2008). His argument had a very modern tone; he wanted to create jobs for his people. This was probably a noble thing to do but its implications for the call to return to traditional systems of managing cultural heritage must be considered.

Power dynamics

Traditional systems of governance operate within a socio-political hierarchy. However, factors such as the separation of powers and duties between the political and religious institutions; the ambition of traditional leaders to enhance their authority through controlling people and resources; and the monetary compensation derived from tasks ascribed to traditional structures, have given rise to political tensions between traditional authorities in Mozambique's Manica Province (Serra 2001). This tension, which may threaten the continuity of the traditional custodianship system responsible for the daily protection of the site, is best illustrated by the relationship between *Mambo* Chirara and *Swikiro* (spirit medium) Mbuya Gondo (the site custodian) over the control of Chinhamapere. Like other contested heritage sites, this example illustrates that the management of heritage is often inseparable from issues of power and ultimately from local and national politics. Places of cultural significance can function as manifestations of power, and all who need power, either to control a small community (or village) or a whole chieftaincy (or district), turn to these places for legitimacy (Jopela 2011; Sinamai 2003). The power dynamics associated with the control over heritage resources are clearly part of local politics and are shaped by power relations amongst members of the community. Disputes between traditional authorities with regard to control of these places exposes the impact of the socio-economic and political factors on these institutions (that is, the increased integration of rural areas into the cash-based economy, the formal state recognition of traditional institutions and the various development pressures). Such changing environments have led some to suggest that traditional leaders are more concerned with re-acquiring powers and economic benefits, rather than with controlling access to and use of natural and cultural resources in ways that ensure their survival into the future (Jopela 2011).

A mixed blessing

Although there are problems with traditional systems, their inclusion in the management of heritage sites remains crucial. Formal management systems cannot effectively protect many aspects of heritage sites, and especially those that are of cultural significance to the communities living around them. In addition, most African countries cannot afford to formally manage all their heritage sites and thus continue to rely on traditional management systems. Even though, in the colonial and postcolonial periods, formal heritage management systems were often imposed on local communities in both Zimbabwe and Mozambique, traditional custodianship systems neither disappeared completely nor remained static. In many cases they shifted so as to remain relevant alongside new models of governance (Jopela 2011). Similarly, traditional custodianship systems exist in many parts of the continent, and local people use these to manage places that are culturally significant to them (Ndoro et al. 2008).

Indeed, traditional authorities, in their various different forms, have demonstrated remarkable levels of resilience. Although their influence varies from place to place, they are critical in areas where they are widely recognised, such as in many districts of Manica Province in Mozambique (Artur 1999; Tornimbeni 2005). Although socio-political factors, including the civil war and consequent population movements negatively affected the integrity of Chinhamapere to a certain extent, it is also true to say that traditional institutions ensured the survival of the Hill's sacred forest, and current practices testify to the survival of other valued aspects of the landscape (Jopela 2011). In fact, Macamo and Sætersdal (2004) point out that, with few exceptions, the absence of deliberate human impact (such as graffiti) on the rock art site and its environs is a testament to community reverence for the archaeological remains.

Thus, although traditional systems and all that they encompass have many weaknesses and imperfections, they also seem to embody constructive strengths and still enjoy legitimacy in many communities (Logan 2008). Therefore any attempt to develop an improved management framework for archaeological sites must include a role for traditional leadership and institutions as part of, or alongside, formal methods, not because these authorities are inherently good, but because, where they exist and have legitimacy, they clearly and effectively enforce 'public authority' on the ground (Kyed 2007). Traditional systems will continue to undergo dynamic and evolutionary changes as factors such as migrations, civil war, and globalisation constantly incorporate new values into people's understanding of their spiritual, social and physical environment (Katsamudanga 2003). Ideally, therefore, there should always be mechanisms to ensure that these changes enhance the management and protection of heritage sites that fall under traditional custodianship.

Conclusions

In this chapter we aim to highlight the advantages and disadvantages of including various players in cultural heritage management in two different socio-political contexts. From the discussion, it is apparent that there is no easy way of ensuring the survival of heritage sites, especially those associated with sacred value systems. Although traditional mechanisms were deployed in the management of these sites before the advent of colonialism, the changes that have taken place since then may militate against their reconstitution at some sites. The loss of knowledge about these systems due to colonial upheavals, and the transformations in social, political and economic dimensions that the modern society has since undergone, need to be seriously considered. Rather than basing our assumptions on an idealised past, we need to consider how this loss of knowledge impacts on the management of heritage sites. We have to acknowledge the modern nature and the modern needs of traditional authorities.

In our view, the most promising way forward would be to incorporate both 'traditional' and 'modern' aspects of heritage management, choosing whichever works best in a particular context – a hybrid approach for our hybrid societies. This does not involve relinquishing all decision-making responsibility to local communities, but rather establishing participatory management systems. Such systems are defined as situations 'in which two or more social actors concerned about a heritage site negotiate, define and guarantee among themselves a fair sharing of its management functions, entitlements and responsibilities' (Taruvinga 2007: 41). This approach recognises the different values, interests and concerns of all stakeholders, thereby allowing the whole community to assume important roles and responsibilities in heritage management. Where traditional systems of management work, as in the example of Chinhamapere rock art site, they should be complemented by modern laws which cater for errant modern members of society who do not respect such systems.

There is also a need to balance reality with people's aspirations. Communities in developing countries are often mainly interested in bread-and-butter issues; they need to ensure that they survive another day if they are to enjoy the benefits of the past. Clearly, archaeological heritage management needs to be beneficial in terms of communities' modern needs, and not only in terms of their traditional heritage. However, this should not be achieved at the expense of cultural heritage sites. The reality is that, in the modern globalised world, most of these sites now have value beyond the immediate community in which they are located. Modern structures should then monitor and intervene where traditional management systems may be detrimental to the wider preservation of cultural heritage. The case of Domboshava is a good example in that the destruction of the sacred Rambakurimwa forest affects a broad spectrum of people, both present and future.

The inclusion of stakeholders other than traditional chiefs and spiritual leaders is essential. For example, urban authorities and schools are crucial stakeholders as they have the potential to give modern urban dwellers, and young people, who may no longer be in contact with traditional authorities, a stake in archaeological heritage management. In Zimbabwe, an archaeological component has been incorporated into junior secondary and more advanced school syllabi. More needs to be done to equip teachers and provide relevant textbooks to ensure that schools effectively teach archaeology material. Other organisations, such as churches and urban cultural groupings, need to be included since they interact with the cultural heritage too.

Note
1   Observed by Ancila Nhamo, 31 July 2009.

References

Abrahamsson H and Nilsson A (1995) *Mozambique: The Troubled Transition from Socialist Construction to Free-Market Capitalism*. London: Zed Books.

Artur DR (1999) 'Estudo de Caso: Província de Manica', in: DR Artur, JC Cafuquiza and A Caso (eds) *Tradição e Modernidad: Que lugar para a Trdição Africana na Governação Descentralizada?* Maputo: PDD/MAE/DAL/GTZ/CIMISAU.

Berkes F, J Colding and C Folke (2000) 'Rediscovery of traditional ecological knowledge as adaptive management', *Ecological Applications* 10 (5): 1251–1262.

Bourdillon M (1991) *The Shona Peoples: An Ethnography of the Contemporary Shona, with Special Reference to their Religion* (third edition). Gweru: Mambo Press.

Buur L and HM Kyed (2005) *State Recognition of Traditional Authority in Mozambique. The Nexus of Community Representation and State Assistance*, Discussion Paper 28, Nordic Africa Institute, Uppsala, Sweden.

Buur, L and HM Kyed (2006) 'Contested sources of authority: Re-claiming state sovereignty and formalizing traditional authority in post-conflict Mozambique', *Development and Change* 37 (4): 847–869.

Bwasiri E (2011) 'The implications of the management of indigenous living heritage: The case study of the Mongomi wa Kolo Rock Paintings World Heritage Site, central Tanzania', *South African Archaeological Bulletin* 66 (193): 60–66.

Chakanyuka C (2007) Implications of 'Fast Track' Land Resettlement Programmes on Cultural Heritage in Zimbabwe. Master's dissertation, University of Zimbabwe, Harare.

Chirikure C and G Pwiti (2008) 'Community involvement in archaeology and cultural heritage management: An assessment from case studies in southern Africa and elsewhere', *Current Anthropology* 49 (3): 1–13.

Chirikure S, M Manyanga, W Ndoro and G Pwiti (2010) 'Unfulfilled promises? Heritage management and community participation at some of Africa's cultural heritage sites', *International Journal of Heritage Studies* 16 (1–2): 30–44.

Cunningham AB (2001) *Applied Ethnobotany: People, Wild Plant Uses and Conservation*. London: Earthscan.

(Direcção Nacional do Património Cultural) (2003). Rock Art Site Management Plan for Chinhamapere Cultural Heritage Site, Manica Province, Mozambique. Maputo.

Garlake P (1987) *The Painted Caves: An Introduction to the Prehistoric Rock Art of Zimbabwe*. Harare: Modus.

Joffroy T (ed.) (2005) *Traditional Conservation Practices in Africa*. Rome: ICCROM.

Jopela A (2006) Custódia Tradicional do Património Arqueológico na Província de Manica: Experiência e práticas sobre as pinturas rupestres no Distrito de Manica, 1943–2005. Bachelor of Arts dissertation, Universidade Eduardo Mondlane, Maputo.

Jopela A (2010) 'Traditional custodianship of rock art sites in central Mozambique: A case study from Manica District', *Studies in African Past* 8: 161–177.

Jopela A (2011) 'Traditional custodianship: A useful framework for heritage management in southern Africa?' *Conservation and Management of Archaeological Sites* 13 (2–3): 103–122.

Katsamudanga S (2003) 'The dilemma of preserving intangible heritage in Zimbabwe', paper presented to the Fourteenth General Assembly and Scientific Symposium of the International Council on Monuments and Sites (ICOMOS), Victoria Falls, October 2003. Available online.

Kessey J (1995) 'Indigenous control of rock imagery in Tanzania', in G Ward and L Ward (eds) *Management of Rock Art Imagery*, Occasional Publication 9, Australian Rock Art Research Association, Melbourne.

Kyed MH (2007) State Recognition of Traditional Authority: Authority, Citizenship and State Formation in Rural Post-War Mozambique. PhD thesis, Roskilde University, Denmark.

Logan C (2008) *Traditional leaders in modern Africa: Can democracy and the chief co-exist?* Working Paper 93, Afrobarometer. Available online.

Lundin IB and J Machava (1995) 'Quadro de conclusões gerais sobre o debate das autoridades tradicionais', in IB Lundin and J Machava (eds) *Autoridade e Poder Tradicional*. Maputo: MAE.

Macamo S (1996) 'The problems of conservation on archaeological sites in Mozambique', in G Pwiti and R Soper (eds) *Aspects of African Archaeology: Papers from The Tenth Congress of the Pan African Association for Prehistory and Related Studies*. Harare: University of Zimbabwe Publications.

Macamo S (2003) 'Projectos SAREC e a participação das comunidades locais na pesquisa arqueológica: O caso do Distrito de Vilankulo, província de Inhambane, Moçambique', *Comunicação apresentada na Primeira Conferencia Nacional da OSSREA*. Maputo.

Macamo S (2006) Privileged places in south central Mozambique: The archaeology of Manyikene, Niamara Songo and Degue-Mufa, Studies in Global Archaeology 4, Department of Archaeology and Ancient History, University of Uppsala, Sweden and Universidade Eduardo Mondlane, Maputo.

Macamo S and T Sætersdal (2004) 'Archaeology and cultural heritage management in Mozambique: Some experiences and some future challenges', in T Oestigaard, N Anfinset and T Sætersdal (eds) *Combining the Past and the Present: Archaeological Perspectives on Society*. BAR International Series No. 1210 Oxford: Archaeopress.

Mamdani M (1996) *Citizen and Subject: Contemporary Africa and the Legacy of Late Colonialism*. Kampala: Fountain.

Maradze J (2003) 'Back to the Old School? Revival of traditional management systems in Zimbabwe', paper presented to the Fourteenth General Assembly and Scientific Symposium of the International Council on Monuments and Sites, Victoria Falls, October 2003.

Marshall Y (2002) 'What is community archaeology?' *World Archaeology* 34: 211–219.

Mataga J (2003) Managing the Intangible Heritage of Monuments and Sites in Zimbabwe: A case study of the National Museums and Monuments of Zimbabwe (NMMZ). Master's dissertation, University of Zimbabwe, Harare.

Milton K (1996) *Environmentalism and Cultural Theory. Exploring the Role of Anthropology in Environmental Discourse*. London and New York: Routledge.

Mumma A (2003) 'Community-Based Legal Systems and the Management of World Heritage Sites', *World Heritage Papers* 13: 43–44.

Mumma A (2005) 'The link between traditional and formal legal systems', in W Ndoro and G Pwiti (eds) *Legal frameworks for the Protection of Immovable Cultural Heritage in Africa*: 22–24. Rome: ICCROM.

Ndlovu N (2009) 'Access to rock art sites: A right or qualification?' *South African Archaeological Bulletin* 64 (189): 61–68.

Ndoro W (2001a) 'Heritage management in Africa', *The Getty Conservation Newsletter* 16 (3): 20–23.

Ndoro W (2001b) *Your Monument our Shrine: The preservation of Great Zimbabwe*. Studies in African Archaeology No. 19, Uppsala University, Sweden.

Ndoro W (2003) 'Traditional and customary heritage systems: Nostalgia or reality? The implication of managing heritage sites in Africa', *World Heritage Papers* 13: 81–84.

Ndoro W (2006) 'Building the capacity to protect rock art heritage in rural communities', in N Agnew and J Bridgland (eds) *Of the Past, for the Future: Integrating Archaeology and Conservation*. Los Angeles: Getty Conservation Institute.

Ndoro W and G Pwiti (2001) 'Heritage management in southern Africa: Local, national and international discourse', *Public Archaeology* 2 (1): 21–34.

Ndoro W and G Pwiti (eds) (2005) *Legal frameworks for the Protection of Immovable Cultural Heritage in Africa*. Rome: ICCROM.

Ndoro W, A Mumma and G Abungu (eds) (2008) *Cultural Heritage and the Law: Protecting Immovable Heritage in English Speaking Countries of Southern Africa*. ICCROM Conservation Studies No. 8. Rome: ICCROM.

Nhamo A, T Sætersdal and E Walderhaug (2007) 'Ancestral landscapes: Reporting on rock art in the border regions of Zimbabwe and Mozambique', *Zimbabwea* 9: 43–62.

Nhamo A (2009) 'From tradition to modernity and back: The use and abuse of cultural heritage in Zimbabwe's post-independence era', paper presented at the Second SANORD Conference on Inclusion and Exclusion in Higher Education, Rhodes University, Grahamstown, South Africa, 7–9 December.

Nyathi P and B Ndiwini (2005) 'A living religious shrine under siege: The Njelelle Shrine/King Mzilikazi's grave and conflicting demands on the Matopo Hills Area of Zimbabwe', in H Stovel, N Stanley-Price and R Killick (eds) *Conservation of Living Heritage*. ICCROM Conservation Studies Series, No. 3. Rome: ICCROM.

Pwiti G (1996) *Continuity and Change: An Archaeological Study of Farming Communities in Northern Zimbabwe AD 500–1700*. Studies in African Archaeology No. 13. Department of Archaeology, Uppsala University, Sweden.

Pwiti G and G Mvenge (1996) 'Archaeologists, tourists and rainmakers: Problems in the management in rock art sites in Zimbabwe. A case study of Domboshava national monument', in G Pwiti and R Soper (eds) *Aspects of African Archaeology*. Harare: University of Zimbabwe Publications.

Pwiti G and W Ndoro (1999) 'The legacy of colonialism: Perceptions of cultural heritage in southern Africa with specific reference to Zimbabwe', *African Archaeological Review* 16 (3): 143–153.

Pwiti G, A Nhamo, S Katsamudanga and A Segobye (2007) 'Makasva: Archaeological heritage, rainmaking and healing in southern Africa with special reference to eastern Zimbabwe', *Zimbabwea* 9: 103–111.

Sætersdal T (2004) Places, People and Ancestors: Archaeology and Society in Manica, Mozambique. PhD Thesis, University of Bergen.

Serra A (2001) *The legitimacy of local institutions for natural resource management: The case of Pindanganga, Mozambique*. Working paper 2, Marena Research Project, School of African and Asian Studies, University of Sussex and Centro de Experimentacao Florestal, Sussundenga, Mozambique.

Sheridan MJ (2008) 'The dynamics of African sacred groves: Ecological, social and symbolic processes', in M Sheridan and C Nyamweru (eds) *African Sacred Groves: Ecological Dynamics and Social Change*: Oxford, Athens, Pretoria: James Currey, Ohio University Press, UNISA Press.

Sheridan M and C Nyamweru (eds) (2008) *African Sacred Groves: Ecological Dynamics and Social Change*. Oxford, Athens, Pretoria: James Currey, Ohio University Press, UNISA Press.

Sinamai A (2003) 'Cultural shifting-sands: Changing meanings of Zimbabwe sites in Zimbabwe, South Africa and Botswana', paper presented at the Fourteenth General Assembly and Scientific Symposium of International Council on Monuments and Sites, Victoria Falls, October. Available online.

Sinamai A (2006) 'Nations and their past: Changing meanings of Zimbabwe sites in Zimbabwe, South Africa and Botswana', *Zimbabwea* 8: 31–41.

Sinclair PJ (2004) 'Archaeology and identity: Some examples from Southern Africa', in T Oestigaard, N Anfinset and T Sætersdal (eds) *Combining the Past and the Present: Archaeological Perspectives on Society*. BAR International Series No. 1210 Oxford: Archaeopress.

Smith L (2004) *Archaeological Theory and the Politics of Cultural Heritage*. London and New York: Routledge.

Sullivan S (2003) 'Local involvement and traditional practices in the World Heritage systems', *World Heritage Papers* 13: 49–55.

Taruvinga P and W Ndoro (2003) 'The vandalism of the Domboshava rock painting site, Zimbabwe: Some reflections on approaches to heritage management' *Conservation and Management of Archaeological Sites* 6 (1): 3–10.

Taruvinga P (2007) 'Community participation and rock art management in Zimbabwe', in J Deacon J (ed.) *African Rock Art: The Future of Africa's Past*. Nairobi: Trust for African Rock Art.

Thebe P (2006) 'Intangible heritage management: Does World Heritage listing help?' in N Agnew and J Bridgland (eds) *Of the Past, for the Future: Integrating Archaeology and Conservation*. Los Angeles: Getty Conservation Institute.

Tornimbeni C (2005) 'The state, labour migration and the transnational discourse: A historical perspective from Mozambique', *Vienna Journal of African Studies* 8: 1–17.

Chapter 10

Steering from a distance: improving access to higher education in South Africa via the funding formula

Pieter le Roux and Mignonne Breier

SOUTH AFRICA'S RAPID POLITICAL TRANSITION to democracy in the early 1990s was a remarkable achievement. Many positive changes have occurred since, but there are ominous signs that the miracle may not last. Poverty, inequality and unemployment remain prominent features of post-apartheid South Africa. Perhaps most ominous of all, educational opportunities for about 75% of black South Africans, specifically African and coloured South Africans, have hardly improved at all.[1] Deracialisation has ensured welcome changes in the top two or three income deciles, but differential access to education has hardly changed for the other seven deciles. A particular cause for concern is tertiary education, where the gross enrolment rate[2] of Africans has improved only marginally since 1994 (mainly because of improved participation rates among female students) and, as we will show in this chapter, the participation rate for African men has actually *deteriorated*.[3]

In our view the existing funding formula, together with myriad attempts at micromanagement by the education ministry, is steering South Africa's higher-education sector down a road that simply perpetuates many of the old inequities. In this chapter we argue for the introduction of a more social democratic approach[4] to higher education. The goals of equity, economic development, and nation building would all be served by a tertiary education system that was able to ensure a significant increase in the numbers of African and coloured students. To bring this about, a new formula that is both more influential and more transformative is required.

In formulating our argument we begin by locating the changes implemented in the South African higher-education sector between the late

1980s and 2012 within a broader international context. Then we provide an overview of trends in black enrolment rates from 1910 to 2009, and show how disappointing these trends have been since the mid-1990s. We argue that four main factors underlie the lack of transformation in enrolment trends, namely:

- the lack of transformation in primary and secondary education;
- a substantial decline in both the proportion of GDP allocated to the higher-education sector and in real funding per student;
- inefficient attempts to steer tertiary education through three-year rolling plans and various ad hoc bureaucratic interventions aimed at micro-managing the sector; and
- the 2004 funding formula, which offers inappropriate incentives.

We believe that the failure to focus on increasing the rate of black enrolment, and on the broad development of citizens' capabilities, is helping to create conditions that have the potential to tear our nation asunder. We therefore discuss the patterns that have emerged in detail, and propose an alternative funding formula, which we argue is capable of bringing about a progressive transformation of the tertiary sector. The alternatives we propose aim to ensure that universities benefit from accepting increasing numbers of disadvantaged students, and that additional resources are invested in identifying students with academic potential and in assisting them to make the transition through higher education.

The nature of the higher education sector since 1980

Since the late 1980s dramatic changes have taken place in the higher-education system, particularly in the Anglo-Saxon regions, and more recently in Europe and in many developing countries. Following a model introduced by Margaret Thatcher in the United Kingdom, governments in the United States, Australia and Canada have abandoned the old collegial system (whereby senior academics effectively ran higher-education institutions) and have instead begun to demand conformity with certain government-defined goals. These include broader admissions policies, higher levels of efficiency in delivery, the meeting of equity criteria, etc.[5] Similar changes implemented in South Africa in recent years are thus not unique, but mirror those introduced in many other countries where performance-related funding, including specific funding formulas, is used by governments to steer universities in particular directions.

Funding formulas were introduced in many countries only in the 1980s and 1990s, but in Canada and South Africa they have long been in place (see

Liefner 2003). In South Africa funding formulas have become increasingly prescriptive as the government has committed itself to steering higher-education institutions in specific directions. For example, after 1993 the South African post-secondary education (SAPSE) formula rewarded universities more for expanding student numbers in the hard sciences, and less for expanding intakes in the humanities and social sciences. Furthermore, since 1996, the government has increasingly tried to micromanage all institutions in a fashion reminiscent of the management style applied to institutions that catered for black students under apartheid.

South Africa's funding formula, introduced in 2004, emphasises certain types of outputs, and provides higher subsidies to universities as they increase their intake of black students. However, the biggest shifts have been: (i) increased funding linked to research output, which, as will be shown later in this chapter, has benefited the more established and historically advantaged universities; and (ii) the provision of (essentially redress) development grants to the historically disadvantaged institutions, where the levels of research output and/or the pass rates are not high enough to warrant adequate research or throughput grants.

Middleton's (2000) review of debates on the modernisation of higher education in Britain is also useful in shedding light on the changes that have occurred in South Africa. Many would argue that the 'creeping state *dirigisme*' identified by Middleton (2000: 543) is evident in South Africa too – see Jonathan Jansen's address at the 2004 TB Davie Memorial Lecture on Academic Freedom, titled 'Accounting for Autonomy, How Higher Education Lost its Innocence'.[6]

Undoubtedly, aspects of the recent reforms in education can be branded or praised, depending on one's bias, as clear evidence of state intervention in how universities are run. Those on the left argue that all funding formulas, including those implemented in South Africa since 2004, are merely an extension of the state's neo-liberal economic philosophy. In the words that Middleton (2000: 543) used to summarise the British debate, what we have is 'state managerialism at the service of the market…a widespread view that higher education is being "marketised"'.

Another view on the process of modernisation in higher education, and one we share, is that it is an approach that uses the market as an instrument of state policy. The kernel of this model is suggested by terms such as 'remote control' and 'steering at a distance' (Middleton, 2000: 547, 548). Bundy (2006: 6), in his discussion of the reforms of the higher-education system initiated by Thatcher, argues that:

At the national level, the defining characteristic of the governance system is 'steering at a distance' – a combination of central control and decentralised authority. Universities are simultaneously deregulated (that is, permitted to become more entrepreneurial and more competitive) and more effectively regulated, through compliance with centrally set norms.

Middleton quotes Hoggett (1994: 44) as giving the following analysis of the processes actually taking place:

It's not so much devolved control as 'remote' control which appears to be superseding bureaucratic control as the preferred method of regulating institutional life. That is why radical processes of internal and external decentralization can occur at the same time as the centralisation of command…

Wherever you look now in the welfare state, semi-autonomous units appear to be springing up. Give managers and staff control over resources, make them accountable for balancing the books, add a framework of performance targets, and perhaps a few core values and mission statements, finally add a dash of competition and there you have it – a disaggregated, self-regulating form of public service production.

Middleton (2000: 551) argues that this 'remote control' or 'steering at a distance' model allows us to understand that the market is not simply managed, but mobilised. However, as he shows, contrary to what free marketers and old-style central planners would argue, this model, depending on how it is implemented, may enhance either uniformity or diversity, and it may either undermine state power, or strengthen it. Thus, in our view, the model is not inevitably part of a Thatcherite agenda, as Bundy (2006) seems to argue. In South Africa, both the old SAPSE formula and the present funding formula introduced in 2004 can be considered forms of 'remote control'. This is true even though the SAPSE formula was part of the collegial regime that Thatcher displaced, and even though the new funding formula's strong *rhetorical* focus on efficiency, throughput and the development of research capacity implies an intention to reform the sector.

Trends in black enrolment, 1910–1996

One of the key promises of the Freedom Charter, which had a strong resonance for students fighting the apartheid regime, was that the doors of learning would be opened to all. In one sense this goal has long since been achieved. The late 1980s and the 1990s saw a dramatic increase in the proportion of black students entering schools, technikons and universities that had previously been reserved for whites. The doors of the finest educational institutions are no longer closed to black South Africans on the basis of race, as they were under apartheid. By 2009, well over 50% of the students at the historically white English universities were black (the University of Cape Town at 54% had the lowest proportion of black students). And at the historically white Afrikaans campuses, at least 40% of students were black, with the exception of the University of Stellenbosch where the proportion of black students was 32% (Department of Basic Education (2010: 28, Table 16).

But as we will show, contrary to expectations, the number of black students in South African higher-education institutions expanded rapidly between 1970 and 1994, and after that the rate of expansion in the numbers of black students dropped dramatically. Indeed enrolment in the years since liberation has grown so slowly that gross enrolment (that is, participation) rates have increased significantly only for Indians, and have actually decreased for white, African and coloured males – a stark reality that has mostly been ignored.

Note that in this chapter we refer mainly to enrolment figures for public higher-education institutions. There is a growing private higher-education system in South Africa but no reliable student data has yet been published.[7] There are indications that private higher education will be encouraged in future as another means of expanding student enrolment.[8] If this occurs, statistics on student intake will be essential for planning and monitoring purposes, and it is hoped that the government will ensure their availability.

Black South Africans on the sidelines, 1910–1950

During the first forty years after the establishment of the Union of South Africa in 1910, a very small number of black South Africans were admitted annually to universities and university colleges. Even among the white population, enrolment rates were initially very low. By the time the National Party took control of the government in 1948, and began to implement its apartheid policies, the total number of students that had graduated since tertiary institutions were first established amounted to far fewer than the number of students who graduate annually from tertiary institutions today. And of those who graduated between 1910 and 1948, less than 4% were black. In 1950 the total number of students registered at universities was 23 122, and of these a mere 1 350 (5.7%) were black, and less than half were African (see Table 10.1). Why was it that nearly half a century after the establishment of the Union, so few black South Africans had enjoyed the benefits of a university education?

Until the late 1950s there was no government decree preventing universities from admitting black students. On the contrary, both JBM Hertzog (prime minister in the 1920s) and Jan Hofmeyr (education minister in the 1930s) rejected requests to prevent universities that were accepting black students (that is, the University of the Witwatersrand, the University of Cape Town and the University of Natal) from doing so. Although situated on different sides of the political spectrum in white South Africa, both men argued that this decision should be at the discretion of the universities, and that the government should not interfere (Moodie 1994). However, their respective governments carry much of the blame for the small number of black students admitted to universities, because they ensured that very few black South Africans had access to secondary schooling and, thus, most never obtained the qualifications needed to access the few universities that might be persuaded to open their doors to them.

The state's early hands-off policy with regard to the composition of the student body came to a dramatic end, however. The 1959 Extension of University Education Act gave the education minister draconian powers, which he used to prohibit existing universities from accepting black students (and academic staff) without a permit. Instead, the Act provided for the establishment of tribal universities in the far-flung rural reserves known as bantustans.

Banished to separate institutions 1960–1970

By 1960, the year after the Extension of University Education Act was passed, the number of black students in the tertiary sector stood at 4 381 (see Table 10.1). Of these 44% were African, 36% Indian and 20% coloured (calculated from Table 10.2). Even though the number of black students had increased threefold (and proportionally from 6% to 10%) between 1950 and 1960, the outlook for black education was bleak. It is no wonder that the Freedom Charter tried to counter these trends by demanding that the doors of learning be opened to all.

Virtually half (46%) of the 4 381 black students registered in 1960 were at the University of South Africa, which is a distance-learning institution. Just under 40% (that is, 72.6% of black students at residential institutions) were at the University of the Witwatersrand, the University of Cape Town and the University of Natal,[9] all of which had been officially closed to black students. And less than 15% were at black institutions – nearly 500 students (11%), were at the University of Fort Hare,[10] and just 161 students (3%) were at the University of the Western Cape, which had just been established for coloured students.

Although the total enrolment of black students more than doubled from 1960 to 1970, the percentage of black students enrolled increased by only about 8% a year, a much lower rate than the more than 12% average annual increase seen in the 1950s (see Table 10.1, which shows tertiary enrolments from 1910 to 2009, excluding teacher-training colleges and the tertiary institutions in the Transkei, Bophutatswana, Venda and Ciskei).[11] Meanwhile, the permit system had brought the number of black students admitted to 'white' universities down to 1550 from the 1728 registered a decade earlier. More dramatically, the number of African students at the University of the Witwatersrand and the University of Cape Town, which amounted to 113 in 1959 when the Act was passed, had been reduced to just four students by 1967 (Reddy, 2004: 14). By 1976 only 7% of black students (see Reddy, 2004: 17), and less than 13% of black residential students, were accommodated at universities reserved for whites. Verwoerdian apartheid succeeded in ensuring that black, and particularly African students, were all but excluded from the universities reserved for whites, and in reducing the growth rate in black student numbers. Whereas black students as a percentage of total enrolments virtually doubled from 5.7% to 10.2% in the 1950s, this percentage crept up to only 11.3% by the end of the 1960s (see Table 10.1).

The era of the *verligtes* and black consciousness, 1970–1996

By the early 1970s the more liberal or *verligte*[12] wing of the National Party were being increasingly successful in challenging aspects of the Verwoerdian approach to tertiary education. The reports of the Riekert (1979) and Wiehahn (1982) commissions made it clear that the country desperately needed black South Africans with the skills and abilities to help manage and run the economy, and that the tertiary education of black South Africans should not merely provide for the needs of managing what Verwoerd called their 'homelands'. The resulting shift in policy is clear from the fact that the growth rate for black students shot up to an average annual rate of 16% during the early 1970s, more than doubling in six years. And during this decade, the proportion of black students increased from just above 10% to virtually 20% of all students.

In terms of black student numbers these statistics signify a significant shift. However, as was the case during the 1960s, virtually all the new black students, except for those registered for distance learning at the University of South Africa, were accommodated in what Reddy (2004) describes as 'tribal colleges'. Thus, although the rapid increase in the number of black South Africans in tertiary education was encouraged to meet the needs of the

TABLE 10.1 Student enrolment and average annual rates of growth at public tertiary institutions (including teacher colleges and the TBVC institutions from 1994), South Africa 1910–2009

Year	Black students	Annual growth rate (%)	All students	Annual growth rate (%)	Black students as % of total
1910			1 160		
1920			3 250	9.8%	
1930			8 269	4.0%	
1940			12 262	6.5%	
1950	1 320	12.7%	23 122	6.3%	5.7%
1960	4 381	7.4%	42 766	6.8%	10.2%
1965	6 273	8.5%	59 365	7.0%	10.6%
1970	9 411	16.0%	83 030	8.2%	11.3%
1975	19 752	15.5%	122 869	8.0%	16.1%
1986	96 665	13.4%	286 736	7.1%	33.7%
1994	273 526		495 356		55.2%
1994	355 811	11.1%	586 003	4.9%	60.7%
1996	439 439	1.5%	644 326	0.2%	68.2%
2001	474 371	5.3%	649 831	4.6%	73.0%
2004	554 044	3.4%	743 001	2.4%	74.6%
2009	656 416		837 755		78.4%

Note: Up to 1976, these enrolments are for universities and university colleges that were recognised and funded by the central government. From 1986, they include enrolment figures for the technikons, established from 1978 onwards, and, from the second estimate for 1994 onwards, they include enrolments at teacher-training colleges and the TBVC institutions. Enrolments at private institutions are not included. Blank cells indicate that data is unavailable.

Sources: Black university enrolment estimates for the period 1960–1976 are calculated from the figures contained in Reddy (2004: 16, Table 2), and for 1950 are extrapolated from the 4.8% Reddy (2004: 10) reported for 1948. The estimates for all students for the period 1910–1975 are taken from Steyn and De Villiers (2006: 24, Table 1.2), those for 1996–2004 from the Department of Education's (2005a) Higher Education Information Management System (HEMIS), and those for 2009 from a report by the Department of Basic Education (2010: 31, Table 19). In total, 70 731 enrolments at teacher-training colleges were added in 1996 (see Hofmeyr and Hall 1995: Table 22). The proportion of the different population groups in teacher-training colleges in 1996 was estimated by extrapolating 1990 and 1992 statistics provided by Bunting (1994: 72, Table 31).

country's economy, this growth took place within the ethnically separated institutions established by Verwoerd.

However, attempts at social engineering often prove counterproductive, and the impact of the establishment of separate black universities, illustrates this clearly. Reddy (2004: 15) describes what happened:

the emergence of black universities marked an important change in white domination...[No longer was there] an insignificantly small number of black students in higher education...At the time of the Soweto uprisings in 1976 three trends, all contributing to the development of student organisations and resistance, are identifiable. First, black student numbers increased...Second, the comprehensive separation of students into ethnic institutions... alienated, angered and frustrated black students... Third, the 'new' institutional vision of the higher education system, designed to reproduce Apartheid social relations...produced new, protest-based identities derived from the spread of black consciousness ideas and practices (Reddy, 2004: 15, 19).

Black consciousness, spread rapidly from one black campus to the other in 1976, and would in all likelihood have been less successful had it not been for the fact that Extension of University Education Act had herded most black students into separate colleges and attempted to bolster their 'ethnic' identities. The very action taken to perpetuate white domination created the conditions under which an increasing number of black South Africans rejected attempts to divide them into different 'ethnic' groups, and they began to discard the dogma, subconsciously accepted by many, that blacks were inferior. It can be argued that this shift in black South Africans' interpretation of social reality was among the most significant changes that eventually led to demise of the apartheid state (see Le Roux 1984).

From the mid-1970s to the mid-1990s, black enrolment in tertiary education continued to grow extremely rapidly.[13] Initially, most of these students were accommodated in universities reserved for black students, and many were trained as teachers or public administrators. However, after 1976 it was obvious that the state's attempts at ethnic mobilisation had been counterproductive and, given the country's skills needs, also misdirected. Based on the recommendations of the De Lange Commission (De Lange 1981),[14] the number of black students admitted to so-called technikons was rapidly expanded – technikons had been established by the state in 1978 to provide technical and commercial skills, and the training received prepared students to serve the needs of the country's economy rather than a specific ethnic group. During the 1980s student numbers at technikons grew more than three times faster than those at the universities (see Steyn and De Villiers 2006: 24, Table 1.2).

In evaluating the delivery of tertiary education during the final 25 years of the apartheid regime, one has to admit that, although the separation of race groups was morally reprehensible and the quality of provision unequal, the expansion of student numbers was impressive. Although it started the process a decade later than the United Kingdom, South Africa moved towards massification even more rapidly than Britain had done. The enrolment rate, which was only 4.1% in the UK in 1961, reached 15% in 1987 according to 'Martin Trow's widely cited measure for a mass system' (Bundy, 2006: 3). In South Africa, the enrolment rate was 4.5% in 1970, and reached 15% in the early 1990s, which is within a shorter time span than the UK. In contrast to the schooling system, where state spending per student was highly unequal, the contribution of state funding to black tertiary institutions per student was on a par with that provided to 'white' institutions up to the late 1980s.

How can the rapid expansion of tertiary education during the latter half of the National Party's regime be explained? It can of course be argued, as Bundy (2006) has done with regard to the delay in scrapping the collegiate system of university governance in South Africa, that it occurred as a result of the country's academic isolation. It is true that the rapid expansion in the number of students enrolled in tertiary education took place in the 1980s and early 1990s, when many African countries were cutting back on tertiary funding based on a rate-of-return analysis propagated by the World Bank.[15] According to this line of argument, South Africa was clearly unaware of the thinking that priority should be given to primary education.

A second possibility, argued by Steyn and De Villers (2006: 41), is that the rapid growth in black student numbers was an unforeseen consequence of the SAPSE funding formula. And there is no doubt that some of the black universities grew far more rapidly in the late 1980s than their bureaucratic minders wished them to.

A third argument, and the one that we find most convincing, is that the rapid expansion of black enrolment was carefully planned by the *verligtes*, led by Prof de Lange, who was an educationist and chair of the Broederbond from 1983 to 1993. Certainly, the outcomes were in line with the recommendations of his 1981 De Lange report, and seem to have been part of a specific strategy. Yet, even during the *verligte* period, when many of the cornerstones of apartheid laid by Verwoerd were being undermined, the *verkramptes* continued to micro-manage the 'tribal universities'. For example, when the senate and council of the University of the Western Cape appointed a very able African academic to the political science faculty in the 1980s, government officials vetoed his appointment on the grounds that an African could not be allowed to teach at a 'coloured' university. Things were changing however, because the following year, when the university reappointed the same candidate, no veto was exercised.

A long tradition of steering via funding formulas

For most of the twentieth century South Africa's tertiary institutions obtained the bulk of their funding from the state. Initially, the universities, and later the technikons too, were given a great deal of freedom as to how they spent this money. From as early as 1922, state subsidies to universities were consolidated into single block grants that could be spent without government approval. Detailed government financial control was temporarily reimposed during the Great Depression when the then education minister, DF Malan, required universities to reduce academic salaries, 'native wages' and other running costs. But, within two years, financial management was returned to the universities (Moodie 1994: 3).

Moodie claims that the funding of South African universities from as early as the mid-1930s was based on broad principles, and not on whether the government agreed with how a specific university was managed. He writes that, in 1933, just after the Great Depression,

> the Report of the Adamson Committee, referring to the 'crippling effects of uncertainty' upon the universities and colleges, proposed the establishment of a stable and predictable system of formula-based funding. The details of the formula were not in fact adopted by the government, but the goals of predictability and of formula funding seem to have remained parts of government policy since that time. (Moodie 1994: 4)

Over the years different funding formulas were implemented on the basis of the Holloway Commission of 1951, the Van Wyk de Vries Commission of 1974, and the Venter Report of 1985 (see Steyn and De Villiers 2007), which all implicitly recognised that government should not get involved in the day-to-day adminis-tration of universities. In line with this principle, the SAPSE formula proposed in the mid-1980s intended explicitly to guarantee this hands-off stance. A commitment was made to:

> a system of financing that can clearly be seen to be immune to manipulation by administrative whim or political caprice. A system of fair and unambiguous rules is required that will allocate the available resources in accordance with both need and merit. (SAPSE I-10, quoted by Moodie 1994: 26)

Regardless of the sentiments expressed by the SAPSE committee in the 1980s, the reality of the preceding 25 years was, as shown, very different. The 1959 Extension of the Universities Act was a blatant and crude attempt at social engineering. In draconian fashion, it interfered with the freedom of universities to decide whom to admit and with the freedom of individuals to choose where they wished to study. Moodie contends that, with this exception, up to the early 1990s, 'All Afrikaans-speaking and black as well as English-speaking universities, mirror the typical British model of internal university government in which authority is shared between lay-dominated Council... and academic Senate' (Moodie 1994: 2). However, as Moodie points out, South African institutions were from the outset subject to far more direct control in certain spheres than their British counterparts:

> All new university statutes were submitted both to the minister and to parliament. Members of academic staff could appeal against dismissal to the minister. And universities are still legally obliged to seek state approval before establishing new courses, departments, or faculties. (Moodie 1994: 2)

Indeed, from the 1950s until about 1996, funding formulas played a crucial role in steering the universities – far more so than Moodie seems to realise. In fact, each of the funding formulas was more specific in terms of what it demanded from the institutions in exchange for the financial support provided. As is clear from the preceding discussion, in terms of increasing enrolments, this approach was highly successful.

Whatever its real motives, the apartheid state, while violently repressing black student activists, expanded opportunities for black tertiary education at an exceptionally rapid rate. It did not succeed in winning the hearts and minds of those educated at apartheid institutions, as those responsible for state security might have hoped. But, ironically, as will be shown in the next section, black enrolment and participation at tertiary level increased far more rapidly during the final decades of apartheid than the democratic government has since been able to manage.

Post-apartheid enrolment trends

Contrary to all expectations, the rate of growth of student enrolments dropped dramatically after the transition to a democratically elected government. At first glance, the rapid increase in the proportion of black students from 55% in 1994 to 68% in 1996 seems to reflect a dramatic improvement (see Table 10.1). However, if one includes the teacher-training college students and students from the TBVC institutions, who are excluded from the SAPSE data, the 1994 percentage rises to 60.7% and the improvement from this to 68% seems less impressive (see Table 10.2). Although, for the first two years after the advent of democracy, the number of black students enrolled increased by nearly 42 000 each year, the overall growth rate in student numbers remained about the same, that is, at an average of 29 000 to 30 000 a year. And in percentage terms, the overall growth rate went down slightly, from an average of 7.1% to an average of 4.9%. The rapid growth in black student numbers during these two transition years relative to the preceding years was possible partly because white enrolment dropped by about 13 000 a year during this period, in contrast to preceding years, during which white enrolment had grown steadily by over 3 000 students a year.

Although the overall growth in enrolment of close to 30 000 that occurred in the eight years prior to 1994 was sustained for another two years, the average number of enrolments for the period 1996 to 2009 was less than 15 000, which is about half that of the eight years preceding 1994. For the period from 1996 to 2009, the previously rapid 7% per year average growth rate fell to a mere 2%. Prior to this, the lowest average annual growth rate (of 4%) was recorded during the decade of Great Depression. Furthermore, whereas black enrolments grew at 8.5% even during the darkest years of Verwoerd, and at 13 to 16% between 1970 and 1994, this rate of growth dropped to an average of only 3.1% after 1996 (see Table 10.2).

TABLE 10.2 Annual changes in student enrolment before 1994, 1994–1996, and after 1996

Year	Enrolments			Average annual change in enrolments			Average annual change (by %)		
	Black	White	% Black	Black	White	All	Black	White	All
1986–	123 106	204 869	37.5%						
1994	335 811	230 192	59.3%	26 588	3 165	29 754	13.4%	1.5%	7.1%
1994–	355 811	230 192	60.7%						
1996–	439 439	204 887	68.2%	41 814	-12 653	29 162	11.1%	-5.7%	4.9%
2009	656 416	181 339	78.4%	16 691	-1 811	14 879	3.1%	-0.9%	2.0%
1996–	439 439	204 887	68.2%						
2000–	436 018	168 000	72.2%	-855	-9 222	10 077	-0.2%	-4.8%	-1.6%
2004–	554 044	188 957	74.6%	29 507	5 239	34 746	6.2%	3.0%	5.3%
2009	656 416	181 339	78.4%	20 474	-1524	18 951	3.4%	-0.8%	2.4%

Note: Teacher-training college students are included for the entire period, but those at TBVC institutions are included only from the second entry for 1994 onwards.

Source: See sources for Table 10.1.

To understand what happened after 1996, it is helpful to consider three different phases. The first phase is the four-year period up to 2000, when actual enrolments surprisingly declined at a rate of 1.6% a year. White enrolment continued to go down, as it had in the preceding two years, by about 5% a year, and during this time, black enrolments also decreased by close to 1% a year. On average, overall enrolments decreased by about 10 000 a year.

The second period is from 2001 to 2004 when an overall annual growth rate of 5.3% was realised. Although somewhat lower than the 7.1% of the eight years before 1994, the higher level of enrolments meant that annually the average number of new enrolments shot up to nearly 35 000, of which almost 30 000 were black students.

In the third period from 2005 to 2009, during which the government introduced a new funding formula and tied universities into a process for negotiating envisaged growth in the sector (discussed in more detail below), annual growth in enrolments was cut back to just under 19 000 a year, which is two-thirds of the annual increases realised before 1994. Black enrolments increased at just over 20 000 a year, and white enrolments decreased by about 1 500 a year (see Table 10.2).

One of the most common measurements of the degree to which a country succeeds in providing its citizens with access to tertiary education is its *gross enrolment rate* (often called the gross participation rate in South African debates). This is the number of students enrolled as a percentage of the total 20–24-year-old age cohort in the population as a whole. In calculating changes in the *gross enrolment rate*, it is crucial to compare apples with apples. South Africa's statistics present a number of problems in this regard. When teacher-training colleges were incorporated into universities and technikons in 2001, these students were included in the Department of Education's data series for tertiary institutions. However, for the years before that, these enrolments were excluded. We therefore added the data from the teacher-training colleges for 1996 and 1986 (see footnotes to Tables 1, 2 and 3 for sources), but not for 1970 or 1960, years for which reliable data was not available. Using rough estimates, the addition of teacher-training college students could increase the overall gross enrolment rate for 1970 to well over 5%, and the enrolment rate for whites to as much as 25%. Another issue that affects South African tertiary enrolment rates is the admission of foreign students. According to the Council on Higher Education (CHE 2009: 27) about 50 000 students from other African countries attended South African institutions in 2009. These students were deducted from calculations of the participation rates for this year. In principle, this type of adjustment should have been made in earlier years too, but no statistics were available. Our assumption is that the proportion of foreign African students was much smaller in 1996.

TABLE 10.3   Higher-education headcount enrolments and gross enrolment rates by population group, 1960–2009

	African	Coloured	Indian	White	Total
1960					
Enrolment	1 871	822	1 516	35 095	42 766
20–24 age cohort	878 100	122 100	41 800	232 200	1 274 200
Enrolment rate	0.2%	0.7%	3.6%	15.1%	3.4%
1970					
Enrolment	4 449	1 921	3 042	64 792	83 030
20–24 age cohort	1 289 300	179 280	67 880	329 390	1 865 850
Enrolment rate	0.3%	1.1%	4.5%	19.7%	4.4%
1996					
Enrolment	360 124	40 014	39 301	204 296	644 326
20–24 age cohort	3 153 083	344 373	103 123	349 102	3 982 353
Enrolment rate	11.4%	11.6%	38.1%	58.5%	16.2%
2001					
Enrolment	391 851	38 493	44 027	175 460	649 831
20–24 age cohort	3 544 596	353 661	102 236	294 030	4 294 523
Enrolment rate	11.1%	10.9%	43.1%	59.7%	15.1%
2004					
Enrolment	453 639	46 090	54 315	188 957	743 001
20–24 age cohort	3 940 965	381 805	108 111	317 611	4 748 492
Enrolment rate	11.5%	12.1%	50.2%	59.5%	15.6%
2009					
Enrolment	497 686	55 101	53 629	179 232	787 755
20–24 age cohort	4 110 200	384 700	104 807	306 600	4 920 900
Enrolment rate	12.1%	14.3%	51.2%	58.5%	16.0%

Note: The participation rates for 1960 and 1970 are underestimated, because data for the teacher-training college students are not available. In the case of Indians in 2009, the 20–24-year-old age cohort estimate was 122 412, which is totally out of line with the 99 303 and 110 310 for the 10–14 and 15–19-year-old age cohorts reported in the 2001 Census. An estimate based on Census data (the average of the latter two age cohorts) was thus used to estimate the number in this age cohort. As a result, the Indian enrolment rate did not drop from 50% in 2004 to 45% in 2009, as seems to be the case should one accept these estimates, but instead increased by 1%. Also in 2009, it was estimated that about 50 000 students from other African countries were enrolled at South African universities (CHE 2009: 27); this figure was thus deducted from the HEMIS totals to obtain South African enrolment rates.

Sources: Enrolments in tertiary education: Subotzky (2003), Department of Education HEMIS (2005a) and Department of Basic Education (2010: 31). Teacher-training college students are part of the HEMIS data from 2001 onwards, because the colleges of education were then incorporated into the universities and technikons. For 1996, the total enrolment in education colleges was based on Hofmeyr and Hall (1995: Table 22), and enrolment according to population group was estimated by extrapolating the changes in enrolment by population group for 1990 and 1992, as provided by Bunting (1994: 72, Table 33). We used Stats SA (2004a: 20, 22, Tables 4.1 and 4.3) for 1996 and 2001 mid-year, five-year-interval age-distribution figures, and Stats SA (2004b and 2009) for the 2004 and 2009 mid-year estimates of the 20–24-year-old age cohort.

As a result of the very rapid growth in enrolments after 1970, the gross enrolment rate (counting only those in publicly funded tertiary institutions) increased dramatically from about 4% in 1970 to 16% in 1996. The enrolment rate then dropped to about 15% in 2001, which reflects the decline in student enrolments in the late 1990s. But from 1999 to 2009 there has been a slight improvement in the growth in enrolments. As a result the gross enrolment rate had again reached the 16% level by 2009 (see Tables 10.3 and 10.4). Comparisons of gross enrolment rates across different years often do not pay due attention to precisely what is being compared. Had we excluded the teacher-training college students from the 1996 figures, the gross enrolment rate for that year would have been only 14.5%.

TABLE 10.4 Headcount and gross enrolment rates by population group and gender in public tertiary-education institutions, including teacher-training colleges, 1996 and 2009

Population group and gender		20–24-year-old age cohort		Enrolment of South Africans		Gross enrolment rate	
		1996	2009	1996	2009	1996	2009
African	Male	1 508 732	2 042 000	173 692	218 385	11.5%	10.7%
	Female	1 644 350	2 068 200	186 432	279 301	11.3%	13.5%
	Total	3 153 083	4 110 200	360 124	497 686	11.4%	12.1%
Coloured	Male	168 867	191 000	21 742	23 434	12.9%	12.3%
	Female	175 506	193 700	18 272	31 667	10.4%	16.3%
	Total	344 373	384 700	40 014	55 101	11.6%	14.3%
Indian	Male	51 295	51 608	19 749	23 356	38.5%	45.3%
	Female	51 828	50 801	18 561	30 273	35.8%	59.6%
	Total	103 123	104 807	39 301	53 629	38.1%	51.2%
White	Male	172 891	155 400	117 294	84 197	67.8%	54.2%
	Female	176 211	151 200	87 002	95 035	49.4%	62.9%
	Total	349 102	306 600	204 296	179 232	58.5%	58.5%
All groups	Male	1 917 918	2 449 400	337 002	350 906	17.6%	14.3%
	Female	2 064 435	2 471 500	302 459	436 849	14.7%	17.7%
	Total	3 982 353	4 920 900	644 326	787 755	16.2%	16.0%

Note: The male and female enrolments for 1996 and 2009 for each population group were estimated by calculating the male to female ratios for 1994 and 2006 from the statistics provided by the Department of Education (2008: 20, Table 5) and applying these to the enrolment data contained in Table 10.3.

Sources: For enrolment figures according to gender, see Department of Education (2008: 20, Table 5). The number of students in education colleges is based on the report by Hofmeyer and Hall (1995). When allocating the students in teacher colleges according to gender in 1996, the gender proportions reported by Stuart et al. (1992: 11) for 1991 were used, that is, 65% female overall, with 75% female in the case of whites, which meant a 63% female proportion for the other groups.

Similarly, had we not subtracted the foreign African students from the 2009 enrolments, the most recent gross enrolment figures would have been 17.1%. This would have indicated some progress towards the target of 20% participation rate in public institutions by 2015, envisaged in the 2001 National Plan for Higher Education (Department of Education 2001). However, our calculations indicate that South Africa has not moved significantly closer to this goal since 1996. There is every reason to assume that, if the funding and enrolment policies implemented in 2004 continue, the goal of a 20% enrolment rate by 2015 will not be reached by the publicly funded tertiary institutions.[16]

Another trend ignored by most analysts, and which is also a cause for concern, is reported in an unpublished paper by Steyn (2008), which we found on the University of Stellenbosch's website. Steyn reported enrolment rates according to gender, and made a startling discovery: the gross enrolment rate for men decreased by 1% from 15.7% in 1996 to 14.7%[17] by 2007. Over the same period the position of women improved significantly, increasing from 13.3% to 17.7%. We subsequently found enrolment data by gender and population group for a number of years in a Department of Education publication (2008: 20, Table 5), and we used this to estimate the enrolment of South Africans by population group (see Table 10.4). Over the period from 1996 to 2009, we estimate that the enrolment rate of males fell from 17.6% to 14.3%, while that of females increased from 14.7% to 17.7%. Again, we added in the enrolment in teacher-training colleges in 1996 (on the assumption that for all population groups, two-thirds of the students in teacher colleges were female), and we subtracted the 50 000 Africans who were not South African from the 2009 data, on an assumption that the gender split was 50/50 – hence the differences between our estimates and Steyn's. The gross enrolment rate for the population as a whole remained at about 16% over the entire period as shown in Table 10.3.

The 13 years from 1996 to 2009 clearly did not offer South African males much on the educational front. As shown in Table 10.4, the enrolment rate among white males went down from 68% to 54%. Although there was a decline of more than 17 000 in the white male 20–24-year-old age cohort during this period, the decline of about 33 000 among white males studying at public tertiary institutions was disproportionate, and resulted in a decline of 14 percentage points in their enrolment rate. Of course, some might argue that this is a positive trend, and that it has brought about more equity given the disproportionately high enrolment rate of white males up to 1996. It is possible, however, that a disproportionate number of white males are now studying in local private institutions or overseas. White females increased their participation rate dramatically from 49% to 63% over the same period, and by 2009 were the group with the highest enrolment rate in public institutions. The net impact of these changes is that the overall enrolment of white South Africans in public tertiary institutions remained fairly stable over the period at between 58% and 59%.

Whereas coloured females had the lowest enrolment in 1996 at 10.4%, they had significantly improved their enrolment rate to over 16.3% by 2009. The enrolment rate of coloured males remained roughly constant at around 12%. Thus the enrolment rate for 'coloureds' as a group increased from nearly 12% to more than 14% over this period. It is worth noting, though, that the gross enrolment rate of this group remained fairly constant up to 2004, and most of the improvement has taken place between 2004 and 2009 (see Table 10.3).

Indians constitute the only group in which enrolment rates of both males and females improved significantly. The rate for males increased by nearly 7% from the 38.5% recorded in 1996, and that for women increased by 14%. In 2009 their enrolment rate of 59.6% was the second highest, just below the white female enrolment rate.[18]

Until shortly before 1996 political power was in the hands of white South Africans, with white males being the dominant group. Hence their very high enrolment rate in 1996 is not surprising. After 1994 African men gained more political power than any other group. One would, therefore expect this to be reflected in improvements in their enrolment rate. However, the enrolment rate for African males decreased slightly from 11.5% to 10.7% between 1996 and 2009, making them the group with the lowest participation rate. The finding that the group that probably has the highest expectation of benefitting from the political transition continues to be so badly prepared for participation in the modern economy, 18 years after the transition to democracy, must surely sound a warning of dangers to come.

Over the same period, the situation of female African students improved marginally by a just over 2% to 14.3%. This means that overall African enrolment has gone up slightly from 11.4% to 12.1% between 1996 and 2009. This is a far cry from what is needed if South Africa is to develop the capabilities of all its citizens, which is a precondition for a common commitment to a shared future. The social, political and economic cost to the country of the failure to transform the African and coloured participation rates more than marginally and particularly the failure to improve the situation of the African males, constitutes a severe risk for the future of our country.

Why the failure to improve tertiary enrolment rates?

Gross enrolment rates in public tertiary education in South Africa have remained stuck at around 16% since 1996, and as we have shown, in the case of South African males, and specifically African and white males, enrolment rates at public institutions actually fell between 1996 and 2009. In this section we examine some of the reasons for these failures.

....

TABLE 10.5 Senior-certificate results and population growth in the 18–20 age bracket, South Africa 1996–2003

Year	Candidates who wrote	Passed without endorsement	Passed with endorsement	Total passes	Population size 18–20 years
1996	100.0	100.0	100.0	100.0	100.0
1997	107.9	97.6	87.6	94.7	101.1
1998	106.7	101.6	87.3	97.5	105.5
1999	98.7	93.3	79.6	89.4	110.2
2000	94.5	107.6	85.8	101.4	115.0
2001	86.7	105.0	84.6	99.2	117.4
2002	85.6	115.7	93.8	109.4	119.8
2003	85.0	120.6	102.5	115.4	121.8

Note: Indexed values with 1996 = 100.
Source: Steyn and De Villiers (2006 138, Table 5.2).

The schooling system: apartheid's poisoned chalice

'Decreasing numbers of first-time entering students as the result of very disappointing Senior Certificate results' (Steyn and de Villiers, 2006: 25) is often put forward as the main reason for the stagnation in student numbers after 1996. There is no doubt that the outcomes produced by the secondary schools are very disappointing, as spelled out in the following report:

> there has been a sharp decline in the number of school-leavers with matriculation exemption, which is a precondition for entry into universities and to a lesser extent into technikons. Between 1994 and 2000, the number of school-leavers obtaining a matricu-lation exemption decreased from 89 000 to 68 626, that is, by 20 374 (or 23%). In comparison, the NCHE's [National Council for Higher Education] enrolment projections were

based on assumptions that the total of school-leavers with matriculation exemption would reach 143 000 by 1999. (Ministry of Education 2005a: 17)

As shown in Table 10.5, by 1999 the number of school leavers who passed their senior-certificate exams with the endorsement that gives them access to tertiary study had declined to about 80% of the 1996 pass rate. By 2003, the 1996 figures had been exceeded by just 2%, by which stage the number of people in the 18 to 20 age group (in South Africa's population as a whole) had increased by 20%. This means that proportionally 15% fewer school leavers were able to gain entrance to tertiary education by 2003. While the pass rate has improved since then, the overall situation has not improved significantly since 1996, if population growth is taken into account.

The schooling system is still in a state of crisis. A breakdown of senior-certificates obtained in 2006 shows that Africans achieved a pass rate of only 62%, compared with 81% for coloureds, 92% for Indians and 99% for whites.[19] In addition, Africans made up just 59% of the school leavers who passed with endorsement (against 83% of those who wrote). Indians constituted 7% of those who passed with endorsement and 2% of those without. Whites constituted 26% of those who passed with endorsement and 8% of those without. Among coloured students the same proportion passed with endorsement as those who wrote (6%). An analysis of results for maths and science show similar trends. Furthermore, a study by Progress in International Reading Literacy (PIRLS) showed that almost 80% of the more than 30 000 South African students in Grades 4 and 5 who were tested did not reach the lowest benchmark in literacy, in contrast to 6% of students in the other 39 countries that participated. If one excludes those who were tested in English and Afrikaans, between 86% and 96% of those tested in the other South African languages failed to reach the lowest literacy benchmark.[20]

These results prove that the legacy of apartheid, which gave Africans the cheapest and the poorest quality education possible, has not been effectively overcome. In fact, for many, schooling has taken a turn for the worse. The PIRLS study shows that the relatively small number of schools formerly reserved for white pupils (commonly known as Model C schools and now comprised of about 50% black students) have shown significant improvements in their scores on international tests between 2004 and 2008. But results on the same tests from most other schools, that is, those still serving the majority of African and coloured schoolchildren, have deteriorated over the same period.[21]

Thus the tremendous differences between the quality of primary and secondary schooling received by most white and Indian children on the one hand, and most African and coloured children on the other, are not being eradicated. The implications of this for equity, economic growth and political stability can hardly be underestimated. Improvements in school quality will not occur overnight, and our contention is that we cannot continue to wait for the schooling system to improve. Tertiary institutions have to admit more students from socio-economically disadvantaged backgrounds into the higher-education system, even if they have not obtained the required senior-certificate results, identifying those who have potential and providing them with the necessary academic and financial support. This will not be easy.

A study by Branson et al. (2009) shows that, among those who do not have the necessary senior-certificate results, there are no easy ways of detecting which students have the potential to succeed at tertiary level. The study finds that the socio-economic circumstances, and the quality of the schools attended by African and coloured students, are far more important in determining how well they do in the senior-certificate examinations (and whether they apply for tertiary education) than their innate abilities reflected in test scores for literacy and numeracy. According to the study:

> individual ability is not able to play a significant role in educational attainment over and above socio-economic context. This result suggests that schools and home environments which are characterised by lack of adequate resources and unfavourable learning environments could be leading to a 'crowding out' of individual ability. (Branson, 2009: 53)

Even though changes introduced into the senior-certificate system may make it easier for students to obtain marks that give them entrance to universities, many able students fare so badly at schools that they may be 'crowded out' of further studies by extraneous factors. This could be disastrous for political stability and economic development in South Africa. As we outline in more detail below, a funding formula that encourages tertiary institutions to identify and provide academic support to able students who fail to reveal their potential through the senior-certificate exams, could increase the enrolment rate of black and, in particular, African and coloured students.

GEAR and the decline in tertiary-education allocations, 1987–2009

Growth in the tertiary sector is clearly dependent not only on the output of the school system, but on a number of other factors, including the funds that are at the disposal of the tertiary institutions and the freedom they have to expand their enrolments.

When considering state funding of the tertiary sector, the percentage of GDP allocated by the state to the tertiary sector is a crucial statistic. The information usually presented for South Africa is contained in Figure 10.1. It combines data provided by Steyn and De Villiers (2006) with data from the Council on Higher Education (CHE 2009) and in a study by Badsha and Cloete (2011: 20). These analyses of changes in government funding for the tertiary sector are based on the SAPSE and HEMIS data. From the graph, one would think that the best years for tertiary-education funding were from 1996 to 2000, the period after the acceptance of the state's Growth, Employment and Redistribution (GEAR) policy. Furthermore it seems as though the proportion of GDP allocated to tertiary education was only slightly higher in the period from 1988 to 1994 than it has been since 2000. However, the data presented in Figure 10.1 is very misleading.

The problem is that the data does not include all tertiary education expenditure for the initial period. It ignores expenditure on teacher-training colleges, which were run by the provincial education governments up to 2001 and then incorporated into the universities and technikons. Furthermore, data related to expenditure on tertiary institutions situated in the TBVC bantustans is included from 1995 onwards only. As already noted in our analysis of the gross enrolment rates, it is necessary to incorporate all the data pertaining to the tertiary sector for the period over which one wishes to compare changes.

In Figure 10.2, therefore, we estimated the percentage of GDP spent on teacher-training colleges in 1987 and 1996, as well as on the TBVC institutions in 1987. We used enrolment estimates from these institutions for those years, and assumed that provincial expenditure per student in the teacher-training colleges, the TBVC technikons and the universities was the same as that in the SAPSE-subsidised tertiary sector. This is a conservative assumption if one accepts the findings of Hofmeyr and Hall's (1995) audit of teacher-training colleges (according to which expenditure per student in teacher-training colleges was much higher than on students in the university and technikon sector), as well as Bunting's (2002: 82) comment that 'funding under the TBVC regimes had been generous in comparison with that...in the old RSA'. Nevertheless Figure 10.2 reveals a dramatic decline in government expenditure on tertiary education measured as a percentage of GDP from about 1% in 1987 to less than 0.7% by 2009.

FIGURE 10.1 The conventional view of government expenditure on higher education, as a percentage of GDP, South Africa 1987–2009

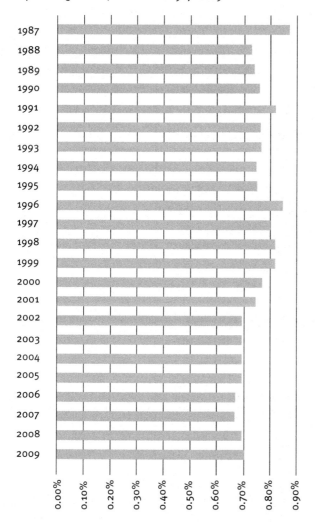

Sources: Steyn and De Villiers, (2006: 89, Table 3.1) for 1987–2003; CHE (2009: 10, Table 2) for 2004–2008; Badsha and Cloete (2011: 20) for 2009.

The 1% of GDP spent in 1987 was an outlier, but the average percentage of GDP allocated to tertiary education for the years 1987 to 1993 was nevertheless a respectable 0.9% (see Table 10.6). However, the slow growth in GDP and the very rapid rate of growth in student enrolment (7.2%) during this period, means that (using 2005 rand values)[22] government expenditure declined from nearly R28 000 per student in 1987 to R15 800 per student in 1993.

FIGURE 10.2 Estimated actual government expenditure on higher education, including teacher colleges and TBVC institutions, as a percentage of GDP, 1987–2009

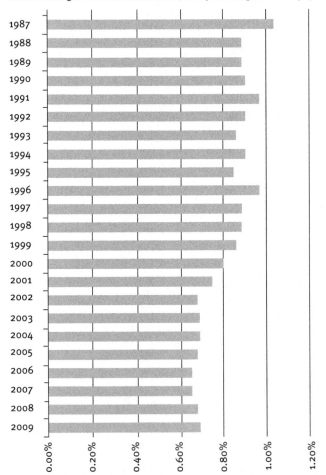

Sources: See Figure 10.1 and Table 10.6.

As shown in Table 10.6, the faster rate of growth in GDP during the transition years, and a once-off increase in the percentage of GDP spent on tertiary education (to 0.94%) in 1996, meant that (even though growth in student enrolment rates remained quite high at 4.9%) average expenditure per student for 1994, 1995 and 1996 went up to R16 200 (from R15 800 in 1993). But this is still much lower than the average of R20 000 per student that was allocated between 1987 and 1993.

TABLE 10.6 The average percentage of GDP allocated to tertiary education, (teacher colleges and TBVC institutions included), the average state expenditure per student and the growth rates of GDP and student enrolment for different periods, South Africa 1987–2009.

Average % of GDP allocated to higher education	Average expenditure per student (at 2005 rand value)	Averages for years	Growth rates for years	Rate of growth in student enrolment	Rate of growth in GDP
0.90%	R20 500	1987–1993	1987–1994	7.1%	1.1%
0.89%	R16 200	1994–1996	1994–1996	4.9%	3.7%
0.84%	R17 000	1997–2000	1996–2000	-1.6%	2.4%
0.70%	R14 200	2001–2004	2000–2004	5.3%	3.5%
0.67%	R14 900	2005–2009	2004–2009	2.4%	3.7%

Notes: By 1996 the TBVC institutions had been reincorporated into the South African system, so their enrolments formed part of South Africa's tertiary-education statistics, and expenditure on them was included in the Department of Education's annual budget. The teacher-training colleges, however, remained separate as many were phased out, and the remaining few were incorporated in the universities and technikons in 2001. Expenditure per student was calculated by multiplying the GDP for the particular year by the percentage of GDP spent on higher education, excluding teacher-training colleges. The result was then divided by the student enrolments excluding teacher-training colleges. For 1987, 1994 and 1996, the percentage of GDP spent on teacher-training colleges (and the TBVC institutions for 1995 and 1996, before they were incorporated into the South African system), was estimated by assuming that expenditure per student was the same as for other higher-education institutions. The average expenditure per student was then multiplied by the number of students in the teacher-training colleges, adding another 10 000 students for 1987 and another 20 000 students in 1994 as estimates of the number of students at the TBVC tertiary institutions. Finally, this product was expressed as percentage of GDP for the specific year.

Sources: GDP in 2005 rand values: Reserve Bank (2011: Series KBP6006Y). Enrolments excluding teachers: Steyn and De Villiers (2006: 24, Table 2.1). Enrolments teacher colleges: 1987: estimated as midpoint between 1986 and 1988 enrolments contained in Table 31 of Bunting (1994: 72); 1994: Pratt (2001: 30, Table 1); 1996: Hofmeyr and Hall (1995: Table 22). See Figure 10.1 for source of % GDP excluding teacher colleges. The other columns were calculated from this data, as explained in the note to Table 10.6.

As mentioned above, changes in the sector can be viewed in three broad phases. In the first phase, from 1997 to 2000, average spend on tertiary education relative to GDP dropped to 0.84% and the economy grew a little more slowly at 2.4% per annum. Nevertheless average expenditure per student increased to about R17 000 because student enrolment decreased by 1.6% a year.

In the second phase, from 2001 to 2004, the average percentage of GDP spent on tertiary education decreased further to 0.7%, and enrolments increased fairly rapidly at more than 5% a year. Thus, even though GDP grew by 3.5% annually, expenditure per student declined to the lowest average for any of the periods. At just R14 200, the amount per student was less than half of what was available in 1987. Not surprisingly, the higher-education institutions took tremendous strain during this phrase.

In the third phase, from 2005 to 2009, a new funding formula was introduced, and three-year expansion agreements were strictly implemented. These measures restricted overall student growth to just 2.4%, and meant that although the average GDP % dropped to an all time low of 0.67%, the average expenditure per student increased somewhat to R14 900 (see Table 10.6).

Thus the three different phases of growth related to student enrolment after 1996 cannot be explained simply in terms of disappointing outputs from the secondary schools. Clearly the decision by the fiscus to reduce the proportion of the GDP allocated to the tertiary institutions played a key role.

The declining percentage of GDP allocated to tertiary education, combined with the growth in student numbers, resulted in a decrease in government's contribution per student (see Figure 10.3).

From directives issued to the tertiary institutions by the Department of Education (2005c), it is clear that a decision was made to keep student numbers down in order to help the state to keep within GEAR's medium-term expenditure framework. Thus the failure to significantly increase enrolment rates between 1996 and 2009 was also a consequence of planning decisions made by the Ministry of Finance and the Ministry of Education, which were committed to maintaining a growth rate in student numbers of about 2% a year to ensure that per student expenditure did not drop any further.

As corollary of the reduction in the per-student funding allocations, student fees increased, as did student indebtedness to the universities. The commitment to macro-economic discipline enshrined in the GEAR policy probably also explains the 'introduction of measures to prevent students with outstanding fees from enrolling' – a factor that, in addition to the poor senior-

FIGURE 10.3   Government expenditure per tertiary student, in rand, South Africa 1987–2009

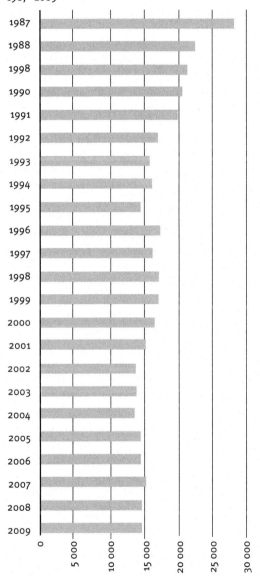

Note: All amounts are reflected at 2005 rand values.

Sources: Our own calculations based on the same sources as used in Table 10.6.

certificate results, Steyn and De Villiers (2006: 25) blame for the surprising decrease in enrolments after 1996. Ironically, the democratic government had the legitimacy (that the apartheid government had lacked) to pressurise the tertiary institutions into suspending students who could not afford fees. Since fee payments were not strictly enforced before and during the transition period, particularly at the universities and technikons previously reserved for black students, the exclusion of students on the basis of their failure to pay fees contributed to a dramatic fall in student numbers at many institutions from 1996 onwards. The SAPSE formula in place at that time based state funding on student numbers adjusted by a growth factor. Thus many institutions would have done much better financially had they stuck to their earlier policy of not insisting on the payment of fees.[23] And, as found by Breier (2010a), financial exclusions have continued despite the expansion of the (often badly targeted) National Student Financial Aid Scheme (NSFAS), which, at best, helps students with their fees but seldom covers their subsistence costs.

The rapid expansion of student numbers that took place between 2001 and 2004 was not sustainable because, by 2003, expenditure per student had reached a low of R13 700. But the situation for tertiary institutions would have been very different if, with the phasing out of the teacher-training colleges, the 0.13% or more of the GDP that was being paid to these institutions annually via the provincial education departments made available to the other tertiary institutions. However, probably because of the strict discipline imposed under GEAR, this did not occur.[24]

As far as the broader question of funding tertiary education is concerned, we feel strongly that, given the real and substantial danger of perpetuating the inequalities created by apartheid, a strong case can be made for significantly increasing the proportion of the GDP spent on tertiary education, thus reversing the marked decline experienced since the mid-1990s. For a wide range of economic, political and social reasons it is vital to ensure that a substantially higher proportion of African and coloured South Africans obtain a good tertiary education. However, we also have to accept the view of the Department of Finance (signalled by the very substantial cutback in the proportion of the GDP allocated to tertiary education) that the steering of this sector needs to improve. Quality control within the sector has to become far more effective than has hitherto been the case.

Government inefficiencies in managing the tertiary sector
From 1996 onwards a series of direct and ad hoc interventions by government negatively affected the expansion of tertiary education. First, as has already

been mentioned, university administrations were pressured not to readmit students who could not pay outstanding fees. This led to a high dropout rate among African and coloured students for financial reasons. Second, following the 1996 Green Paper on Higher Education Transformation, some universities came under pressure to disband their traditional degree offerings and replace them with programmes that it was claimed, would better prepare students for specific careers. Anecdotal evidence suggests that the fact that some 'black' universities (such as the University of the Western Cape) did away with certain degrees, such as a BA in History and English in favour of programmes such as Tourism Studies, further contributed to a shift away from such institutions. A third initiative was the merging of a number of institutions – a process from which there have been no clear benefits, and which incurred very significant direct and indirect costs (see OECD 2005 for a discussion of these). Finally, from the late 1990s, the tertiary institutions have been required to put much energy into new systems of reporting and planning, often apparently mainly for the sake of window dressing.

Thus, very under-resourced and often only partly informed bureaucrats in the Department of Education got involved in far too many ad hoc intervention measures. One is reminded of central planners in the Soviet Union who tried to manage the Soviet economy in great detail, and failed in most of their attempts. Instead of effectively steering the broad direction of transformation in the tertiary sector from a distance, the Education Department has tried to bureaucratically manage universities – a tendency that has been compounded by the planning processes it has imposed.

However, it is our conviction that there are two further key factors that explain the government's failure to steer tertiary institutions in the direction it intended: (i) the introduction of an inappropriate funding formula in 2004, and (ii) the fact that far too much reliance is placed on micro-managing universities via three-year rolling agreements. For the remainder of this chapter we outline some of the problems with the government's approach and propose an alternative that has the potential to enable universities to meet the challenges South Africa has to face far more effectively.

The potential role of tertiary education in South Africa and the development of a compatible funding formula

In this section we first consider the role that tertiary education ought to play in South Africa and we argue for what we call a social-democratic approach to tertiary education. By this we mean that tertiary education has as its goal the optimal development of the capabilities of all citizens. Given the broader social and political challenges facing South Africa, this is an important objective in itself, over and above the goal of meeting the skills needs of the economy, or, as is some times emphasised, the skills needed to participate in the knowledge economy. Against this background we consider the limitations of the existing funding formula, and broadly outline an alternative that has the potential to bring about the much-needed changes in the tertiary sector.

In the 1997 White Paper on Higher Education (Department of Education 1997: 1.3) tertiary education was seen as helping the nation to realise a variety of objectives:

- To meet the learning needs and aspirations of individuals through the development of their intellectual abilities and aptitudes throughout their lives. Higher education...is...a key allocator of life chances and important vehicle for achieving equity...among South African citizens.

- To address the development needs of society and provide the labour market, in a knowledge-driven and knowledge-dependent society, with the ever-changing high level competencies and expertise necessary for the growth and prosperity of a modern economy...

- To contribute to the socialisation of enlightened, responsible and constructively critical citizens...

- To contribute to the creation, sharing and evaluation of knowledge. Higher education engages in the pursuit of academic scholarship and intellectual inquiry...through research, learning and teaching.

In most subsequent documents on tertiary education in South Africa at least two additional broad objectives are put forward, namely, to enhance equity and economic development. For us a more fundamental goal incorporates both of these objectives; that is, tertiary education needs to play a key role in nation building. Whereas Verwoerd saw tertiary education as preparing individuals to serve different ethnic groups, we argue that tertiary education should help create a united nation in which the development of the capabilities of all South Africans takes priority.

It is often argued that the goals of equity and economic development are in tension with one another – equity may require giving priority to black South Africans to access tertiary education, whereas economic considerations emphasise giving access to higher education to those students who obtain the best results in the senior-certificate examinations. We argue that nation building requires a widening of these two objectives. In our view, South Africa should place the same emphasis on tertiary education, and attempt to develop the same broad-based access, as exists in the social democracies of Scandinavia for the same reasons. In other words, the development of human capabilities must be the primary goal, and not (in the first place) the needs of the economy.

Seen from this perspective, the most important failures of tertiary education during the post-apartheid years are: (i) the failure to significantly increase the overall enrolment rate of African and coloured students, and, (ii) the decline in the enrolment rate of African men, which as noted above was 1% lower by 2007 than it was in 1996.

Although a significant number of black South Africans now theoretically have access to a good tertiary education, the vast majority have no opportunities to acquire the capabilities that would enable them to participate in the higher education sector. Among the few who do actually gain access to universities, a strong urban and class bias is evident. As Branson et al. (2009) show, the chances of a very bright young African man from a subsistence-farming household in a rural area (say Mpumalanga) gaining entry into tertiary education are only a fraction of those of a young African man of average abilities, whose middle-class parents send him to a Model C school in an urban area such as Cape Town. It is hardly surprising that disempowered young men and women, many of whom who have the ability to succeed in tertiary education, and have been given no opportunity to obtain even the rudiments of a proper secondary education, are becoming increasingly disenchanted and seeking ontological security in superficial populism.

If South Africa sees its highest priority as being the development of the capabilities of all its people, significantly more funding must be directed to improving the entire education system, and the Department of Education must urgently put in place a funding formula capable of steering the tertiary education sector towards accommodating the tens of thousands of bright and able young African and coloured people who have so far been failed by the system. A common refrain in South African policy documents is that

The higher education system...needs to be steered to meet national goals and priorities through a combination of instruments, namely, planning, funding and quality assurance (Department of Education, 2005c: 1).

In principle there is no problem with these sentiments. However, when one considers what happened on the ground between 1995 and 2012: (i) the planning process, as argued in the preceding section, often fails to address the most serious problems of the tertiary sector; (ii) in spite of time-consuming quality audits, very little empirical evidence is available on the quality of the outputs of different programmes, departments and institutions; and (iii) the existing funding formula does little to incentivise the realisation of the outcomes that government claims to be committed to.

More macro-planning and less micro-management

South African tertiary institutions have to put a massive amount of work into developing three-year rolling plans, which along with other projects[25] are seen as important by bureaucrats in the national education department. In other words, instead of relying on incentives in the funding formula to steer the universities from a distance, the department has relied on central enrolment planning, often with little rhyme or reason (See Steyn and de Villiers, 2006). What is more, although their other plans usually envisage desirable changes, they tend to be unrealisable. For instance, all institutions have made a commitment to transforming their academic staff complement. This assumes a significant increase in the number of Africans obtaining master's and PhD degrees but statistics reveal an overall decrease in the number of postgraduate degrees being awarded (see CHE 2009: 60, Table 20).

Unfortunately the CHE, which has the task of advising government on tertiary education, has often failed to play the monitoring role it should, and has, at times, made serious blunders. For example, it has not raised the alarm about key trends in the system, including the decrease in male enrolment rates since 1996. It is possible that this oversight is due to the frequent emphasis placed on improving female enrolment numbers, a key policy of the 1990s. But gender parity in enrolments (other than at post-graduate level) has long been achieved, and the decline in male enrolment rates is of serious concern. The CHE was also clearly out of touch when it reported glowingly on NSFAS in its October 2009 publication on the state of higher education, stating that 'NSFAS is one of the success stories of South African higher education' (CHE 2009: 28). Yet just a few months later, NSFAS was called before the responsible parliamentary committee to explain audit disclaimers, and a year after that, the education minister had to restructure the NSFAS board 'so that it could deliver on its mandate'.[26]

Instead of attempting to micro-manage the universities in a fashion similar to that employed with regard to economic planning by the Soviet bureaucrats of yesteryear, the Department of Higher Education should put far more effort into ensuring that sensible macro-parameters are put in place. In particular it should give far more thought to the effective steering of the tertiary institutions from a distance by devising and implementing an appropriate funding formula. Much of the remainder of this chapter is devoted to how the funding formula should be reconstituted to ensure that tertiary institutions are effectively transformed.

Quality control of articles published and qualifications awarded

The massive relocation of funds to published research (discussed further below) clearly indicates the state's intention to encourage research. The problem is, as Walwyn (2008) points out, that all articles published in recognised journals qualify for this funding, regardless of whether they are read or have any impact whatsoever. There certainly is a case for rewarding institutions that deliver world-class research, but, as Walwyn convincingly argues, rewards should depend on the quality of the research, not simply on the quantity.

In the case of the grant for student throughput (discussed further below) there is, as Walwyn also warns, another risk related to simply rewarding quantity. Quality is essential, particularly now that (because of the concerns raised by Walwyn) development grants based on pass rates are being phased out.

Quality control can sometimes be monitored effectively through reviews, as was evident from the CHE review of MBA programmes in 2004, and some external monitoring is necessary to determine whether students who pass a course or are awarded a degree actually have the skills that their success implies. Some centrally controlled testing, along the lines of that introduced in Brazil (see Cloete et al. 2002), should be introduced to ensure that pass rates are not artificially inflated by institutions more concerned about securing the next year's funding than about the impact that badly qualified graduates might have on their reputations. This type of quality control will be crucial if the revised funding formula we propose in the final sections of this paper are accepted.

Restructuring the funding formula implemented since 2004/2005

The existing funding formula was first implemented in the 2004/2005 financial year. In this section we discuss its main features, highlight a number of its short-comings and make some proposals as to how it can be improved.

Reinstate the teaching input aspect of the formula

The government provides two types of grants to tertiary institutions: 'Firstly, block grants, which are undesignated amounts to cover the operational costs of higher education institutions linked to the provision of teaching and research-related services. Secondly, earmarked grants, which are designated for specific purposes' (Steyn and De Villers 2006: 51). When the current funding formula was first implemented in 2004, just over two-thirds (64.1%) of the block grant comprised of an input element that depended on the numbers of students, the courses, and the degrees or diplomas for which they registered. Courses such as education, law and public administration receive the basic subsidy. The subsidy for students registered for degrees such as the health, life, and physical sciences is 3.5 times higher. The subsidy for subjects, such as languages, social sciences and commerce is 0.5 times higher than the basic, whereas subjects such as engineering, industrial arts and mathematical sciences receive a subsidy 2.5 times that of the basic amount.

However, after the first year, this part of the formula was no longer applicable because the rate at which student numbers were allowed to grow was determined by the department after discussions with each institution (see Steyn and De Villiers 2006 and Department of Education 2006). In such negotiations the department consistently restricted growth in the numbers of arts and social science students.

If, as suggested earlier, the funding allocated for tertiary education is increased to 0.9% of the GDP, it should be possible to actually reinstate the teaching input element of the funding formula and to reward institutions that expand their student enrolments. This would lead to a more rapid growth in students registered. But even if funding is not increased, we strongly recommend that the limitation on the proportion of students allowed to do arts and social sciences be lifted.[27] The reason for this is that many of the students from more poorly resourced schools are more likely to achieve an arts or social science degree than one for which a background in mathematics is needed. Thus, while we acknowledge that there may be a case for retaining a differential in the subsidy paid for different types of courses, we suggest that the policy of subsidising arts students as long as they do not constitute more than 40% of the total student body be scrapped. Between 2002 and 2012, the number of social sciences and arts students (excluding the education students) grew at only 0.5% (see 2012: 38, Table C). This slow growth deprives many first-time university applicants of real opportunities for admission to higher degrees.

Reconsider the formula in respect of teaching-output grants

The teaching output subsidy, which, under the SAPSE formula, depended on the successful completion of a particular course, have, since 2004, been awarded only for degrees or diplomas completed. In 2004/2005 the output subsidy for successful completion of the degrees constituted less than a sixth (16%) of the block grant. We believe there is a compelling case for returning to the principle of awarding output subsidies per course completed, rather than on graduation. Breier et al. (2007) have shown that many students 'stop out' in the course of their studies to earn money or attend to family concerns, but they do often return. In our view, universities should not be penalised for accommodating such students, yet this is the effect of the department's current approach to rewarding graduation rates.

An ideal funding formula would encourage every department and lecturer to strive for the goals set by the central planners, but the current formula makes it very difficult to calculate the teaching output of individual lecturers or specific departments. Thus, although a lecturer or department may have a very good pass rate, the output subsidy accrues only when all courses have been passed. This makes it virtually impossible to use the existing funding formula to determine the micro-level contribution of a particular department or a staff member, or to provide incentives for improved output. However, if success rate is rewarded per course, this output could be monitored and incentivised at departmental level, rather than according to the graduation rate per degree or diploma.

In principle, too, the assumption that an institution produces a teaching output only when a student has completed a degree is open to question. As shown in Breier et al. (2007), students who drop out of higher education after successfully completing a number of courses are relatively successful in obtaining employment. Prospective employers recognise that an employee who has completed several higher-education courses is better qualified than one who has completed no post-school studies.

Thus, on both pragmatic and principled grounds there is a case for linking output subsidies to success rates in specific courses. Of course, an additional incentive for completed degrees or diplomas could also be provided. But even if the education department decides to stay with the present system, fairness requires that it calculate success rates more accurately. Instead of considering pass rates against the number of students enrolled for a particular diploma, the department should consider pass rates against the original age cohort that enrolled for a degree or diploma. This would avoid the danger of punishing faculties when interest in a degree or diploma is growing, or rewarding them when enrolment is shrinking, as was the case at the time of writing. Similarly, when students are studying part time, longer periods should be allowed for completion, as is the case for many distance students.

Redesign the research-output grant
Research-output grants are paid out, based on the research output from higher education institutions two years previously. In 2004/2005, this amounted to nearly an eighth (13.1%) of the block grant.

As noted in Le Roux and Breier (2007), although some South African tertiary institutions have both low throughput and low publication rates, they still receive development grants, ostensibly to improve their research and student output levels. Thus, instead of earning funding by, for example, finding better ways of teaching students who have been badly prepared or increasing their research output, these institutions receive funding regardless, and had, as Steyn and De Villiers (2007) and Walwyn (2008) also argue, no particular incentive to improve. Whereas 'the redress allocation' of the late 1990s was seen as disappointing by some historically black institutions, far larger and less well-motivated redress transfers have taken place since 2004 in the form of development grants. Funds that are paid from year to year, regardless of what institutions deliver, clearly perform no effective steering function. Instead, these grants probably reflect the lobbying power of these institutions within the education ministry – that is, their ability to steer the ministry, rather than the ministry's readiness to steer them.

Allocations to higher-education institutions for research publications and research grants have increased from about R120 million per year in 1999 to approximately R1.5 billion in 2009; the reward for publishing in one of the many recognised journals increased from R22 000 to about R103 000 per article over the same period (CHE 2009: 66). There has been, as the CHE notes, a very significant increase in the number of articles published, but primarily by those universities that don't receive development grants. Thus, while the funding formula in respect of publications worked for those institutions to which it applied, as Walwyn (2008) argues, it could not have any impact on the universities where the grant was paid out regardless of publication levels.

Give equal weight and funding to master's programmes
Unfortunately the funding formula has also had a negative effect on the output of master's graduates. As we warned in an earlier publication (see Le Roux and Breier 2007), lowering the subsidy for standard master's degrees (consisting of a 50% thesis component and a 50% course-work component) to be equivalent to that of a honours degree, as was done in the funding formula promulgated in 2004/2005, became a disincentive for institutions to enrol this type of master's student. In the five years from 2004 to 2009 the number of registered master's students decreased from 6.1% to 5.2% (calculated from, Department of Higher Education and Training 2012: 42, Table D). Given the dire need for more African postgraduates, this outcome is out of line with the stated aims of the education department, but it was to be expected,

given the nature of the funding formula. To maintain the master's enrolment level at 6.2%, about 7 000 more master's students should have been registered between 2008 and 2010.

While there is no doubt that some departments have allowed students to obtain master's degrees on the basis of small dissertations (perhaps too similar to an honours paper), our conviction is that this problem should be addressed through quality control, rather than by trying to reintroduce a research master's degree. In addition, the international trend, as witnessed, for example, by The Bologna Process in Europe, is overwhelmingly towards coursework master's programmes.[28]

In South Africa, students accepted into research-based master's programmes tend to be from more privileged backgrounds, and those that opt for coursework master's programmes are more likely to be from disadvantaged backgrounds (or mature students admitted on the basis of the recognition of prior learning). We would argue that any master's programme in which at least half of all the credits are earned via a thesis should earn a full master's subsidy. This might contribute to reversing the proportional decline in registrations for master's courses since 2004. Without such an adjustment, universities are unlikely to produce sufficient PhD candidates for the development of future academic cohorts.

The key to a transformative funding formula: rewarding institutions that enrol students from disadvantaged backgrounds.
In our view the most fundamental weakness of the existing formula is not, as Walwyn would have it, that it gives too small a benefit to the institutions that conduct quality research, but that it gives no incentives to tertiary institutions to identify and absorb the many black students with potential who come from destitute households and inadequate schools. We agree that good research should be better rewarded than it is at present, and that poor research that somehow lands up being published should not be rewarded at all. But for us the most crucial need is to find a funding formula with the potential to increase the admission rates of impoverished and underprepared but potentially capable students, particularly from the rural areas.

The differences in the quality of schooling received by the students who exit from South African high schools are, ironically partly because of the end of apartheid, even greater than in the days when the apartheid system was in force. Black students from middle- and upper-class homes now have options. They no longer have to stay in schools designated for their particular racial group, and can choose to attend better schools. The Western Cape province, for example, has schools in which all students pass their senior-certificate examinations, virtually half obtain a distinction average, and almost all obtain the endorsement needed to access university. Meanwhile, in the same province, other schools receive the same or even more government funding per student, yet very few of their students pass the senior-certificate exams and even fewer obtain the marks required for access to university. Many middle-class black students, and many of the better teachers, have moved to the Model C schools (where government funding is supplemented by substantial financial contributions from parents), and although there are cases where good principals have managed to create a new culture of teaching and learning, township schools have generally deteriorated.

Thus while 'race' was a fairly good indicator of 'under-preparedness for higher education' in 1994 (Ministry of Education 2003: 3.3.4), with the many changes that have taken place since then, 'race' is no longer an unambiguous indicator of deprivation, nor does it neatly coincide with socio-economic class. African and coloured students who have attended, Model C, or private schools tend to do well at university and cannot be considered educationally disadvantaged. Nevertheless, in terms of the existing funding formula, these students are regarded as 'disadvantaged', and the institutions they attend receive the same additional subsidy per black student (once the number of black students exceed 40% of the total) as those that draw their student body from contexts that are truly disadvantaged, both socio-economically and educationally. Since universities receive additional funding for successful throughput, the existing formula thus encourages institutions to favour black South Africans who have benefited from better schooling over those who may even be more capable but who attended poorly managed schools. Given our country's history, and the low enrolment rate of African and coloured South Africans, a strong case can be made for retaining some incentives for institutions that increase the proportion of black students regardless of the type of school they attended, but,, as we have shown strong incentives are needed to ensure that students who are socio-economically disadvantaged are increasingly absorbed into the system.

Thus the crucial question is, what kind of funding formula would offer real incentives to higher-education institutions to identify students with genuine potential from socio-economically disadvantaged situations, get them to apply, equip them with the appropriate academic skills, and see them through to graduation? In our view, an appropriate funding formula would enable the Department of Education to steer the sector in this direction without having to engage in often-inefficient bureaucratic management such as the three-year rolling plans.

The details of which parameters should inform a new funding formula call for a modelling exercise to establish the impact of various different options. This exercise has to be undertaken by the education department since it has access to all the relevant HEMIS data. Using this data the department of education could easily determine what type of school a student attended. Was he or she the only student who passed the senior-certificate examinations with an endorsement for tertiary study (which might mean an access rate for that school of as low as 0.7%)? Or, at the other extreme, was the student at a school where 90% or more of learners passed with endorsements? The pass rates of the different schools, which vary across the entire spectrum, are indicative of two things: the quality of teaching the students receive, and the socio-economic status of the students. We propose that, for the purposes of institutional grants, whether a student is considered disadvantaged should depend on how well the student has been prepared for higher education, that is, on the quality of the school attended by the student, rather than on whether students are 'African and coloured students who are South African citizens' (Ministry of Education 2005a: 11).

Exactly what the level of the grant should be, and how it should be increased if the pass rate of the school attended is low, can only be worked out with the statistics necessary to run simulation models. But for illustrative purposes, consider the following possibility: institutions receive a standard grant for students admitted from schools that obtain 100% pass rates with university endorsements, and a maximum additional grant (as much as 50% to 100% more of the basic subsidy) for students admitted from schools with very low pass rates and where only 1% or 2% of the students pass with endorsements. The total additional subsidy could be adjusted downwards in a straight line, either as pass rates improve, or as additional weighting factors are incorporated. Thus we propose that a socio-economic indicator, based on the success rate in the senior-certificate exams of the school the student attended, be added into the process of determining the per-student subsidy.[29] We do not wish to propose a specific formula at this stage, but, to illustrate how this idea could be implemented in practice, we outline one possible approach.

Let us assume that 100% of students at a few outstanding schools pass with endorsements. The subsidy for students from these schools would not be adjusted at all (although, if government wishes to retain race as a criterion, the present formula for increasing the overall subsidy for institutions when they increase the proportion of black students from 40 and 60%, could also be retained). On the other hand, the subsidy would be increased substantially for students admitted to university from schools where the endorsement rate is substantially lower – that is, the lower the exemption rate, the larger the adjustment factor per student. The percentage (k) by which the subsidy is to be increased could be calculated as follows: k = (100-x)/2, where x is the percentage of students from the relevant school who attained the necessary senior-certificate endorsement.[30] This means that the subsidy tertiary institutions would receive when admitting students from schools where no one obtained marks high enough to qualify for access to university, would be adjusted upwards by 50%. The subsidy for students from schools with a 50% success rate would be adjusted upwards by 25%, etc. The actual formula used could, of course, work differently and depend on all sorts of considerations. For example, one simple modification would be to double the subsidy increase for any specific success rate, as shown in Option 2 in Table 10.7.

TABLE 10.7 Possible subsidy increases depending on the percentage of pupils from an applicant's school who obtain senior-certificate passes with endorsements for admission to university

Percentage of students who pass with endorsements (x)	Percentage increase in subsidy Option 1: k = (100-x)/2	Percentage increase in subsidy Option 2: k = (100-x)
100%	0%	0%
75%	12.5%	25%
50%	25.0%	50%
25%	37.5%	75%
0%	50.0%	100%

A number of potential benefits arise when using a socio-economic criterion to determine the degree to which a student is disadvantaged. First, and most fundamentally, it destroys the neo-liberal flavour of some other versions of the 'steering from a distance' approach. If implemented, this system would no longer bestow more benefits on the economically better off. In fact, given a sufficiently progressive grant, this system could load the dice in favour of the socio-economically disadvantaged as the potential reward for a university that enrols a student from a poorly resourced school who eventually obtains a PhD would be significant, as the subsidy for this student would continue to be higher for all years of study than the subsidies obtained for students from well-resourced secondary schools. Second, it creates the possibility of free or lower education costs for students from socio-economically disadvantaged backgrounds, without them having to take onerous loans. Finally, if correctly constructed, the system would enable the government to fund a diverse range of higher-education institutions without having to resort to options such as development funds.

Reducing or scrapping fees on the basis of socio-economic indicators

The case *for* student fees in the South African context has been argued by Steyn and De Villiers (2007). Their arguments are similar to those put forward by economists worldwide, including Nicholas Barr (1993). The greater the income equality in a country, the more valid these arguments become. However, South Africa has one of the most unequal income levels in the world: the most affluent quintile (20%) of households receives 62.2% of household income and the least affluent quintile receives only 3.5%. Various studies (see, for example Breier et al. 2007, 2010b) have confirmed that low-income students are dropping out of South African universities for financial reasons, even when they are academically successful. Even if they receive NSFAS support, their loans or bursaries seldom cover anything more than fees, and students find that they have to cover all other costs (accommodation, food and other personal expenses, as well as books and other study resources). In addition, poor families often tend to regard bursaries as a source of household income, thus placing a further burden on students. In this context it is unsurprising that students often work part-time to support themselves or enter full-time employment and 'stop out' temporarily. Many other school-leavers avoid tertiary study entirely, partly because they see no way of affording it and are reluctant to trap themselves in a seemingly endless debt cycle.

At the same time, as noted earlier, higher-education institutions in South Africa are under tremendous pressure as a result of the significant increase in student numbers and the cut backs in the government's contribution to the sector (from about 1.01% of GDP in 1987 to 0.69% in 2009 as shown in Figure 10.2).

Institutions have thus been forced to increase their fees, and the more prestigious ones have increased fees quite dramatically. In an insightful paper on the dynamics of competition amongst universities Van Vucht (2007: 15) points out that:

> Even though student-aid policies are designed to create opportunities for the least advantaged, increased competition leads institutions to focus either on those students who have the financial resources themselves, or on those who have the highest abilities (and who can be offered grants).

Since an important determinant of how well students cope with the higher-education system is how well they are prepared, the present funding formula is thus likely to lead to exactly the consequences Van Vucht warns against. Hence our proposal that, until the overall quality of schooling improves, universities should be rewarded for admitting students who show potential from schools that generally have bad results.

In addition, we suggest that, while providing progressively higher grants for students from disadvantaged schools, the government should also require, or, at the very least, permit institutions to charge much lower or no fees to socio-economically disadvantaged students. In fact, using the funding formula suggested, this would work in the universities' own interests because they would receive much higher subsidies for accepting those students. In our view, if students from the worse-off schools did not have to pay fees, or paid progressively lower fees as a form of compensation for the poor schooling they received, they may well seek entry to tertiary education in increasing numbers. Were this proposal accepted, NFSAS funding could provide for the costs of study not supported by the subsidy (including accommodation, food, etc.). It could also contribute towards the fees of less well-off students who attend schools that obtain good results.[31]

Scandinavia's social-democratic stratagem was and still is not to have any fees at all. We are not suggesting that this would be appropriate in the South African circumstances as it would deprive the universities of an important source of funding. Given the high private returns on education, the financially privileged are willing to pay a significant premium for their right to study. Instead, the changes we propose would allow institutions to continue to raise funds through fees from students in the more affluent socio-economic quintile, while exempting or giving significant discounts to those in the less well-off quintiles. Not only would this bring additional resources into the higher-education arena than would be the case if all fees were scrapped, but it could also, as Adam Habib (2006) argues, offer a better guarantee of academic freedom than would be the case if the institutions were dependent solely on state funding.

Applying the same formula to diverse institutions

The unsuitability of the existing funding formula for the diversity of institutions that need to be supported, has led some to argue for a return to the situation South Africa had before, and which is still in place in many other countries where different funding regimes cater for different types of institutions. Our contention is that, if the existing formula were appropriately modified, it would be sufficiently flexible to support different types of institutions and a uniform regime could be maintained.

In principle, the existing funding formula rewards institutions that obtain high pass rates, good publication records and an adequate throughput of master's and PhD students. However, the many institutions in South Africa that attract students that are badly prepared for university tend to be unable, without drastically lowering standards, to maintain the same pass rates, generate the same number of publications or have the same throughput of master's and PhD students as institutions that attract the better-prepared students. Therefore, in recognition of the fact that they need funding, these institutions receive development grants, but the grant system does not reward those universities that deliver or censure those that do not. In other words, the grants are but a form of handout and offer no real incentive to more effective delivery.

If institutions that that cater disproportionately for disadvantaged students were to obtain additional subsidies as we have proposed, they should earn enough to be able to afford the academic development resources needed to support these students, and the need for development grants would fall away. And where these institutions improve their publication and graduate-throughput records, they would then earn funding for these outputs, rather than face having their development grants cut, as is currently the case.

Meanwhile, institutions that are already academically successful would be motivated and financially supported to develop better ways of identifying which students from disadvantaged schools have the potential to succeed at tertiary level.

Considering a diversity grant
With the exception of one traditionally Afrikaans university where the language of instruction has remained an issue, most historically white universities now have a very substantial number of African and coloured students. However, except where they were merged with historically white institutions, virtually all the black universities have remained black. What is more, in the case of some of the rural institutions, they predominantly draw their students from a specific ethnic group. Is it not time for the government to consider a diversity grant, which would encourage an institution to diversify its student body? We recommend that this be given serious consideration.[32]

Conclusion
Three types of change are needed if higher education is to live up to the expectations of raising enrolment rates to 30% proposed by the National

Education Commission in 1996 or even the more modest 20% of the National Plan (Department of Education, 2001: 36). Firstly, the schooling system needs to be improved dramatically. However, this is a long-term goal, and is unlikely to be realised soon. In the short to medium-term, the tertiary sector will, therefore have to do more to accommodate students who are badly prepared.

Secondly, the ability of the tertiary sector to deliver in this respect would be much enhanced if the funding formula were changed. And finally, as noted, the government's contribution to higher education as a proportion of the GDP, and in terms of the real contribution per student, was significantly higher in 1987 than it is today. If South Africa is really committed to successfully entering the information age, it is essential that this decline be reversed at the very least, and that the government's contribution be increased to about 0.90% of GDP (from 0.69% in 2012). Should the changes in the funding formula we proposed be introduced simultaneously, significantly more black students with the potential to succeed could be accommodated in the country's tertiary institutions.

Far too small a proportion of black South Africans are being properly prepared for the twenty-first century; apartheid inequalities are still with us. Van der Bergh (2010) provides a number of indicators of this: in 2000, the average per capita income among whites was nearly nine times that of black Africans. Since 1994, inequality overall has worsened, he says, but its racial dimensions have 'softened' with an increase of inequality within racial groups, largely as a result of the rapidly growing black middle class, which, in turn, are largely the result of black-economic-empowerment policies.

The potential for racially divisive conflict remains high although the picture is perhaps more complicated than it was in 1994. Nowadays, a groundswell of unemployed youth, largely male, and largely without tertiary education, are being led by other youth, with the same gender and educational profile, who have, nonetheless, managed to enrich themselves greatly through deals that accrue to, for example, senior members of the ANC Youth League.

Would tertiary education make a difference to the lives, aspirations and political consciousness of the youth? It is our contention that it would, and that restructuring the funding formula combined with a small increase in the proportion of GDP allocated to higher education may be all that is needed. The inability to extend numerical and 'epistemological access'[33] to tertiary education to a far greater proportion of South Africans, together with an inability to significantly improve the primary and secondary education, might well turn out to be the greatest failure of government in the first two decades of democracy.

Notes

1   In this chapter we refer to the population categories African, coloured, Indian and white. The term 'black' is used to denote all the population groups other than white. While we do not wish to perpetuate the practice of racial categorisation that underpinned South African society under apartheid, the use of these terms is still necessary to understanding South Africa's history and to monitoring the effects of attempts to achieve equity and redress.

2   'Gross enrolment rate' is the term used in the international literature for what in South Africa is commonly referred to as the gross participation rate, that is, the percentage calculated by considering all tertiary students, regardless of age, as a proportion of the 20–24-year-old age cohort in the population as a whole. Enrolment rates (not preceded by gross) are, strictly speaking, the proportion of only the 20–24-year-old cohort in tertiary education (see Steyn and De Villiers 2006: 26). In this chapter, although the word gross is sometimes dropped, as is mostly the case in South African policy documents, both enrolment rate and participation rate refer to the total number of tertiary students of all age groups relative to the 20–24-year-old age cohort.

3   This chapter develops and refines arguments first put forward in a paper delivered at the first Annual Conference of the the Southern African–Nordic Centre on 6 December 2007. An edited version of the chapter was published by the Friedrich Ebert Stiftung as an occasional paper in late 2012 in an effort to make the content more widely available. We would like to thank SANORD and the editors of the this volume for granting permission for us to do this.

4   In particular, we argue that South Africa should strive to develop the same broad-based access to tertiary education as exists in the Scandinavian social democracies. Given the realities of South Africa, however, we argue that fees should not be scrapped for the better-off students, but that the higher subsidy given to students from disadvantaged backgrounds should enable institutions to scrap or significantly reduce fees for this section of the student body.

5   Bundy (2006) provides an excellent overview of the reforms in the United Kingdom, and considers the possibly ominous consequences, were South Africa to follow this route.

6   For the often critical response from various academics to Jansen's lecture, see Hoadley (2004). And for an interesting take on the views of various participants in the South African debate, and on the importance of a degree of financial independence to maintaining academic freedom, see Habib (2006). Of particular importance, although only indirectly relevant to this chapter, is Habib's argument that the higher-education system 'must also reflect a plurality of ideological voices including those that are intellectual dissidents in our society' (2004: 3).

7   The only estimate we could find of enrolment in private tertiary institutions was in a presentation by Cloete (2011: Slide 41) which provides 'provisional headcounts'

for the South African higher and post-secondary education, and indicates that there are 81 596 students in private institutions. If one excludes the post-secondary colleges and considers only the 23 public tertiary institutions and the 98 providers of private higher education, this means that private providers enrolled approximately 8.4% of students in 2010.

8   See Kruss (2004) and Subotzky (2003) for analyses of the private sector.

9   At the University of Natal, black students were, however, taught separately from the white students.

10   The University of Fort Hare, located in the small rural town of Alice in the Eastern Cape province, was the premium black university in southern Africa until 1950, when the government intervened and prohibited the acceptance of Africans from outside South Africa. Under apartheid the institution was earmarked to become a tribal college for Xhosa-speaking Africans by the late 1950s.

11   Commonly known as the TBVC states, these were 'homelands' or 'bantustans', which (between 1976 and 1981) accepted the nominal independence on offer during the apartheid era. Their population statistics, enrolment data and also their budgets were not incorporated into South African statistics until after 1994, when the new democratic government reincorporated them into South Africa. None of these territories were ever recognised by any other state as independent, but many of the official statistics for South Africa simply exclude these areas for the period during which they were nominally independent.

12   The word *verligte* was first coined in the South African context by Wimpie de Klerk, then editor of the Transvaler and brother of FW de Klerk. It refers to someone who is enlightened; it carries positive connotations in contrast to the term 'liberal', which was used by the National Party to brand any Afrikaner who deviated from apartheid dogma, and the term *verkrampte*, which refers to conservatives.

13   The figures usually quoted, by Steyn and De Villiers (2006) for example, exclude the students undergoing teacher training up to 2001, and the students in the TBVC institutions up to 1994, after which they are included. Furthermore the figures include the students enrolled at the technikons from 1986 onwards, but not for the preceding years. This makes comparisons over time misleading. In Table 10.1 we have included both these groups in our second set of figures from 1994 onwards, and in Table 10.2 we have included estimates of the students receiving teacher training from 1986 onwards. Whichever set of figures one uses, the growth in the number of black students from the mid-1970s to 1994 was clearly quite phenomenal. If one uses the conventional data (see Table 10.1), black tertiary enrolments increased 14-fold from 19 752 in the mid-1970s to 273 526 by 1994. This means that black student numbers in this period increased from less than a sixth (16.1%) of the total number of students in 1975 to over half (55.2%) by 1994. Using these figures, the overall annual growth rate in student numbers for this period was about 7.5% and black enrolment grew at about 14%. In fact, if one

includes the students in teacher-training colleges and the TBVC institutions, the proportion of black students was already over 60%, by 1994.

14 When the De Lange commission reported in 1981, it attempted to put forward a new educational policy and ideology. Making a sharp break with the overtly racial discourse of the Verwoerd period, it took a technocratic approach, focusing on the need for education to underpin economic development. The commission recommended that the government should aim to provide equal educational funding for all, and allow tertiary education and private schooling to be racially integrated. It also proposed that technical education be given more emphasis, and that industry be encouraged to participate in funding educational projects and providing in-house training (Morris and Hyslop, 1991).

15 Work by Psacharopoulos (cited in Steyn and De Villiers, 2006: 10) and others concluded that the rate of return from tertiary education in sub-Saharan Africa was about 11 as against a return of 25 for primary education. In OECD countries the return on tertiary education was only 8.5, but the figure for primary education was the same – hence the conclusion that, given its much higher rate of return, Africa should prioritise primary education. Since estimates for South Africa were returns of 12 and 22 respectively, the same logic would have applied, had the World Bank been giving us advice at that time; South Africa's international isolation might have prevented this kind of pressure from being applied.

16 No reliable data are available on enrolment in private institutions, apart from an estimate of total enrolment for 2010 in Cloete (2011, Slide 41). If this estimate is correct, and if one accepts the same number for 2009 as 2010, the enrolment rate for 2009 would have been 1.7% higher. We do not know the numbers or population groups of these students for the earlier years.

17 We use the rates as published by Steyn, but given problems with the data, it seems specious to give estimates to the second decimal as he does.

18 It should be noted that given the age distribution of the 2001 Census, we adjusted the mid-year population estimates for 2009 for the Indian 20–24-year-old age cohort downwards by about 15 000 as discussed in the note to Table 10.3. Should one accept the 2009 age cohort estimates, the Indian enrolment rate was 45%, not 51%, in 2009.

19 This information was obtained from figures supplied by the Department of Education's Higher Education Management Information System (HEMIS), see Breier and Mabizela (2007).

20 See 'SA pupils fail literacy tests, complex reading skills are introduced too late', Pretoria News, 30 November 2007. Available online.

21 Ditto Note 20.

22 Average government expenditure per student is given at 2005 rand values throughout this chapter to ensure that real values can be compared.

23　Another reason for the fall in student numbers at the institutions formerly reserved for black students was that the historically 'white' institutions were now open to black students.

24　In fact, although the closing of the teacher-training colleges was recommended in an ill-conceived report to the Department of Education (Hofmeyr and Hall, 1995), some observers argue that GEAR should also carry part of the blame for this process. As noted by Pratt (2001:12), 'The GEAR policy emphasised new goals of efficiency, effectiveness, and affordability over developmental objectives, and ushered in a new climate of competitiveness. Provincial Treasuries were constrained by the national Departments of Finance and State Expenditure to conform to GEAR principles and guidelines in their respective budgeting processes...Teacher-training colleges were perceived to be a high-cost activity, and witnessed a greater degree of rationalisation as provinces grappled with huge deficits, and diminishing allocations in real terms. Initial expectations of substantial investment in capacity-building and human-resource development soon dissipated, and in teacher-training colleges, the conviction grew that economic exigencies driving rationalisation had supplanted educational and developmental considerations.'

25　Replacing academic degrees with the skills-oriented programmes mentioned earlier is one example of such projects.

26　See 'NSFAS moves from audit disclaimer to unqualified audit', press statement issued by Blade Nzimande, Minister of Higher Education and Training, 10 October. Available online.

27　The argument favouring this restriction is that the labour market offers more opportunities for students with commerce or science degrees than for those who obtain an arts degree (see Pillay 2003). In our view, this is very short-term perspective. In 1956, with respect to the integration of Afrikaners into the management structures of the economy, Prof Jan Sadie argued that this was a long-term process. He said the first generation getting tertiary education usually have to become teachers (with arts degrees), the second generation might become professionals, and the third generation will become leaders in commerce and industry (see Thom, 1956).

28　Prof David Cooper from the Department of Sociology at the University of Cape Town brought this point to our attention. See also the 'Conclusions and recommendations of the Conference on Master-level Degrees' from The Bologna Process, Helsinki, 14–15 March 2003. Available online.

29　It is possible that if this system is implemented some students might choose to attend schools where the overall pass rate is lower in order to become more attractive candidates to universities. They would risk being less well prepared, but if they succeed they may, if some of our other proposals below were accepted, be liable for much lower fees or no fees at all. This could, in fact, be beneficial, not only for the individuals who adjust their behaviour to benefit from the system, but also for society as a whole. More middle-class children, some of them in all likelihood white, may move into the black schools that have been denuded of students from middle-class backgrounds.

30 See Department of Education (2009: 21, 24, Table 11) for a provincial breakdown of this percentage.

31 For example, the children of domestic workers whose parents live at their employers' premises and attend Model C schools.

32 To quote the NCHE (1996: 1.2.1), 'There has been a tendency for higher education institutions to replicate the ethnic, racial and gender divisions of the wider society. This has limited the role of higher education in constructing a critical civil society with a culture of tolerance, public debate and accommodation of differences and competing interests.'

33 Wally Morrow (1992) distinguished between mere physical access to higher education and access that ensured the successful acquisition of knowledge and skills.

References

Badsha N and N Cloete (2011) *Higher Education: Contribution for the NPC's National Development Plan.* Cape Town: Centre for Higher Education Transformation. Available online.

Barr N (1993) 'Alternative funding resources for higher education', *The Economic Journal*, 103 (418): 718–728.

Branson N, M Leibbrandt and TL Zuze (2009) *The Demand for Tertiary Education in South Africa.* Cape Town: Southern Africa Labour and Development Research Unit.

Breier M (2010a) 'From "financial considerations" to "poverty": Towards a reconceptualisation of the role of finances in higher education student dropout', *Higher Education* 60: 657–670.

Breier M (2010b) 'Dropout or stop out at the University of the Western Cape?' in M Letseka, M Cosser, M Visser and M Breier *Student Retention and Graduate Destination: Higher Education and Labour Market Access and Success.* Pretoria: HSRC.

Breier M and M Mabizela (2007) 'Higher education', in A Kraak and K Press (eds) *Human Resources Development Review 2007.* Cape Town: HSRC Press.

Breier M, M Letseka and M Visser (2007) *Pathways Through Higher Education to the Labour Market: Factors Affecting Student Retention, Graduation, and Destination. Case-Study Report on the University of the Western Cape.* Cape Town: Human Sciences Research Council.

Bundy C (2006) 'Global patterns, local options? Changes in higher education internationally and some implications for South Africa', in *Kagisano 4: Ten Years of Higher Education Under Democracy*. Pretoria: Council on Higher Education.

Bunting I (1994) *A Legacy of Inequality: Higher Education in South Africa*. Cape Town: UCT Press.

Bunting, I (2002) 'The higher education landscape under apartheid', in N Cloete et al. (eds) *Transformation in Higher Education: Global Pressures and Local Realities in South Africa*. Cape Town: CHET. Available online.

Chisholm L (1983) 'Redefining skills: Black education in South Africa in the 1980s', *Comparative Education* 19 (2): 357–372.

Cloete N (2011) 'Differentiation: Reasons and Purposes, Systems and Methodologies', PowerPoint presentation to the Centre for Higher Education Transformation. Cape Town, July 2011. Available online.

Cloete N, R Fehnel, P Maassen, T Moja, H Perold and T Gibbon (eds) (2002). *Transformation in Higher Education: Global Pressures and Local Realites in South Africa*. Cape Town: CHET. Available online.

CHE (Council on Higher Education) (2006) *Kagisano 4: Ten Years of Higher Education Under Democracy*. Pretoria.

CHE (2009). *The State of Higher Education in South Africa*. Higher Education Monitor, No. 8. A report of the Council on Higher Education's Advice and Monitoring Directorate. Pretoria.

Darling AL, MD England, DW Lang and R Lopers-Sweetman (1989) 'Autonomy and control: A university funding formula as an instrument of public policy', *Higher Education* 18 (5): 559–583.

De Lange JP (1981) *Provision of Education in the RSA: Report of the Main Committee of the HSRC Investigation into Education*. Pretoria: HSRC.

Department of Basic Education (2010) *Education Statistics in South Africa, 2009*, Pretoria.

Department of Education (1996) *Green Paper on Higher Education Transformation*. Pretoria: Department of Education.

Department of Education (1997). *Education White Paper 3, A Programme for the Transformation of Higher Education*. Pretoria. Available online.

Department of Education (2001) *National Plan for Higher Education*. Pretoria.

Department of Education (2005a) HEMIS (Excel File), www.education.gov.za. (Accessed: 17 June 2008)

Department of Education (2005b) 'Information on the State Budget for Higher Education', August 2005. Available online.

Department of Education (2005c). *Student Enrolment Planning in Public Higher Education*. Available online.

Department of Education (2006) Ministerial Statement on Higher Education Funding: 2006/7 to 2008/9. Available online.

Department of Education (2008) 'South Africa: National Report on the Development of Education', report presented to the 48th International Conference on Education, 25–28 November, Geneva. Available online.

Department of Education (2010). *Trends in Education, Macro Indicators Report: South Africa 2009*. Pretoria.

Department of Higher Education and Training (2012) Green Paper for Post-School Education and Training. Pretoria.

Habib A (2006) 'The Practice of Academic Freedom in South Africa', Paper presented to the Council on Higher Education's Regional Forum on Government Involvement in Higher Education, Institutional Autonomy and Academic Freedom, Pretoria, 24 March and Bloemfontein 4 May. Available online.

Hoadley U (ed.) (2004) *Accounting for Autonomy*. Report of a seminar jointly hosted by the Cape Higher Education Consortium, the Centre for Higher Education Transformation, and the Centre for the Study of Higher Education.

Hofmeyr J and G Hall (1995) *The National Teacher Education Audit: Synthesis Report*. Johannesburg: Centre for Education Policy Development.

Hoggett P (1994) 'The politics of the modernisation of the UK welfare state', in R Burrows and B Loader (eds) (1994) *Towards a Post-Fordist Welfare State?* London: Routledge.

Jansen JD (2004) 'Accounting for autonomy: How higher education lost its innocence', lecture given at the 41st Annual TB Davies Lecture, University of Cape Town. Available online.

Kruss G (2004) *Chasing Credentials and Mobility, Private Higher Education in South Africa*. Cape Town: HSRC Press.

Liefner I (2003) `Funding, resource allocation, and performance in higher education systems', *Higher Education* 46 (4): 469 -489.

Le Roux P (1984) 'The theory of structuration and racial domination in the South African context', paper presented to the Conference on Economic Development and Racial Domination, University of the Western Cape, Cape Town, 8–10 October.

Le Roux P and M Breier (2007) 'Steering from a distance: Funding mechanisms and student access and success in higher education in South Africa', paper presented to the 1st Annual SANORD Centre Conference, University of the Western Cape, Cape Town, 6 December. Available online.

Liefner I (2003) 'Funding, resource allocation, and performance in higher education systems', *Higher Education* 46 (4): 469–489.

Melck A (2001) *Indicators and Benchmarks for Universities and Technikons*. South African Universities Vice-Chancellors Association.

Middleton C (2000) 'Models of state and market in the "modernisation" of higher education', *British Journal of Sociology of Education*, 21 (4): 537–554.

Ministry of Education (2003) 'Funding of Public Higher Education', Government Notice, November. Available online.

Ministry of Education (2005a). Draft National Plan for Higher Education in South Africa. Pretoria. Available online.

Ministry of Education (2005b) Ministerial Statement on Higher Education Funding, 2005/06 to 2007/08, 15 April 2005.

Moodie GC (1994) 'The state and liberal universities in South Africa: 1948-1990', *Higher Education* 27 (1): 1–40.

Morris A and T Hyslop (1991) 'Education in South Africa: The present crisis and the problems of reconstruction', *Social Justice* 28 (1/2): 259–270.

Morrow W (1992) 'A picture holds us captive', in S Pendlebury, L Hudson, Y Shalem and D Bensusan (eds) *Kenton-at-Broederstroom 1992: Conference Proceedings.* Johannesburg: Education Department, University of the Witwatersrand.

NCHE (National Commission on Higher Education) (1996) 'An Overview of a New Policy Framework for Higher Education Transformation'. Available online.

OECD (Organisation for Economic Co-operation and Development) (2005). *Reviews of National Policies of Education.* Paris.

Pillay P (2003) 'The South African experience with developing and implementing a funding formula for the tertiary education system', a paper presented at a Regional Training Conference on Improving Tertiary Education in Sub-Saharan Africa: Things That Work! Accra, 23–25 September.

Pratt E (2001) 'Remodelling teacher education, 1994–2000: A perspective on the cessation of college-based teacher education', a paper commissioned by the Council for Higher Education Transformation, Cape Town.

Reddy T (2004) *Higher Education and Social Transformation: South Africa Case Study.* Council on Higher Education.

Reserve Bank (2011) 'National accounts: December 2011' (online data), *Quarterly Bulletin* 262 (December). Pretoria.

Riekert PJ (1979) *Report of the Commission of Inquiry into Legislation Affecting the Utilisation of Manpower.* Pretoria.

Stats SA (Statistics South Africa) (2004a) *Census 2001, Primary Tables South Africa: Census '96 and 2001 Compared.* Report No. 03-02-04. Pretoria.

Stats SA (2004b) *Mid-year Population Estimates for 2004.* Statistical Release P0302. Pretoria.

Steyn AGW (2008) 'Measuring student participation in the higher education sector in South Africa', Institutional Research and Planning Division, Stellenbosch University. Available online.

Steyn G and P De Villiers (2006) 'The impact of changing funding sources on higher education institutions in South Africa', *Higher Education Monitor*, No. 4. Pretoria: Council on Higher Education.

Steyn AGW and AP de Villiers (2007) 'Public funding of higher education in South Africa by means of formula', in *Review of Higher Education in SA 2007*. Pretoria: Council on Higher Education. Available online.

Stuart W, P Dzvimbo, W Fanslow, B Figaji, P Hunter, S Jones, J Kennedy, T Lodge and PN Pillay (1992) *South Africa: Tertiary Education Sector Assessment*. A report produced by the Academy for Educational Development for the US Agency for International Development. Available online.

Subotzky G (2003) 'Public higher education', in A Kraak and H Perold (eds) *Human Resources Development Review 2003*. Cape Town: HSRC Press.

Thom HB (ed.) (1956) *Volkskongres oor die Toekoms van die Bantoe: Referate en Besluit, Volksongres, Bloemfontein, 28–30 Junie 1956*. Stellenbosch: Pro Ecclesia Press.

Van der Bergh S (2010) *Current Poverty and Income Distribution in the Context of South African History*. Working paper 22/10, Department of Economics and Bureau for Economic Research, Stellenbosch University.

Van Vucht F (2007) 'Diversity and differentiation in higher education systems', paper presented to the anniversary conference, Centre for Higher Education Transformation, Cape Town, 16 November.

Walwyn D (2008) 'An analysis of the performance management of South African higher education institutions', *South African Journal of Higher Education*, 22 (3): 708–724.

Wiehahn NE (1982) *South Africa: Commission of Inquiry into Labour Legislation*. Johannesburg: Lex Patria.

PART IV: CRITICAL PERSPECTIVES

Chapter 11

Cultural heritage and social context: research and management in Mozambique

Anne Bang and Tore Sætersdal

This chapter explores some of the challenges and possibilities related to researching Africa's cultural heritage – as well as the ways in which its conservation, and dissemination is put to popular and political use. In the context of this chapter, we define the terms 'dissemination' and 'conservation' in their broad sense. In other words, we understand conservation to be the processes involved in looking after a *place*[1] so as to retain its *cultural significance,* including its past and present aesthetic, historic, scientific, social and spiritual value. Thus we see cultural significance as being embodied in a place through a whole range of elements that represent tangible and intangible heritage.[2] We also acknowledge that places can have a range of values for different individuals or groups of people. We understand dissemination as the promotion of knowledge and awareness about the cultural significance of aspects of heritage, and we see dissemination as a prerequisite for conservation.

Knowledge production concerning African cultural heritage (such as surveys of archaeological sites and the interpretation of written material or cultural practices) is typically conducted by research institutions (and often in collaboration with international partners). Yet dissemination and conservation are typically left to the local authorities. In many cases, these authorities lack the practical skills, academic insight or political influence needed to adequately fulfil this mandate. This leaves the field open for political and other forms of interference, and this in turn affects which aspects of cultural heritage are selected for dissemination and conservation, as well as the means and modes through which this is carried out.

In some cases, if tackled at all, archaeological and historical research is guided by political motives, and conservation is made to suit these ends. In Eritrea, for example, archaeological research is prohibited so as not to risk evidence emerging that the country has any shared history with neighbouring Ethiopia. After independence, the Eritrean state also decided to co-fund the Red Sea Press to ensure the publication of material demonstrating Eritrea's history as distinct from that of Ethiopia. Sudan has similar initiatives showing its history to be independent of that of Egypt. Meanwhile Rwanda's national museum mentions no ethnic groups in its displays, even when iron-age migrations are presented – Rwanda's post-colonial and post-genocide realities make ethnicity something to be avoided, and so the present is imposed on the past.

With reference to archaeological and historical studies in Africa, and with a special focus on two examples of research projects underway in Mozambique, this chapter aims to highlight the importance of independent research on cultural heritage in all its forms. In our view, while heritage conservation is certainly a matter of resource allocation that requires an emphasis on research and good management, it is also a matter of human rights – the right to *correct information* about your own historical and cultural heritage.

Archaeological and ethnographic research

Archaeological research in Africa has always been uneven. Countries such as South Africa, Egypt and some of Britain's other former colonies have a strong tradition of archaeological research, management and dissemination: archaeology is a prominent discipline in the universities, and national museums and antiquities services disseminate and manage many aspects of cultural heritage. Furthermore, national legislation on cultural heritage inherited from the former colonial power tends to remain in place. This ensures that major road works, as well as city and agricultural development projects, have to present environmental impact assessments before development can begin; and when archaeological excavations prove necessary, the developer is expected to cover these costs. Countries such as these are the exception in Africa, however. In far more cases, antiquity services have little access to power or resources, universities don't offer archaeology degrees, and national museums lack both funding and conservation expertise.

One of the reasons for this situation is the lack of importance accorded to 'culture' in the discourse of development. Culture and heritage are seldom mentioned in countries' development plans or in priorities agreed between donors and recipient countries. Development priorities tend to be set by donor nations, and culture is decidedly not among their major objectives. We are not arguing that culture should be accorded a higher priority than health and education. However, the need to compare and prioritise between obviously worthy causes tends to be overstated when budgets are being calculated. It is also worth noting that while Western countries place strong emphasis and importance on their own cultural heritage, similar focus is seldom accorded to development interventions. Thus donor countries blithely allocate millions dollars of state support to protecting and developing their own 'culture' in its many forms (in museums, dissemination and cultural tourism), yet virtually always overlook this element when addressing the needs of African countries. Debates about how culture and heritage may contribute to development and national unity in aid-receiving countries are seldom heard, despite the efforts of programmes such as Africa 2009,[3] which aimed to include cultural heritage in the development agenda and build competence in heritage management.

Historical studies: towards a corpus of written sources of the African past

The first conference on African history took place in 1953, and presented, according to Vansina (1994: 51), 'information derived from archaeology and oral traditions'. By the 1960s, African history, as a scholarly discipline, stood on the threshold of unprecedented expansion, both in Africa and elsewhere. Driven by initiatives such as the Fontes Historiae Africanae (FHA)[4] initiated in 1962, historians began orienting themselves towards written sources – European, African and, increasingly, Arabic. A series of projects grew focusing on the publication of non-European sources for African history. The Centre for Arabic Documentation in Ibadan, Nigeria is one example; established in 1964, it soon began to issue regular bulletins on written sources of African history. These bulletins, alongside those of other similar undertakings, made it clear that written sources existed in abundance, not only in Arabic but also in local languages written in Arabic script. In sum, as John Hunwick once observed, it became evident that *'l'Afrique ne seulement danse, il pense'*.[5]

In other words, the efforts of researchers in the 1960s and 1970s disproved the claim that Africa's written tradition began with the arrival of European colonialists and missionaries. Rather, it became clear Africa's scriptural traditions began centuries earlier, and dated back to the arrival of Islam in various regions between the eighth and nineteenth centuries. With Islam came cultural practices, architectural styles, and the Arabic language and Arabic script – all of which now form aspects of African cultural heritage. As the basis of religious worship, Arabic and Arabic letters were essential as the language of prayer, and mastering them became a religious duty usually undertaken by community leaders. However, Arabic did not remain solely a language of ritual nor of inter-ethnic communication. Arabic script became the means through which several African languages, including Hausa, Fulfulde, Songhay, Yoruba, Swahili and Malagasy, were first written down. In other words, Africans modified the Arabic alphabet for their own use, adding sounds that were lacking or changing letters to fit their needs. These adaptations are known collectively as *ajami* script – that is Arabic script used for languages other than Arabic.[6]

Thus, by the time European mission schools and colonial administrations were established in the nineteenth and early twentieth centuries, literacy – understood as a system for presenting one's language in writing – was already an established social fact in many parts of the African continent. Despite their omnipresence – and repeated attempts – colonial education systems did not fully replace these pre-existing modes of writing. Rather, knowledge transfer using *ajami* took place well into the colonial and post-colonial periods. Indeed, the practice of writing (manuscripts, letters, ritual/magic texts, and text-based ritual performances) continued in the face of both colonial rule and the growing presence of print culture as well as radio and film.

Ajami texts are widely distributed across the African continent. Perhaps the most famous collection is the one in Timbuktu, Mali, where an estimated 300 000 manuscripts are deposited in family-owned libraries, containing texts in a wide range of languages (including many in Arabic) (Diagne and Jeppie 2008).[7] Beyond Timbuktu, several towns in Mali, Nigeria, Niger, Senegal and Ghana have major collections. Further east, *ajami* texts are held in privately held family collections throughout Ethiopia (see Kawo 2008), while in Kenya, Tanzania/Zanzibar, Mozambique and the Comoros Islands, a rich tradition of Swahili/Comorian *ajami* exists in several private and public collections that are yet to be fully documented. Although several of these scripts, including substantial *tendi* (narrative poems) and chronicles, have been transliterated, edited and translated (see, for example, Allen 1971; Knappert 1964), much remains unexplored. In Madagascar, the presence of the *sorabe* script (literally meaning 'large writing' but referring to the Malagasy language in Arabic script) became an object of study for early European missionaries and scholars, and its origins are still debated (Munthe 1982; Versteegh 2001). Perhaps the most surprising case of *ajami* is to be found in Cape Town, South Africa, where so-called Arabic-Afrikaans texts are among the oldest examples of written tradition among Cape Muslims (Davids 1991; Jappie 2011; Van Selms 1951).

In more recent decades, various initiatives have raised the profile of the *ajami* tradition as a whole, focusing on traditional Islamic scholarship.[8] In addition, the 'rediscovery' of Timbuktu's large manuscript collections spurred further efforts at conservation, digitisation, research and publications, and this highlighted Africa's written heritage to some extent. Nevertheless, the fact that Africa's long history of reading and writing predates European colonisation (by several centuries in some areas) remains relatively unknown.

Parallel to the development of African historical studies from the 1950s to the 1970s, came the establishment of new archives and museums for the conservation and dissemination of written material. However, academic research on the role of *ajami* in Africa has, since the 1960s and again in the 2000s, become a focus within the disciplines of history, and religious, literary and museum studies. Admittedly, some research was conducted from the point of view of philology during the colonial period. However, wider studies of the fundamental role of writing, the educational systems that formed the basis of textual production, the economy of texts, linguistic transfers from other languages (notably Arabic), the materiality of book-making, alphabetic adaptations into local scriptural traditions and the elaboration of written expressions remain largely unexplored. The study of African writing culture has the potential to address a whole range of questions pertaining to material, intellectual and political history, and to offer a view into Africa's pre-colonial past.

Several research paths have opened out which will all certainly lead to new knowledge about the history of African knowledge production. For example, there is a need to investigate *ajami* script itself and its uses in African contexts – *madrasas* (mosque schools) where writing was taught and where texts were studied and produced are of particular interest. In addition, more needs to be know known about how books were produced and distributed, and about the repositories of these texts – who owned libraries and private collections, who used them and why?

Given these lacunae, it is not surprising that the conservation of Africa's written cultural heritage has received comparatively little attention at local, regional or national levels. The major exception here is Timbuktu in Mali, and also Nigeria and Niger,[9] which have established specialised research facilities for the study and conservation of *ajami* manuscripts. In Timbuktu, although the current political situation renders the future of the manuscripts themselves highly insecure, several research and conservation programmes have digitised irreplaceable pieces of scriptural heritage.

Further south, in sub-Saharan Africa, *ajami* manuscripts and books have received especially low priority, both as historical sources and as cultural artefacts. One of the reasons for this is clear: reading and understanding these documents requires an expertise that very few people possess. *Ajami* is dying out in many local communities, having been supplanted by the Latin alphabet introduced by the colonial authorities and since favoured by post-colonial education systems. In addition, a renewed emphasis on standardised Arabic among Muslim communities generally (linked to the orientation towards Salafism, and sometimes a requirement for funding from the Middle East), is undermining these traditions among Muslims in Africa. In terms of Western scholarship, the marginalisation of *ajami* texts can also be partly explained by the fact that Arabic-language training and research has been closely tied to Middle Eastern studies, which has given little attention to sub-Saharan Africa. Furthermore, since Muslims find themselves in a minority in several sub-Saharan nations, it is perhaps understandable that there are few specialists in post-colonial administrations with the competence – or the will – to initiate research or conservation on this aspect of their countries' national heritage. Essentially, a real lack of resources has prevented conservation efforts in this field, as in many others.

The case of Mozambique: archaeological and scriptural research and management

Mozambique was ravaged by two wars, waged between 1964 and 1994, and is now home to one of the world's most impoverished nations. It has, however, launched a dynamic process of reconstruction, and is considered one of the region's success stories. It also holds one World Heritage Site – the colonial buildings of Mozambique Island.

The National Directorate for Cultural Heritage's (2003) strategic plan for 2003 to 2007 devotes particular attention to the intangible aspects of Mozambique's cultural heritage, arguing that these have been neglected in the past. There is also an increased awareness of the country's pre-colonial heritage. The so-called intangible aspects are particularly important when applied to rock art. However as shown below, aspects of rock art found in Mozambique that are often defined as intangible, are as tangible to local communities as any of the physical aspects of these sites.

Archaeological sites and studies

In 2003, an initiative of the Centre for Development Studies at the University of Bergen led to a three-year project supported by the Norwegian Agency for Development Cooperation, whereby archaeologists and students from the University of Bergen in Norway, Eduardo Mondlane University in Mozambique, the University of the Witwatersrand in South Africa, the University of Zimbabwe and the Malawi Department of Antiquities joined forces to conduct research in the Manica and Tete provinces of Mozambique and in the adjacent border areas within Zimbabwe and Malawi. Staff and students from all the institutions took part in the fieldwork, and field training for students was integrated into the process. The project was the first to include co-operation between South African and Mozambican archaeologists, and the first to arrange joint fieldwork between the four participating countries. The aim was to record and document elements of both tangible and intangible cultural heritage in the study areas (Sætersdal 2009). In Zimbabwe, the project worked closely with another ongoing project known as The Ancestral Landscape of Manyikaland, being run by the University of Bergen and the University of Zimbabwe's Archaeology unit, which is funded by the Norwegian Programme for Development, Research and Education.

Archaeological activity since 2000 has increased our previously sketchy knowledge regarding the hunter-gatherer communities and original authors of the San art in the area. Research has revealed the presence of hunter-gatherer groups in this border region for the last 7 000 years. The earliest migration of Bantu-language speaking farmer groups into the area is dated to around 2 000 years ago (Phillipson 1993, Pikeray 1993). Archaeological surveys carried out in the Manica district of Mozambique's Manica province and on the Zimunya communal lands of Zimbabwe's Manyikaland province, have revealed over a hundred sites containing San rock paintings. Sites with finger painted images in the Bantu tradition are also found, but these are vastly outnumbered by hunter/gatherer art. At present we have no certain knowledge about the meeting and subsequent coexistence of hunter/gatherer and farmer groups in the area. Portuguese colonial documents make no reference to hunter/gatherers south of the Zambezi. The arrival of the present Shona-speaking population in the Manica area can be dated to approximately AD 1700. According to oral tradition the newly arrived groups quickly established control of the area (Beach 1980: 167)

At present, communities on both sides of the colonially imposed national borders speak a common language, a dialect of Shona also known as Manica, and they have incorporated certain San rock art sites within their ritual practices. Unlike in many other parts of southern Africa, the people of Manica were not moved off their ancestral lands during Mozambique's colonial period. Apart from a short period of local movement during the civil war, the people have lived on the same land for generations; they have strong ties to the landscape in which their kings and ancestors are buried. While the post-independence government of Mozambique initially tried to rein in the traditional authorities and curb traditional religious practices, this did not succeed, and in more recent years traditional leaders have been officially recognised by the state as community leaders. In Manica, the paramount Chief Chirara is the eleventh chief of his dynasty. He resides near the royal burial caves of his ancestors in the Vumba Mountains, which lie on the border between Mozambique and Zimbabwe. The chiefdom of Zimunya was also previously under Chief Chirara but became a separate chiefdom under an elected chief on the Zimbabwean side of the border when the modern state boundaries were drawn in 1891. The demarcation of the national boundary was negotiated between the Bristish and the Portuguese, and local people had no say in the matter. Although it meant that any formal ties that the chiefdom had with Zimbabwe, or Southern Rhodesia as it was known at the time, were broken, the two chiefdoms continued to work very closely, and still often meet to rule in matters that concern people on either side of the border.

The ritual and religious life of the population is closely linked to the landscape and their ancestral beliefs exist alongside the Catholicism brought in by missionaries. Ancestor spirits are believed to dwell in the land and in the waters (streams, lakes or springs) and to be approachable at certain places in the landscape – such as the burial place of someone important, an ancestor tree, or a place linked to a particular story or experience. Trees are thought to reach into the world of the ancestors, and springs to deliver water from deep within the ancestral world. Crevices and cracks in rock shelters are seen as places where snakes and lizards enter the ancestral dwellings. The rock art found in many such sites is perceived to be a form of communication from the ancestors, and it is held that if proper rituals are not observed when approaching or entering these sites the ancestors may choose not to display the paintings.

Ancestral sites are often linked to annual rainmaking and healing rituals. Some of the most prominent San rock art sites are used for such rites, and function as communication points with the ancestors. While the main activities of feasting and praying may not take place at the actual archaeological sites, beer is brought to the site and offered to the ancestors in front of the painted panels.

The Manica spirit world is seen as being as dynamic as the real world, and a mirror image of our reality. When a person dies he or she becomes a *mudzumi* (pl. *midzimu*), an ancestor spirit. A whole lifetime of accumulated knowledge and experience it believed to be available to the living via ancestor sprits who are seen as a resource to be drawn upon and consulted when guidance, protection or divination is needed (Abrahams 1966; Lan 1985). Since worldly worries and problems no longer hinder the dead, they are thought to devote their whole attention to guiding and protecting their families. They are believed to be capable of seeing into the future and may offer advice on how to avoid impeding dangers and be called upon to cure illnesses. Having no material form, the ancestors are not bound by time or space, and can be at all places at all times in the form of *mweya*, (breath or air). However, the spirits are believed to have sensory experiences, eyesight, hearing and emotions (Lan 1985). Since the spirits exist in a mirror image world of our own, it is thought they too age and fade away as new spirits are 'born' – that is, when younger relations die into the spirit world. Elders die and younger people take over as spiritual leaders, which is the dynamic of any such elder-based knowledge system. Older spirits die and new ones take their place, as *midzimu* or ancestor spirits. Hence the two spheres of humans and spirits are constantly changing. Yet when the community gathers for rainmaking ceremonies, or their spirit mediums carry out divination rituals in front of the paintings, their own oral tradition is key. And placing the rock-paintings in the realm of the spirits gives the images an authenticity that is accepted by all present.

Archaeology and anthropology go hand in hand in many places, not only in Africa. However, working in Mozambique made us realise that such sites are not 'dead' places void of current meaning but 'live' sites imbued with meaning for local people and with layers of stories accumulated through time.

Archaeological research in Manica and Zimunya is therefore carried out in accordance with the traditional systems of knowledge and governance; researched areas are entered only with the chief's permission and in the company of an appointed guide who can perform the appropriate ancestor rituals. This close contact with the local communities means that their intimate knowledge of the area, its ancestral sites and rock art sites, is shared. The researchers and villagers are slowly building a relationship of trust and collaboration, and it is hoped that this will feed into joint planning for the future management and conservation of the rock art sites and the traditions associated with them.

Thus, the aim of the research projects is not to simply identify the sites and leave the local communities to look after them. Instead, the rock art sites are conceptualised as falling within the larger scope of *cultural heritage*. This involves expanding the framework of our research beyond the usual archaeological concerns with images, sites and particular readings of arts and contexts, to include a much wider set of relevant meanings and values. These multiple meanings and values are generated by the actions and perceptions of different *stakeholders*, whose multiple agendas may at times be conflicting, and among whom we find ourselves as archaeologists.

Written historical sources: Mozambican *ajami*

When it comes to sources for historical studies, the northern provinces of Mozambique are home to an *ajami* writing tradition. For centuries, the region was an integrated part of the Swahili cultural continuum, frequented by dhows from the trading centres to the north, the Comoros Islands, as well as from the coastal cities of Yemen and Oman (Alpers 2001; Bonate 2010b; Hafkin 1973; Newitt 1997).

From the point of view of Islamic history, the interconnections between the coastal mainland of Mozambique and other centres in the Indian Ocean have received scant research attention when compared to better-known sites in Tanzania and Kenya (including Lamu, Mombasa, Zanzibar and Kilwa). Since 2000, however, research has emerged that places the Muslim communities of northern Mozambique within the cultural, historical and religious continuum of the Swahili coast and its interconnections in the Indian Ocean. At the time of writing, Bonate's (2007) study of the Sufi brotherhoods in the region was the most complete analysis of religious and family networks. At the same time, preliminary studies conducted on *ajami* material from the region point towards a scriptural Islamic culture that communicated in Arabic, Swahili and local languages.[10] However, as Bonate has pointed out, historical, ethnographic and linguistic research is still severely lacking when it comes to the histories of these communities. Earlier research has hesitated to characterise coastal, Muslim communities in northern Mozambique as 'Swahili', with the definition of 'Swahili' constructed in terms of language and networks. Yet the question remains as to what influences were present in the coastal regions of northern Mozambique.

A substantial collection of letters in Mozambique's National Archives bear witness to the use of *ajami* for communication among KiMwani, Ekoti, Esangaji, Yao and Makua speakers. In addition, some people of the region wrote in Swahili using Arabic script. Bonate and Mutiua (2011) carried out a preliminary study of this collection, and included the correspondence that was sent to the Portuguese government from local rulers and other stakeholders, all written in *ajami* script. A total of 782 documents were studied, and of these, 568 originated in the district of Cabo Delgado and the remainder from Nampula province. The majority of the documents date from the mid-to-late nineteenth century, that is, the period that saw increased Islamic missionary activity and the expansion of Sufism in East Africa.

Textual material may also be privately held throughout northern Mozambique, but this remains entirely unexplored. As far as can be ascertained, private collections are likely to contain information on genealogy and family histories, and may thus shed light on transformations with local and regional power alliances, and on the emergence of new lineages and chiefdoms through the processes of migration and conquest. Furthermore, such documents may also shed light on important aspects of the local cultural practices and traditions. Islamic history is a very neglected field in Mozambique and there is simply no overview of documents that may be in private hands. However, as has been shown by studies in Tanzania, such material can provide valuable insight into religious life, literary and linguistic developments, healing, divination, dream reading, amulet writing etc. Like the San rock art sites discussed, these traditions are still very much alive, and must be understood in the context of both localised forms of Islam as well as of the specific local meanings attached to the Arabic alphabet and language, including formulas and symbols.

The varied contexts in which these texts must be understood, pose many challenges and underscore the value of multi-disciplinarity. However, they also pose problems on the basic level of interpretation, as knowledge of the *ajami* form is fast disappearing. Even in Kenya and Tanzania, where the most widespread *ajami* form is Swahili (a much more widely understood and researched language), there is not enough competence in either country to survey, catalogue and preserve (let alone conduct historical interpretations) of the known material. In Mozambique, where *ajami* sources exist in lesser-researched languages, competent staff are extremely scarce – a fact that challenges research and conservation efforts. As noted by Bonate (2007; 2008), traditionally trained scholars are essential to the interpretation of these documents – both in the literal sense, and in terms of securing what Lambek (1990) calls the full, local hermeneutics of the texts. Efforts are being made to train at least one master's student in the reading and interpretation of northern Mozambican *ajami*, and hopefully more scholars will be trained in the near future to interpret and disseminate information about this aspect of Mozambique's written heritage.

Cultural heritage and the post-colonial nation state

Cultural heritage is a complex and context-dependent concept. It may mean very different things on very different scales in different contexts.

The rock paintings of Manica undoubtedly form an important national cultural resource that may be used to symbolise a proud pan-Mozambican, pre-colonial, past. However, they also form part of the specific cultural heritage of the people of Manica, and it is their cultural right to use them in building their own more specific cultural identity. Conversely, the *ajami* writings of the north may be construed as being specifically part of a Muslim tradition (and as such, religious in nature and conceivably of little interest for nation building). Indeed, in some situations, the presence of a transnationally oriented population, with extensive historical links to cultural and religious centres beyond the nation, may even be construed as harmful and actively suppressed. In the case of Manica, both the Portuguese colonialists and the early independent government under Samora Machel tried unsuccessfully to curb the traditional cultural and religious system of the region; the Portuguese by a policy of invisibility and Samora Machel with radical socialism. When it comes to the *ajami* writings, the most enduring management policy to date has been indifference from archives, museums and research institutions; a tradition only recently broken by the renewed interest in written sources relating to Africa's pre-colonial past.

However, when looking at Mozambican cultural heritage and its role in nation building, it is important that the past should build a bridge towards the future. Development is closely connected with the past, and may be legitimised with reference to the pre-colonial history. On another level, it is important for Mozambique to try to reconstruct the pre-colonial past without denying that the last 500 years were of any consequence. The present independent state of Mozambique is, of course, a completely different entity conceptually, physically and culturally to anything that existed prior to 1498. Hence the importance of cultural heritage will be the extent to which it comes to represent the remains of what existed 'on the way to becoming what Mozambique is today'. Cultural heritage is what we inherit from those who may have been like us in some respects but who were also very different from us in other respects.

The 1992 ICOMOS New Zealand Charter for the Conservation of Places of Cultural Heritage Value states that 'undisturbed constancy of spiritual association may be more important than the physical aspects'.[11] This underlines the importance of indigenous spiritual association with certain sites and areas. Archaeology must avoid being seen as an alien and potentially dangerous university discipline, removed from the real context that it encounters in the field. As Trigger (1994: 31) states:

If archaeology is to play a useful role in a democratic society, it must seek to provide a more accurate understanding of the past that will enable those who wish to do so to derive enjoyment from archaeological findings and to draw their own conclusions about human history and human nature.

People may have their own understanding of their own past which, with proper care and knowledge, should not compete with archaeology and the management of cultural resources and heritage. Rather these understandings should inspire communities to value and respect all aspects of their cultural heritage.

It is hoped that in future, the increased dissemination of knowledge about the physical heritage of Mozambique – and other African countries – will lead to the realisation that this heritage is a common one, and not exclusive to any one group or community. It is hoped that this will promote understanding and thus a deeper awareness of current social structures and traditions within and between groups locally, translocally and internationally.

Notes

1   Place here means 'site, area, land, landscape, building or other work, group of buildings or other works, and may include components, contents, spaces and views' as defined in Article 1.1 of Australia's 1999 Burra Charter (more formally known as The Australia ICOMOS Charter for Places of Cultural Significance). Available online.

2   'Intangible heritage' refers to the cultural fabric of a place, its setting, use, associations, meanings, records, related places and related objects.

3   See www.africa2009.net

4   The FHA was initiated after the United Nations declared the 1960s the 'Decade of Development. The International Academic Union, consisting of national academies of science worldwide was charged by UNESCO to set up Africa-related activities, and the FHA was one such initiative.

5   Personal communication, RS O'Fahey, 16 December 2010.

6   The word *ajami* derives from the Arabic word for foreign or stranger.

7   For an overview of conservation efforts in Timbuktu before 2012, see contributions by Abdel Kader Haidara, Ismaël Diedié Haidara and Haoua Taore, Mukhtar bin Yahya al-Wangari and Muhammd Ould Youbba in *The Meanings of Timbuktu*, edited by Jeppie and Diagne (2008). In 2012, at least one of the major conservation institutions, the Ahmed Baba Institute, was ransacked and looted by rebel forces. It is unclear whether the manuscripts are safe or not. The question remains open as to what will happen to these conservation efforts in the current troubled situation in northern Mali.

8   Among the most exhaustive reference works are *Arabic Literature of Africa*,
    Vols 1 (1993), 2 (1995), 3 (2002) and 5 (forthcoming) by John O Hunwick and
    RS O'Fahey, published by Brill.
9   Department of Arabic and Ajami Manuscripts, Human Sciences Research
    Institute, Abdou Moumouni University of Niamey.
10 See Bonate (2008; 2010a); and Bonate and Mutiua (2011) – the documents in
    Arabic script form part of an extensive collection (most of it in Portuguese) that
    exists in the Mozambqiue National Archives and which concerns this region.
11 See the revised 2010 edition at http://www.icomos.org.nz/docs/NZ_Charter.pdf.

References

Abrahams DP (1966) 'The roles of "Chaminuka" and the mhondoro-cults in
    Shona political history', in E Stokes and R Brown (eds) *The Zambezian Past*.
    Manchester: Manchester University Press.

Allen JWT (1971) *Tendi: Six Examples of a Swahili Classical Verse Form with
    Translations and Notes*. Nairobi and London: Heinemann.

Alpers EA (2001) 'A complex relationship. Mozambique and the Comoro Islands in
    the 19th and 20th century', *Cahiers d'études africaines* 161: 73–95.

Beach DN (1980) *The Shona and Zimbabwe, 900–1850*. London: Heinemann.

Bonate L (2007) Traditions and Transitions. Islam and Chiefship in Northern
    Mozambique c. 1850–1974. PhD thesis, University of Cape Town.

Bonate LJK (2008) 'The use of Arabic script in Northern Mozambique', *Tyskrift vir
    Letterkunde* 45 (1): 120–129.

Bonate, LJK (2010a) 'Documents in Arabic Script at the Mozambique Historical
    Archives', *Islamic Africa*, 1 (2): 253–257.

Bonate LJK (2010b) 'Islam in Northern Mozambique. A Historical Overview',
    History Compass 8 (7): 573–593.

Bonate LJK and C Mutiua (2011) 'Duas Cartas de Farallahi', *Estudos Mocambicanos*
    22 (1): 91–106.

Davids A (1991) 'Abubakr Effendi: His creation of the Afrikaans "e" in Arabic
    script', *South African Journal of Linguistics* 9 (1): 1–18.

Hafkin NJ (1973) Trade, Society and Politics in Northern Mozambique. PhD thesis,
    Boston University.

Jappie S (2011) From Madrasah to Museum. A Biography of the Islamic
    Manuscripts of Cape Town. Master's thesis, University of Cape Town.

Jeppie S and SB Diagne (eds) (2008) *The Meanings of Timbuktu*. Cape Town: HSRC
    Press.

Jakobson-Widding A (1989) 'Notions of heat and fever among the Manyika of Zimbabwe', in A Jakobson-Widding and D Westerlund (eds) *Culture, Experience and Pluralism. Essays on African Ideas of Illness and Healing*. Uppsala: Department of Cultural Anthropology, University of Uppsala.

Kawo HM (2008) The Contribution of Muhammad Jaju (Abi al-Mahasin) (1849–1956) to Arabic Literature in Arsi. Master's thesis. Addis Ababa University.

Knappert J (1964) *Four Swahili Epics*. Leiden: Luctor et Emergo.

Lambek M (1990) 'Certain knowledge, contestable authority: Power and practice on the Islamic periphery' *American Ethnologist* 17 (1): 23–40.

Lan D (1985) *Guns and Rain: Guerrillas and Spirit Mediums in Zimbabwe*. London: James Currey.

Munthe L (1982) *La tradition Arabico-Malgache vue a travers le manuscript A-6 de Oslo et d'autres manuscript disponibles*. TPFLM: Antananarivo.

National Directorate for Cultural Heritage, Mozambique (2003) *Plano Estratégico 2003–2007: Celebrando a diversidade cultural*. Maputo.

Newitt M (1997) *A History of Mozambique*. London: Hurst.

Phillipson DW (1993) *African Archaeology*. Cambridge: Cambridge University Press.

Pikeray I (1993) 'The archaeological identity of the Mutapa State: Towards an historical archaeology of northern Zimbabwe', *Studies in African Archaeology* (Volume 6). Uppsala: Societas Archaeologica Uppsaliensis.

Sætersdal T (2009) 'Manica rock-art in contemporary society', in Terje Oestigard (ed.) *Water, Culture and Identity*. Bergen: BRIC.

Trigger B (1994) 'Archaeology and social responsibility', *Boletin Museo Arqueologico de Quibor* 3: 25–35.

Van Selms A (1951) *Arabies-Afrikaanse Studies I: 'n Tweetalige (Arabies en Afrikaanse) Kategismus*. Amsterdam: Nooord-Hollandse Uitgevers.

Vansina J (1994) *Living With Africa*. Madison: University of Wisconsin Press.

Versteegh K (2001) 'Arabic in Madagascar', *Bulletin of the School of Oriental and African Studies* 64 (2): 177–187.

Walderhaug Sætersdal EM (2000a) 'Ethics, politics and practices in rock-art conservation', *Public Archaeology* 1 (2): 163–180.

Walderhaug Sætersdal EW (2000b) 'Some reflections on the complications of form, context and function in rock art studies', in D Olaussen and H Vandkilde (eds) *Form, Function and Context. Material Culture Studies in Scandinavian Archaeology* (Acta Archaeologica Lundensia Series in 8° No. 31). Stockholm: Almquiest & Wiksell.

Chapter 12

Academic co-operation in a bipolar world: where does SANORD fit in?

Tor Halvorsen

WHEN SANORD WAS FOUNDED, the hope was that it would contribute to the growth of an open and democratic dialogue between academics across cultures. SANORD was created by universities, is governed by universities, and aims to promote research between universities that would otherwise not happen or not be possible. SANORD also aims to enhance co-operative research-based teaching relationships, ideally drawing on the findings of SANORD-generated research.

In the following pages I discuss five reasons why such co-operation is difficult to achieve, but also advance five counter-arguments as to why those involved with the SANORD project should try to make the organisation fulfil the goals for which it was formed.

However, I begin by identifying some of the general societal trends that have penetrated the thinking of both the Nordic and the southern African regions. These trends create similar challenges for their universities, despite the different contexts within which they are situated.

Democracy and capitalism

In the early 1990s, Africa experienced a wave of democratisation (Hydén 1998), which paralleled the fall of the Berlin Wall, and what is seen as the political and economic liberalisation of Eastern Europe (and later Russia).

To many, not only in the West, this spread of democracy in both the North (Europe) and in Africa south of Sahara, including South Africa after 1994, symbolised the final victory of *liberal capitalist institutions*. What had emerged seemed to be a single global system for economic development. Some assumed that globalised capitalism, in line with the new democratic developments, would in time lead to a democratic order worldwide. Behind this thinking lay the theory of *rational choice*. This theory builds on presuppositions about human behaviour to argue that the same human choices that promote the market economy also promote democracy. The theory has little respect for the old school of social thinking whose prominent figures (ranging from Max Weber to Joseph Schumpeter) had as their main research question exactly this: what is the link between capitalism and democracy when these institutions derive from different motives and require actions that are not easily reconciled? Building on these classics, Rueschemeyer et al. (1996) suggest that capitalism's options in times of crisis are not clear; it can tend equally towards dictatorship or democracy.

It is, however, rational choice theories that have hegemony at present. It seems to be accepted that *rational choice* motivates our actions in politics and in economics. We make political choices, as if we were consumers. And as consumers, we tend to see capitalism and democracy as one and the same, or as part of the same development. Put colloquially, the same factors that motivate our shopping motivate our voting. This view is proposed by Amadae in his book, *Rationalizing Capitalist Democracy: The Cold War Origins of Rational Choice Liberalism* (2003), in which he discusses the global victory of this way of thinking.

But with the advent of the financial crises since 2008, and the domination of politics by the financial institutions, a new debate about the relations between economics and democracy has emerged, as predicted by Rueschemeyer et al. (1996). Developments in both Europe and southern Africa, where democratic institutions seem to be under attack, have led to a renewed questioning both of the hypothesis that capitalist development is the result of rationally motivated human choice, and the idea that capitalism necessarily strengthens democracy. As I write (in 2012), Greece is not the only case in Europe where 'economic technocrats' play the role of the proverbial 'House of Lords' whose task it is to discipline popular democracies. The World Bank, as all readers will recognise, plays this role in a number of African countries. Analysing the conflicts within democratic capitalism, Wolfgang Streeck argues that Europe's financial dramas are the result of democratic states being turned into debt-collecting agencies on behalf of a global oligarchy of investors:

> More than ever, economic power seems today to have become political power, while citizens appear to be almost entirely stripped of their democratic defenses and their capacity to impress upon the political

economy interests and demands that are incommensurable with those of capital owners. (Streeck 2011: 29)

The situation in southern Africa and, in particular, in South Africa is similar. As Marais (2011: 130) argues,

Neo-liberalism continues to provide the organizing framework and ethical compass points for South Africa's transition. This is especially stark in relation to the state's obligation towards citizens.

Marais also argues that the state disciplines its people to become consumers of public services, rather than to act as 'debating citizens' who attempt to solve collective problems. And neo-liberalism, which justifies this by deploying its theories of 'rational choice', has not been consigned to the past but continues to prevail.

A neoliberal development path was adopted, and has been maintained, because the balance of forces within the ANC alliance, and between it and corporate capital, favours such a course [of action]. (Marais 2011: 139)

So, the domination of the concept of rational choice seems to serve an ideology that permits economic interests to take precedence over democracy. This is particularly evident in southern Africa (Hydén 1998) where the competitive dimension of democracy has developed into a process of 'shopping' for votes – with party bosses rewarding voters and dispensing with public processes, such as debate and deliberation, through which citizens arrive at decisions and act upon these. These two understandings of democracy – *the voter as consumer of political promises* and *the constitution of a political community through discourse* – build upon two different understandings of human action. This is contrary to Amadae's (2003) argument that the social sciences and the humanities can build on only one view of human action, namely the one that leads to rational-choice liberalism. But it is Amadae's view that penetrates much of modern economic thinking and legitimises neo-liberalism.

Whereas *rational-choice* theories emphasise the voter as a consumer, an alternative understanding of democracy, which I build on below in my discussion of neo-liberalism, assumes that people do not have stable opinions and preferences. Instead, they are

in flux and constantly being formed, reproduced, validated, tested, abandoned, adapted, revised, upgraded, and reflectively enriched in the light of new information and experience [thus] the process of opinion and preference acquisition is not exclusively an internal and monological one, but always takes place in a communication and interactive dialogue with others. (Offe 2011:4)

So, the fact that democracy has been weakened by the veto posed by the global reach of economics, illustrates that economic governance and democracy can part ways. And given that democratic forces are still more embedded in the nation state, or are, at least, less global than the economy, the power of neo-liberal economics as a conditionality for national democracies is growing. But the global victory of rational-choice liberalism, which has been celebrated as successful globalisation, prevents many of us from problematising the international and global economy as an anti-democratic movement. Expertise (as represented by the neo-liberal global economy) vetoes national democracies. According to the many think-tank promoters of neo-liberalism, as analysed by Mirowski and Plehwe (2009), democracy is instead 'recreated' as a decision-making process worthy of global capitalism. As Streeck (2011) argues, democracy legitimises a state bureaucracy that transforms global pressure into national policies. This bureaucracy transforms public institutions, including universities, in line with 'new economic demands'. The state then secures quasi-markets – the services sector in South Africa being a good example – as the arena in which citizens can exercise rational choice.

Those who have expressed these ideas most forcefully point to its success in the United States and, since the fall of the Berlin Wall, have urged its global penetration as the only policy for 'handling public space':

Any attempt to understand the phenomenal success of rational choice theory within the social sciences must acknowledge the interconnections between rational choice as a decision tool for government policy initiatives and as an explanatory device for predicting the outcomes of human action. (Amadae 2003: 28)

Thus the ability of national democracies to generate rational decisions is increased by the insights offered by what Amadae (among others) calls 'new social science' on decision making. These are based on the self-same epistemologies as decision making within global capitalism. As a result, a common 'explanatory device' is has been created and, happily for capital, the problem of how to democratise the global public space vanishes.

As the global economy has become detached from national democracies, it has also become concerned to detach knowledge institutions from nation-state democracies by, for example, transforming them into service-delivery-type institutions within the global market. This is most clearly expressed in the negotiations within the General Agreements on Trade in Services (GATS). GATS is an agreement within the World Trade Organisation (WTO) that promotes free trade within service industries of all kinds. In line with new public-management ideals, public institutions are being transformed into private service providers, and the services sector has become the fastest growing part of the global economy (Tilak 2011). Typically, there is little, if any, concern about how knowledge institutions could enhance the creation of a global public space, or a global democratic discourse.

Neo-liberal ideas, based on theories on rational choice, which conflate democracy and capitalism, on the one hand, and theories of democracy as a way of giving meaning and ranking to our preferences on the other, also leads us to different ideas about knowledge and the role of knowledge-creating institutions. In this controversy SANORD, as argued below, sees itself as a tool for a broadening of democratic values, even when these may contradict the expertise of the global economy.

Knowledge for democracy and knowledge in times of neo-liberalism

The notion of knowledge as a science is a hundred or so years old. It became a tool of economic growth after the Second World War. Since then not only technology and market analysis but also decision making and education have become science based. The role played by knowledge in the process of capitalist accumulation is obvious, and the degree to which knowledge can be used as a means of improving competition, promoting innovation, changing the direction of economic priorities, as well as reproducing (or transforming) social relations within the economy, are topics that deserve analysis.

But knowledge as science, that is, research-based knowledge, has another role: that of critical reflection. In historical perspective, this is not just an auxiliary role; it is the primary purpose of knowledge. Universities have come to accept knowledge as a basis for dialogue and argument in order to support the goal of democratic development. Consequently, universities have become involved in all forms of opinion making, the formation of judgements, the shaping of preferences and, through discourse and social interaction, the presentation of opinions and arguments which are perceived as a voice of 'cognitive rationality'. So universities have become involved in shaping national democracies, not only by teaching citizens to vote in a narrow technical sense but, more importantly, by creating the basis for public discourse, and shaping opinions that may make voting meaningful beyond individual 'rational choice', particularly when democracy is under threat.

As drivers of global knowledge – knowledge knows no borders – universities have been eager to exchange ideas and insights, results from research, and to encourage colleagues to move (relatively) freely across borders. As an international 'movement', they have become closely linked to the project of democratic development (Kalleberg 2011, but see also Vale 2010 on the idea of the *volksuniversiteit*). As a distinctive form of 'international organisation', spread across most of the world, and with tremendously increasing cross-border networking, universities have demonstrated how internationalisation can strengthen nation-state democracies and embed democratic processes internationally at the same time.

However, with the growing involvement of the academic community in processes of accumulation that are governed by economic interests beyond the influence of the nation state, there is less space for the university's traditional calling – the development of critical discourses and informing public debate. Instead, as noted earlier, universities have been transformed into more or less privatised service-delivery mechanisms (as advocated by the WTO and GATS). For example, knowledge is made into commodities by patent systems, the Trade Related Intellectual Property Right agreements under the WTO, and by being locked up in agreements with transnational companies. Put bluntly, if universities start to behave as rational-choice actors, and if governments treat them as such within an internationally competitive context – as the present regime of ratings, rankings and rewards requires – the decisions made by universities will increasingly align with pre-set choices determined by the forces outside universities that define their success. The forces in question are the strong economic actors and the political elites – what Streeck (2011) has called the global oligarchs. The role of the university, as an arena that problematises strategic choices, and questions goals and decisions, is wholly insecure; and universities that aim to make broad public debate a vital part of public choice and participation are hardly valued.

The role of SANORD

In what follows SANORD is discussed in the light of the dichotomies between capitalism and democracy, national and international. The emphasis falls on the role SANORD could play as an international organisation that promotes a role for universities in inter-democratic discourses. The question is how cross-border, post-national and globally oriented networks of academics can strengthen the ability of citizens of nation states to formulate well-founded opinions about important issues of common concern, such as poverty, multiculturalism, economic oppression, public underfunding, private inequality, environmental degradation, unemployment and the like.

The formation of SANORD was inspired by hopes for a new, open, and socially just South Africa. After the end of apartheid, free and open academic co-operation across numerous borders were mobilised, and close political affiliations were quickly transformed into academic networks. Research co-operation also grew out of the interest expressed by leading academics in South Africa in gaining a deeper understanding of the Nordic development model. Typically enough, when I first met my co-editor for this book in 1995, it was at a conference in Cape Town to which he had invited me to talk about the Nordic experience. More specifically, the focus of the conference was on how to distribute power across society through democratic institutions, and particularly how to strengthen their discursive and deliberative roles (Halvorsen 1995).

In my introduction to this chapter I undertook to offer five reasons why SANORD will find it difficult to defend its place within the field of academic internationalisation, and also to provide five counter-arguments as to why we should try to make the organisation a sustainable alternative to the dominant model already described. The exercise of presenting 'for and against' arguments draws on the broader debate about capitalism and democracy explored above. Although this debate is one of the oldest in social science (Rueschemeyer et al. 1996), it is given new meaning by the emergence of academic capitalism, which has followed from the enormous success of neo-liberal economics – a phenomenon that seems to be, as argued above, on the verge of overruling democracy, both in Europe and southern Africa.

As noted, higher education and research has always had an international character, and in the past this was driven by the understanding that knowledge knows no borders. However, during the 1990s, the decade during which globalisation may be said to have peaked, internationalisation within the academic community suddenly gained a new and different meaning – we might call this 'new internationalisation'. The idea that universities should be linked internationally was sucked into the vacuum created by the end of the Cold War and by the victory of neo-liberalism and rational choice epistemology. For universities, this ushered in an age of increasing student and knowledge mobility, as a global search for so-called 'relevant knowledge', transformed thinking about where to go and who to co-operate with internationally. Steered by emerging global economic regimes, competition grew fierce within emerging academic capitalism for the best brains, the most reliable fee-paying students, more patents, intellectual-property rights, and the highest international rankings. Academic co-operation became an instrument through which to gain traction in competitions for 'academic honour' and resources, where this 'honour' translates as a tool for further resource acquisition. Thus, for example, Nobel Prizes are no longer valued for their contribution to new knowledge, but are counted as guarantors of future income.

Shortly after apartheid ended, South Africa signalled that it saw education and research as a kind of public co-operation. For example, in 2002 Kader Asmal, who was then minister of education, moved to prevent private and for-profit higher education enterprises from establishing themselves in the SA 'market'. This is reflected in an important discussion document by Asmal entitled, 'The Idea of a South African University: Higher Education in a Transforming Society'.[1] Asmal starts out by restating the wholeness of the sector and asking: 'How do we understand the very idea of a South African University? What is its role in transforming society, and, how does SA keep the market at a distance?' He then goes on to state: 'Higher education is a public good, engaged in a social compact, which includes all our people'.

Asmal explores the idea of an African university – going back to the early 1970s and beyond South Africa with reference to Nigerian economist TM Yesufu who advocates a strong role for universities in national development and growth. Yesufu (1973) writes that universities must be committed to social transformation, economic modernisation, and the upgrading of the human resources of a nation. By anchoring its idea of a university within debates about African universities (that is, outside its own history as a European institution transplanted to Africa, but within African regionalism), Asmal laid the basis for the 'Africanisation of higher education'. He argued that the central issue for South African universities is to provide for the production of knowledge that recognises the African condition as historical and defines its key tasks as one of coming to grips with it critically. This means decolonising and Africanising higher education and thus providing a new paradigm and a new approach in knowledge seeking. Asmal went on to state that 'if it is democratic, inclusive and sensitive to historical realities, it will give rise to a notion of Africanisation that will necessarily repudiate racism and, along with it, the "racialised" notion of "African" inherited from the colonial period'.

Norway, for its part, at first shocked many by trying to use WTO regulations to open up a market in South Africa, but withdrew from this role when it was publicly criticised by Asmal and several Norwegian critics (Mathisen 2005). This context is provided to illustrate that SANORD was created in an atmosphere of strong publicly oriented values, despite the powerful influence of neo-liberal forces in both the Nordic and southern African countries – paradoxically, in this case, stronger in South Africa than in Norway (despite Asmal's position). Although the picture is uneven in other regions: in India, for example, Norway collaborated with the liberal Anglo-American countries to push for global academic capitalism (Tilak 2011), 'public values' are the basis on which higher education institutions in both Norway and South Africa supports the goals of SANORD.

As we have seen, an understanding of higher education as part of the public realm is embedded in the organisations that created the basis of 'old internationalisation' and are now influential in shaping the present debates about the global knowledge regime. But 'new internationalisation' also has 'defenders' and 'rational-choice proponents' in strategic places. All over the world, governments are setting up and funding 'internationalisation offices' to foster growth in the neo-liberal higher education market. In Europe, governments joined forces to establish coordinating agencies, such as the Academic Cooperation Association and the European Association for International Education to promote European interests in competition with (the seemingly more successful efforts of) the United States.

However, for the purposes of this chapter, I will focus on the oldest such organisation, the International Association of Universities (IAU), which was shaped by 'old internationalisation'. The reason for this focus is the similarity in the values that lie behind the creation of both the IAU and SANORD. As a result, both face the challenge of how to promote democracy and foster critical knowledge in these times in which neo-liberalism dominates the global regime.

From the start, the IAU developed a global and co-operative approach to its work. Founded in 1948, and so a child of the post-Second World War period, one of the IAU's core values was the defence of academic freedom. Its purpose, was thus to secure the promotion of academic values worldwide. In a book published on its sixtieth anniversary, Dorsman and Blankesteijn (2008: 48) noted that:

> It is interesting to see how nearly all specific items of the [founding] Utrecht conference remained on the agenda during the following decades and in that sense the 1948 conference is still of topical interest. In 2008 after 60 years, another IAU conference took place in Utrecht discussing virtually the same themes: the debate has come full circle.

The purpose of SANORD is not to promote the EU as the most 'competitive knowledge economy in the world', nor does SANORD aim to be a European co-operation project like Erasmus Mundus, which is striving to become a successful brain gain initiative; nor does SANORD seek to co-ordinate the behaviour of national actors in WTO negotiations about GATS' educational services. Rather, SANORD seeks to express a dimension of the co-operation that exists between two culturally distinct regions that have developed fairly free and open academic contacts, and believe that strengthening this contact may also contribute to widening the space for global public knowledge.

Since SANORD was established in the same spirit as the IAU, and because it shares the same goals of promoting academic co-operation for a better world, it seems proper that topics from the IAU's founding conference in 1948 – five in number – should guide this discussion (Dorsman and Blankensteijn 2008). The topics are first listed and then discussed in more detail below.

- The changing role of the university;
- Academic standards;
- Financing and providing basic services for higher education (with a sub-theme on the relation between higher education and the state);
- University education and international understanding (or the university as a force in world co-operation);
- Means of continuing international co-operation among universities.

The changing role of the university

It was clear to the participants at the IAU founding meeting in 1948 that the role of the university had to change, not only from being elitist in a selective way, but also in relation to being part of a '*Bildungsbürgertum*' – an educational bourgeoisie. This was necessary because, at the time, politicians in many countries were trying to capture higher education for the sake of their own agendas. SANORD faces the same kind of challenge, but this time from an alliance between politicians and the new global economic powers.

Arguments against the form of internationalisation that SANORD stands for from representatives of the alliance between politics and economics, is that SANORD presupposes both a type of co-operation and a form of university that no longer exist. It might also be argued that SANORD does not promote the new role of universities, the 'new globality' (Albrow 1995) that emerged after the fall of the Berlin Wall. The 'free universities', namely those that have been 'deregulated from state control and ownership', and 're-regulated by neo-liberal policies of reward and punishment' through ratings, rankings and rewards, are celebrated as part of a post-national environment.

This represents a clear break with the ideas that created the IAU; that is, ideas characterised by a worldview that saw academic co-operation as integral to mutual understanding, dialogue and academic competition in the sense of 'who has the best argument'. When the formative narrative is that the university is a 'strategic actor' that must forge its own future, the centrality of the notion of dialogue in university and intellectual life, suffers. And if there is a growing autonomy, this is in relation to an environment that rewards knowledge outputs and gives status to the organisation delivering this knowledge. This shift in focus away from the academics who are at the centre of the research to the centrality of the organisation itself has taken place over the past twenty years. The shift has seen increasing calls for organisational 'accountability' at all levels and for evaluations based preferably on numerical measurements of outputs. The rankings, rating and rewards that emerge from this, or are made possible by these measurements, are in turn used to promote the organisation, in competition with others in the education market. At some, but not all, universities internationalisation offices have been drawn into this kind of competitively motivated promotion of, say, logos and symbols of success to generally enhance the reputation of the organisation. Most surprisingly, perhaps, has been the quick adoption of universities of the global ranking system that now seems to be a permanent feature of the higher-education landscape. It is interesting to note that the growth of institutional bureaucracies has never been stronger and this growth often occurs demonstrably at the cost of academics. As debates in Denmark show, not only does new public management create additional bureaucracy, but wage differences and the role of administrative oversight linked to highly rewarded positions undermine academic initiative and space for creativity (Harste 2011)

Social science theory sees these changes as shifts in form; that is, universities that used to be what the academic literature called loosely coupled organisations, anarchies or even 'systems of non-decision' or arbitrary decision (see below) are now all classifiable under the broader theory of 'rational decision making'. The paradox is that the management and organisational theory that created these categories (which seem a bit condescending) have legitimised the new regime, which boasts of its ability to make ordered and clear decisions thanks to rational choice theories of organisational behaviour. Given these new leadership strategies, universities are not only changing their organisational form, but also their content, thereby becoming an entirely different kind of organisation. As notions of universities' accountability towards society have changed, institutional goals and identities have changed too, from being centred on the nation state, to focusing on the post-national context. This is where the new governance impulses come from and it has led to a move away from the idea of a 'government of colleagues' to the notion of 'management-based' governance. Essentially, universities are now institutionalised differently: academics become employees (effectively white collar workers), the organisation is run by managers, the 'products' are valued in terms of their contribution to users (and not to society as such), and the general institutionalisation of the organisation occurs within the sphere of economics as opposed to the socio-cultural setting occupied by the 'old universities'. SANORD's constitution, however, takes for granted the idea that the academic community must – and indeed will – decide on what is good knowledge, identify the most creative researchers with whom to communicate and work, and determine how to value the academic process itself. It is assumed that the academic members of the organisation will value input into scholarly debates sought by SANORD even if these do not fit the different ranking and rating bureaus' institutionalised classifications of 'good knowledge' or 'networks' that currently drive the neo-liberal university governance system and the competition it promises.

Rooted in history, universities must look back at the different academic traditions upon which present-day knowledge rests. Through this retrospective lens, what organisational and management theory calls 'anarchy', etc. stand out as some of the most valuable aspects of academic life: disciplinary continuity, consistency in theoretical reasoning, and the understanding that we – as colleagues across politically and economically created borders – build on each other's work over time and honour ethical commitments to the independence of knowledge. Ivar Bleiklie, who heads up the Transforming Universities (TRUE) project[2] on the implications of this thinking, argues:

> In the 1960s and 1970s universities were sites of important academic studies that made path breaking contributions to Organisation theory by developing concepts such as 'loosely coupled' Organisations, 'organized anarchies' and 'garbage-can models' of decision making (Meyer and Rowan 1977; Cohen, March and Olsen 1972; Weick 1976). The studies demonstrated how universities could be portrayed as a specific kind of Organisation, with loosely coupled, decentralized structures, weak leadership capacities to govern decision-making processes from the top down (Brunsson and Sahlin-Andersson 2000; Musselin 2007). Since then university reformers around the world have tended to base their reform attempts on an assumption that is diametrically opposed to that of these Organisation theorists: universities are not a specific kind of Organisation, they are just poorly managed. (Bleiklie 2009: 3)

The stable 'old' organisations have inspired SANORD's co-operation efforts more than the new 'organisation theory' that has – perhaps unintentionally –

legitimised increasing managerialism with its focus on ridding universities of bad governance. Using historical sociology to research academic discourses, and to understand and explain the basis of independent academic work, would probably have been more useful than introducing new managerial techniques that are anchored in bureaucracy.

So, in case you did not know, anarchistic co-operation between academics, flowing from a number of loosely coupled creative projects, that are both disciplinary and cross-disciplinary and which provide meeting points between cultures that are otherwise worlds apart, may not always create rational decisions but is more useful now than ever before. In particular, this kind of academic work helps us understand both how theories evolve within a context, and how they are transformed by the meeting of new contexts. Globalised ideas about the universal victory of 'rational-choice liberalism', such as those suggested by Amadae (2011) for example, find no defenders among those who are empirically sensitive to the limits of such universalism. SANORD stands out as an important counter to the exaggerated emphasis on universities as *strategic actors* in a global rankings game – a game that is only possible in a framework that accepts universalised ideas about 'good knowledge'. Within this game, a process of standardisation seems to be ongoing, not only related to the standards set by evaluation systems but also to the standardising effect of competition. Happily, SANORD does not fit any of the contemporary evaluation criteria. It therefore escapes many of the demands on the organisation to adjust to 'global' standards. Rather the kinds of co-operation it fosters, the networks it builds and the knowledge potential it offers promotes variation rather than standardisation. The variety of academic cultures and the plurality of topics meeting each other within the SANORD agora is creating new knowledge. Thus SANORD does not seek to continuously adjust to the new governance system that funnels all academics into the same research areas so as not to lose out in the global competition for resources.

Academic standards

The issue of 'academic standards' has become highly politicised because they have become external to the academic community. This is most clearly expressed through the focus on the idea of 'excellence' which is a particular way of organising research in centres within universities where the decision as what is excellent – and what is not – is provided by a political/academic selection process. Universities make arenas for research centres that seek to distance themselves from teaching. Thus they are not judged 'excellent' through how they renew and invigorate a field of knowledge, but by living up to preset expectations about results, in line with a pre-determined promise made in an application to become 'a centre of excellence'. For universities to improve their position in the international rankings system, it is necessary for them to have centres of excellence *and* to make these into nodal points of international co-operation. Only excellent centres that work with other even more excellent (or highly ranked) centres are thought to truly enhance the status of a university. Fostering centres of excellence has become a strategic imperative for a new kind of university management which, ironically, often has no intrinsic idea about how to evaluate or foster the development of new knowledge (which, after all, is a creative process and therefore cannot always be known beforehand). The reality is that managers may have an understanding of how funding and governance may create an organisation that looks like it is 'excellent', but, in fact, this is often based on a template.

Another category used to indicate the new and external ways of governing knowledge is the issue of 'quality'. Indeed, a veritably global quality-assurance industry aims to protect the 'consumers' of higher education. Quality assurance is said to secure value for money and, together with rankings, is thought to make selection easier for potential customers. Like banks and credit institutions can buy their ratings (AAA+ at best) from private assessment bureaus that they more or less own, so too can also education businesses buy their quality evaluations from private quality assurance agencies. The purpose is of course to secure better competitive positions. This is particularly prevalent in the MBA world, but it is spreading to the rest of the higher education system. But, whether quality assurance is publicly or privately authorised, it often acts as a form of 'window-dressing' to make external powers reward quality that has been pre-packaged for them in ways that they recognise and appreciate.

SANORD is, of course, not a product of the hype around the idea of 'excellence', nor is it part of quality-assurance profiling aimed at 'enhancing' the quality of teaching programs or staff based on external criteria. So, SANORD is out of sync with the criteria for 'good internationalisation' developed in Europe. Instead, SANORD can be seen as reaction to the kinds of internationalisation and prioritisation of resources that both the drive towards 'excellence' and the criteria of 'good internationalisation' represent. SANORD's goal is to seek out broad co-operation wherever there is initiative and originality, whether or not these are selected by external forces – such as ministries, research councils or other funding bodies. SANORD's mandate is to foster co-operation created by mutual interests, whatever the topic. This rests on the idea of learning one from the other, and of researching together, rather than being located in outcome-oriented groups selected by standardised criteria of what makes a good researcher and what is acceptable knowledge. Pierre Bourdieu might have said that these kinds of centres deliver work according to a taste that is ritualised, that they miss out on the originality of creative processes (Hess 2011). SANORD's goal is to counter the elitism proposed by new approaches to university management. It aims to accomplish this via its North–South orientation, its combination of research with or without reputation, and in its internal academic criteria for what is good and what should be counted as new knowledge.

On occasions when the IAU has taken the initiative to ignite a global debate and to discuss anew the value basis for internationalisation, many of the arguments strongly support the SANORD model. Indeed, within this debate SANORD may be ahead of its time (IAU 2012) The 1948 IAU founding meeting invited participants with very diverse experiences, thus cutting through both the East–West and the religious–secular divides in a body that was then standing at the edge of the Cold War. Although few recommendations were made regarding the role of funding as a key to the future of universities, academic freedom was then, as today, considered the critical issue. Two conditions around funding emerged as important – first, to keep the influence of funders at a distance and, second, to make sure that funding improved the general economic situation of the university. For example, even if the state is the funder, it needs to legally legitimise and safeguard the academic freedom of the university to conduct research in any and every place.

As used here, freedom means 'legal, financial and material autonomy' (Dorsman and Blankesteijn 2008: 33). The notion of funding has since turned into a discussion about 'project requisition' and 'customer relations' legitimised by cross-disciplinary ideas about ' usable knowledge' or the value of 'robust knowledge' that needs to prove itself through use. Thus the new autonomy of the universities seems to be autonomy only to act in relation to the market for research funding, with the consequences this raises for forms of client dependency. If universities were interpreted to be suffering from poor management forty years ago, this must be even more the situation today as external funding sources decide not only what research should be conducted but also how and when. The university, as an institution building on *cognitive capacities*, as Parsons et al. (1973) argued it should be, has instead become an organisation searching to mediate so called 'robust knowledge' to its users, that is, knowledge that has proven to be useful. Even 'centres of excellence' that are supposed to build on the basic values of the university, are often partly owned and controlled by external organisations such as research councils, and legitimised by their relationships with particular users or clients.

The success of a university is thus measured mostly by its project-acquisition abilities. A strong indication of this is the tendency to create project-acquisition synergies that promote competition in line with 'useful knowledge' as determined by political or developmental priorities. Thus if, for example, European Union money is acquired through a research application, the national research council and the local university often automatically reward the applicants for having succeeded in the competition for funding. This enormous concentration of research money leads not only to the emergence of research oligarchs (with large numbers of unemployable doctoral and post-doctoral assistants), but also to the gradual homogenisation of academic culture and the concentration of academic power outside of the universities.

Of course, SANORD may be a source of collaboration related to project acquisition and, indeed, it should be. However, as a broad-based organisation promoting a variety of cross-border and cross-cultural links, it should primarily be an arena for generating independent knowledge and new ideas; it should be a place where academic ingenuity can blossom. As such it needs to be dependent on basic funding from member universities to make possible meetings between like-minded scholars and researchers; it should also be dependent on a funding system that is open to unexpected forms of creativity. The enormous growth of programs and projects pre-defined for specific research money does not easily fit the SANORD model of academic interaction which, as noted, leans on the ideas that shaped the IAU in 1948. And, again as noted, it is contrary to the contemporary trend of university funding policies.

University education and international understanding: 'the university as a force in world co-operation'

'Internationalisation strategies' are now considered essential in orientating universities towards improving their competitive position. Research money or bright students (and in some countries, rich students) are resources that a specific internationalisation strategy may help to attract. But co-operation with other universities is part of this strategy, too: especially a strategy for building reputation in order to gain access to the 'research front'. The purpose here is to climb the rankings ladder, obtain good evaluations and the like.

SANORD's goal, however, is more akin to the ideas of international *understanding* through which, in 1948, universities were considered integral to a world peace movement. And as institutions with their own histories, universities were often able to detach themselves to different degrees from commitments to the nation state in which they found themselves. This 'alienation from immediate concerns' often made co-operation with 'the stranger' easier, and assisted institutions in developing the common interests that new knowledge requires. The tendency now, however, is to see universities as integral to a country's foreign policies, particularly when these are aimed at promoting economic interests and co-operation. SANORD works against policies that try to 'use' national university systems for narrow purposes, as well as the strategic orientation that sees universities as agents in an increasingly internationalised competitive market. SANORD offers North–South co-operation that seeks to be independent of external rankings, ratings and foreign policy commitments. It seeks to promote understanding between two cultural regions; one marked by extreme forms of European imperialism with all the tragedies this implies, and one that has been more or less spared the influence of the big powers, and whose small democratically governed nations have largely retained their independence.

Means of continuing international co-operation between universities

The mechanism for continuing international co-operation among universities in 1948 was the creation of the IAU. It was open to all universities and 'university-like' organisations that emphasised research and teaching, and were willing to foster the crucial links between their institutions. The role of UNESCO in helping to create and subsequently support the IAU underscores the cultural orientation of the organisation.

Today, however the global knowledge regime is not dominated by IAU, because it bases its membership – as does SANORD – on individual universities. By contrast, the international university system is dominated by multilateral organisations, the power of which rests on the support of member states (Bøås and McNeill 2004). Their interests influence international co-operation between universities more than the ideas embedded in the IAU and in UNESCO. Martens et al. (2007) argue that the hegemony of the global knowledge regime is located in organisations like the World Bank, the OECD, the WTO and in neo-liberal economic ideology. Thus the world has at least two 'ministries of higher education'. If UNESCO embodies the official one, an alternative ministry resides within the World Bank which presently enjoys the strongest power of co-ordination over reform strategies for this sector in the so called global South. Undoubtedly an important supporter of this 'ministry' would be the OECD, which with its increasingly global reach aims to co-ordinate the reform of higher education and research, even outside its own membership. As the 2009 UNESCO/IAU World Conference (the second of its kind) showed me and other participants, UNESCO represents an arena for debate and for the development of alternative ideas around what could be called (in contrast to the 'knowledge economy') the 'knowledge society' model, but with little or no formal influence on practices driving global trends towards the new university model (see also (Altback 2009).

The overarching issue of 'co-operation and mutual understanding' that emerged after the Second World War has been replaced with one dominating value, namely: how knowledge can contribute to economic innovation. The integration of universities in the 'innovation economy' has gradually been streamlined by quantitative measurement systems developed since 1996. The key factor in the transformation from qualitative to quantitative understandings of knowledge, or from human development and nation-state identities to human capital and global capitalism, has been the essentially moving target called *best practice* (Bøås and McNeill 2004; Carroll and Kellow 2011; Martens et al. 2007). This is part of the new kind of governance conceived within the OECD (Trondal et al. 2010). Hegemony in the production of numbers and statistics has shifted from UNESCO to the OECD. Best practice, as now statistically interpreted by OECD, also creates uniformity, convergence and commitments, and most of all conformity. If there is a 'war' between faculties, disciplines or academic cultures, it is no longer fought on grounds of epistemological criteria or *cognitive rationality*, but on measurements of output. And this is of course how the politicians like it to be. Ruling via measurements of best practice contributes towards (as the World Bank and OECD see it) the transformation of society (or nation states) into a system of competing organisations, which, through tautology, seek to approach what is considered best practice within the confines of neo-liberal governance. As Keynesian economics and much else was left behind during the 1980s, the research university was reshaped in the image of the market.

It is not surprising that SANORD hardly fits the new global knowledge regime built around the idea of a university as an organisational actor constantly adjusting to a changing environment based on external evaluations. Instead SANORD represents a kind of practice that evolves from below, from the trust that develops between fellow researchers who seek to make society grow from little histories. These histories are important and valuable as cases for learning, if not action. But SANORD does not stand alone. A UN initiative to develop sustainable higher-education policies has been underway since about 2003. A global campaign with clear local commitments, the Education for Sustainable Development (ESD) programme attempts to link local actions with the fundamental global value of sustainable development and the related Millennium Development Goals. The UN declared the decade 2005 to 2014 the Decade of Education for Sustainable Development, hoping to create a powerful movement of nations, communities, and households towards a more sustainable future. The programme is linked to a series of regional initiatives that will be followed by national and particularly local practice and policies that place the responsibility for sustainable higher education on higher-education institutions themselves (see McKeown and Hopkins 2004).

If this UN initiative is taken seriously, it will be difficult for universities in Europe to continue their search for 'excellence' without reflecting on the consequences of this on the environment and the use of resources, on the social redistribution of knowledge throughout populations, and on poverty and the redistribution, of the global power balance, and many other issues. This kind of approach to higher education has the potential to make universities in the South far more relevant for collaboration. Without knowing it, perhaps, SANORD has become an alternative to massive global capitalist ideas about how knowledge and competition should combine, and as such, it is an organisation that everyone concerned about sustainability and mutual respect should strongly support.

The 'Accra Declaration on GATS and the Internationalisation of Higher Education in Africa', that was adopted at a representative conference in April 2004, calls on African governments and other African role players

> to exercise caution on further GATS commitments in higher education until a deeper understanding of GATS and the surrounding issues is developed and a more informed position is arrived at on how trade related cross-border provision in higher education can best serve national and regional developmental needs and priorities on the African continent.[3]

So, plainly, it is not through trade with knowledge as a commodity or through private providers that Africa wishes to expand its system of higher education. The Accra Declaration supports internationalisation, but in line with a series of global values that have the potential to benefit regions other than the rich and dominant ones. First of all, therefore, it is necessary to remove obstacles to knowledge creation, knowledge exchange and knowledge application, and to base these instead on forms of co-operation and collaboration. In this respect SANORD stands out as an example.

A final word

It is challenging to expand democracy, both as a practice and as a value, beyond the nation state. This is particularly so when democracy as a value ranks after the universalism of neo-liberal economics. Yet universities, in line with their own history, have a particular responsibility to face the challenge. Both the IAU and UNESCO, as well as a number of other UN initiatives, are supportive of such endeavours. SANORD has the potential to contribute to the ideas and values of democracy both within nation states and beyond, and it now up to SANORD to live up to its commitments in a world where, together and across borders, we create our preferences through the discourses we contribute to.

Notes

1 Discussion document presented by Kader Asmal to the Ministerial Working Group on Higher Education, 13 December 2003.

2 See TRUE – Transforming Universities on the UiB website.

3 The Accra Declaration was published by Association of African Universities and is available at http://www.aau.org.

References

Albrow M (1995) *The Global Age*. Cambrige: Cambridge University Press.

Altbach PG, L Reisberg and LE Rumbley (2009). *Trends in Global Higher Education: Tracking an Academic Revolution*. Paris: UNESCO

Amadae SM (2003) *Rationalizing Capitalist Democracy. The Cold War Origins of Rational Choice Liberalism*. Chicago and London: Chicago University Press.

Bleiklie I (2009) The TRUE Research Programme. Department of Administration and Organisation Theory, University of Bergen.

Bøås, M and McNeill MB(2004) *Global Institutions and Development: Framing the World*. New York: Routledge.

Carroll P and A Kellow (2011) *The OECD: A Study of Organisational Adaptation*. Cheltenham and Northhampton, MA: Edward Elgar.

Dorsman L and A Blankesteijn (2008) *'Work With Universities': The 1948 Utrecht Conference and the Birth of IAU*. Utrecht: Stichting Matrijs.

Halvorsen T (1995) 'Parliaments, committees and foreign affairs', in *Parliaments and Foreign Policy, The International and South African experience: A Conference Report*. Cape Town: Centre for Southern African Studies, University of the Western Cape.

Harste G (2011) Dansk universitetsledelse: Tilbage til enevælden', *Politiken/Kroniker*, 27 April 2011. København.

Hess DJ (2011) 'Bourdieu and science studies: Toward a reflexive sociology', *Minerva* 49 (3): 333–348.

Hydén G (ed) (1998) *Demokratisering i tredje världen*. Studentlitteratur. Lund: Författarna och Studenlitteratur.

IAU (International Association of Universities) (2012) *IAU Horizons: World Higher Education News* 18 (2).

Kalleberg R (2011) 'The cultural and democratic obligations of universities', in T Halvorsen and A Nyhagen (eds) *Academic Identities, Academic challenges: American and European Experience of the Transformation of Higher Education and Research*. Newcastle: Cambridge Scholars.

Marais H (2011) *South Africa Pushed to the Limit: The Political Economy of Change*. Cape Town: University of Cape Town Press.

Martens K, A Hurrelmann, S Leibfried, K Martens and P Mayer (eds) (2007) *Transforming the Golden Age of the Nation State*. New York: Palgrave.

Mathisen G (2005) 'Chasing quality, WTO and UNESCO: Mulitlaterals at work', in T Halvorsen, T Skauge and G Mathisen, *Identity Formation or Knowledge Shopping?* Bergen: SIU Norwegian Centre for International Cooperation in Higher Education

McKeown R and CA Hopkins (2004) 'New challenges and roles for higher education in education for sustainable development', a paper presented at the IAU's 12th General Conference, São Paulo, Brazil 25–29 July.

Mirowski P and D Plehwe (2009) *The Road from Mont Pelerin: The Making of the Neoliberal Thought Collective*. Cambridge and Massachusetts: Harvard University Press.

Offe C (2011) 'Crisis and innovation of liberal democracy: Can deliberation be institutionalised?' *Sociologický časopis/Czech Sociological Review* 47 (3): 447–472.

Parsons T, G Platt and NJ Smelser (1973) *The American University*. Cambridge, MA: Harvard University Press.

Rueschemeyer D, E Huber Stephens and JD Stephens (1996) *Capitalist Development and Democracy*. Oxford: Polity Press.

Streeck W (2011) 'The crises of democratic capitalism', *New Left Review* 71: 5–29.

Tilak JBG (2011) *Trade in Higher Education: The Role of the General Agreement on Trade in Services (GATS)*. Paris: International Institute for Educational Planning, UNESCO.

Trondal J, M Marcussen, T Larsson and F Veggeland (2010) *Unpacking International Organisations*. Manchester: Manchester University Press.

Vale P (2010) 'The humanities and social sciences: Orphaning the orphan', in *The State of Science in South Africa*. Pretoria: ASSAF.

Yesufu TM (ed.) (1973) *Creating the African University*. Ibadan: Oxford University Press.

Chapter 13
Whatever happened to imagination?

Peter Vale

> Imagination is more important than knowledge. For knowledge is limited to all we now know and understand, while imagination embraces the entire world, and all there ever will be to know and understand.

> *Albert Einstein*

THE QUESTION IN MY TITLE should not be considered deliberately provocative although, as will become plain, I do aim to provoke a response from the reader. Nor, and this must be made abundantly clear, does what appears in these pages refer to any individual or group of people: instead, the accusatory tone of the argument is directed at all who call themselves academics, whether they chose to connect with the SANORD network or not.

As Stanly Ridge says in his contribution to this book, the SANORD network was conceived at the end of apartheid when the creative energies of both Nordics and southern Africans were focused on what to do next in a relationship which, though dating back to the age of Linneaus, had just passed through one of those rare moments in history when people can hope for better times (see Sellström 1999; 2002). Broadly speaking, both sides – southern African and Nordic – considered how they might build on the work of their predecessors, and continue to make the world a better place by recommitting themselves to the emancipatory goals that can still be tapped from the Enlightenment project. They imagined a better world than the one that was ending.

It is no surprise that university people, who above all treasure the realisation of human potential offered by the search for the truth, should have been persuaded that deep-seated ties of support for the liberation cause could easily translate into university co-operation. The result was the formation of SANORD with its inclusive spirit, its networked organisation and the compelling appeal of its North–South axis. So, using Darwinist language, one might safely say that SANORD was a natural development from the trust that had been built between a southern Africa which was finally free and the Nordic people who had done so much to bring this about.

But, if hard truth be told, the moment that was seized upon by SANORD's visionaries was not a good one to explore the great potential promised by the changes taking place, even if many considered it to be a hinge of history. Rather than being a time when both politics and minds thawed after the deep freeze symbolised both by apartheid and the Cold War, the very best of hopes were soon dashed and the best of intentions seemed to close off – and quickly, too. Provocatively, I want to suggest that SANORD, for all the undoubted successes illustrated in the essays in this book and in the organisation's Annual Reports, has been similarly hamstrung by a discourse (and practice) of social control that has closed minds instead of freeing them.

How was this closing possible at a time when (to quote Irish poet, Seamus Heaney) 'hope and history rhymed'? Answering this question is the business of this chapter. Although a difficult undertaking, understanding the answer is essential if, as all involved in the project hope, SANORD is to fulfil the emancipatory promise of its founding.

Carbon dating

Although it is difficult to explain, as we will see, carbon dating the moment at which minds closed is easy – the year was 1989; the month, November; the iconic instant, the breaching of the Berlin Wall on that city's famous Friedrichstrasse. The overarching historical phase was the ending of Communism – first in Eastern Europe, then in the Soviet Union, and later elsewhere too. What caused the collapse of this dominant global system remains to be answered clearly and with confidence. Was it, as neo-liberal economists claim, the success of Thatcherism initially, and later of Reaganism? Did these leaders, and the economic system they unabashedly espoused, press the Soviet Union to compete beyond its capacity? Or was it that the United States (and perhaps its allies too) simply believed that they no longer had anything to fear militarily from the Soviet Union and its allies? Perhaps it was the ultimate recognition of the common-sense significance of the famous challenge in Franklyn Delano Rooosevelt's inaugural address as America's thirty-second president: 'the only thing we have to fear is fear itself'. Or, to bring the explanation forward in time, was it the growing force of electronic technology – beginning with the humble fax machine – that finally ended the capacity of states to successfully corral populations and, more importantly, control the flow of ideas?

Whatever the explanation, the fall of the Berlin Wall was a catalytic moment in international politics and in the way in which lives were lived across the world. Afterwards, although everything looked the same, almost everything had changed. As a result, what was once unthinkable became almost commonplace. How else, dare one ask, could a country like Germany which was once divided by bricks, barbed-wire fences and (especially in late 1961) the crack of bullets, reunite again and, given the extent of the ideological antagonism that had divided the country, join NATO, a quintessential Cold War institution? If explaining these events presented one set of puzzles for what would later be grandly called 'global change', the political side-show in southern Africa was equally perplexing.

So, to use an apposite example, how do we explain that, even prior to the crumbling of the Berlin Wall, the almost century-long conflict over Namibia ended with the country achieving its independence? That country's liberation movement, SWAPO (South West Africa People's Organisation), which had long been the beneficiary of much Nordic largesse, came to power after a transition presided over by apartheid South Africa, which was effectively the colonial power, and the United Nations which had long been the ward of the disputed territory. With this shift, the 30-odd-year serial war in Angola ended. And with it, Castro's courageous Cubans returned home, apartheid's external war machine was slowly wound down, and this is too often forgotten, its soldiers returning to barracks.

Then, and almost in quick succession, an apartheid president made a speech of both hope and history which set in motion a transition in South Africa itself. It was not to be easy but, in the end, instead of facing the fire that had long been predicted as its fate, South Africans took hands to move forward. Here, too, a liberation movement – and the ANC (African National Congress) especially – which had also enjoyed Nordic munificence, was elected to power. But, and this is at the centre of the SANORD story, the southern African region which had itself been held captive by the wars in South Africa and Namibia, could begin life anew. In some places, Mozambique is a good example, South Africa ceased its surrogate war against that country's people while elsewhere – Zambia most famously, perhaps – long-standing presidents yielded to the power of democracy.

But, and this is in the form of a brief research agenda, the complexity of the link between the fall of the Berlin Wall and the freeing of southern Africa has not yet been well explained. Using the counter-factual as a point of entry, we can ask a few suggestive questions about the possible links. Would apartheid have ended if the Berlin Wall had not come down? What was the link between the ending of apartheid and Mikhail Gorbachev's twin strategies of *perestroika* and *glasnost*? How are we to understand these ideas (and the outcomes they unleashed) against the backdrop of what American political theorist Samuel P Huntington called the 'Third Wave of Democratization' (1993: 3)? Or, less ambitiously but, probably, more appropriately in domestic South African terms, what are we to make of the role of a powerful counter-cultural movement of Afrikaner youth, known as, *Voëlvry*, on the ending of apartheid? This was the rise and revolt of the Afrikaner youth – their Paris 1968, if you like – against their parents and the political party that had nurtured them. Then, and crossing only one of South Africa's many divides, what was the role played in both the ending of communism and apartheid by Olivier Tambo's 1985 call to 'make apartheid unworkable, make South Africa ungovernable, prepare the conditions for the seizure of power by the people' (Tambo 1985)?

We don't really yet know the answers to these (and a myriad of other) questions; indeed, we must accept that it is possible that we will never fully answer them because partial understandings and explanations are often all that is on offer, no matter how hard academics try to find the truth. To get there, if that is our goal, will require language that will enable us to grasp the interwoven strands of economics, politics, sociology, cultural studies (and several more disciplines, besides) in order to ask both the kinds of new questions that will forge answers that remain illusive. So, part of what academics have to do is exercise patience, which is in short supply in a busy materialist world, and in the now seemingly mindless pressure to publish. Scholars must wait for knowledge and, most importantly, language to catch up with the questions that need to be answered – or, to put it slightly differently, intellectuals must create the space so that society can fashion answers to the questions still to be asked. To appreciate these issues, all scholars need to understand (following the lights offered by Ludwig Wittgenstein) that the limits of our knowledge are decided by the limitations of vocabulary and, its corollary, that knowledge is a prisoner of language.

One of the explanations for the end of the Cold War (and indeed of apartheid) has held water for the best part of a decade, and was advanced by Huntington's student, the Japanese-American theorist, Francis Fukuyama. His controversial neo-Hegelian explanation is best known by the catch-phrase, 'the end of history' which carried his ideas into both popular culture and everyday analysis. This is not the place to disentangle the myth from the reality of Fukuyama's argument nor, indeed, to survey the rich literature – a veritable cottage industry – that has grown up around his explanation. Instead, my interest is to use some of Fukuyama's thoughts to anchor some ideas about the evolution of SANORD's work, in the hope of explaining what has happened to higher education since the end of the Cold War and apartheid, and in an effort to explain the effects of this on the work of those involved in what (these days) is fatuously called the 'knowledge economy'.

Interestingly, Fukuyama, believed that the post-Cold War period would be a very, very sad time. He wrote that 'the struggle for recognition, the willingness to risk imagination, and idealism would be replaced by economic calculation, the endless solving of technical problems, environmental concerns, and the satisfaction of consumer demands' (1989: 18).

While many serious minds have contested, and correctly so, the extravagance of Fukuyama's claims, especially the idea that history, in its epic condition would (or, indeed, could) simply end, few who have lived through the past two decades could fault the clairvoyance of this claim. The years since the ending of the Cold War have been a dreadfully dull time in which the prosaic seems to have triumphed over the politically important; in which the economic imperative rather than the socially relevant has marked the course of public debate throughout the world; and in which violence in all forms has been visited on the poor on every continent. It has also been an age in which mindless consumerism has largely conquered the deep consciousness required to build a more equitable and accessible world. These, of course, were the very high-minded ideas that first drew the Nordic people into supporting the southern Africans. This switch in thinking has made it more difficult to secure a peaceful, prosperous and planet-friendly future. It is not, therefore, surprising that the creative energy of the humanities, which should awaken humankind to alternative ways both to live and understand, have been driven into the corners of campuses across the world. Looking at the countries through which SANORD's writ runs – the southern African region and the Nordic countries – we might ask how this came to pass, especially since it was the humanities – with its free-thought and commitment to emancipation – that delivered the end of apartheid and freed southern Africa's people; outcomes for which so many on all sides sacrificed so much.

So, it remains a great irony that whilst solidarity, political support and education were the great 'instruments' of the Nordic–southern African partnership, they feature today as a minor part of the terrain in which SANORD may have to chart its future course. It is as if the achievements of the past – and the ways of making and building upon the successful earlier partnership – have been obliterated by foreign ways of knowing, of explaining, of understanding. In the place of human-centred ways of knowing, experimental science and business studies have made an impressive stand, even occupying the idea of the 'knowledge economy'.

Why has this happened?

Drawing on the fragmentary technique that has already been used, my argument advances by considering not the politics and the contemporary history that has brought us to this point, but by trying to understand the kinds of words that have trapped scholars in these bleak times. Indeed, these words have become the hallmark of the phase that Fukuyama so presciently suggested would follow the end of the Cold War.

Let me be clear, however: the argument that follows is not original; it draws from a wide range of thinkers and, as will be immediately clear, from the ideas of the Australian writer (and one-time prime ministerial speech-writer), Don Watson. In particular – and, arguably, this is original – I will focus on one word: *innovation*. This is certainly a word of our times: a fact that is confirmed by the number of times it is inserted into conversations about higher education's role in understanding and exploring the second decade of the twenty-first century. It is, however, a word which, for all its promise, lends little real opening to the broader exploratory goals of academia – the kind of knowledge that needs an open mind. Instead, it calls forth forms of social control over the essential, and intrinsically open, calling of scholarly work.

Before, the argument fully turns in this direction, I want to set a goal which lies beyond the critique that will carry the first. This takes the form of a plea – a plea not for *relevance*, though plainly that is important in a region like southern Africa where problems range from A to Z (AIDS to Zimbabwe), but rather a plea for a return, in the academic world, to an old-fashioned word, *imagination*. This of course explains the title of my chapter, but only by understanding what follows will readers understand why it takes the form of a question.

On the power (and powerlessness) of words

Shortly after the Cold War ended, a friend and sometime collaborator, Ken Booth, of Aberystwyth University, wrote a line that captured the disquiet then being experienced by most involved in the study of international relations, the discipline that he and I share. Here is Booth's sentence, 'Our work is words, but our words don't work anymore' (1991: 313). In important ways, these ten words capture the hopelessness of explanation that occurs when an epoch ends as it did when the Berlin Wall came down. But, and this is the important bit, his words also teed-up the conceptual challenges of a new world waiting to be born. In the proverbial nutshell, Booth's phrase drew closer the challenge over words – of which words could (perhaps, should) be used in crossing the multiple divides between one epochal moment and an unknown future.

Booth's point was this: words and phrases die with one epoch, and only words and phrases still to be imagined can describe and, indeed, make the next.

At this juncture, many turned to Antonio Gramsci's maxim, 'the old is dying, and the new cannot be born; in this interregnum a great variety of morbid symptoms appear', to explain the changes that were taking place (quoted in Hoare and Nowell-Smith 1971: 276). It was, of course, not the first time that words had had to catch up with the times: at the end of the Second World War, British cultural theorist Raymond Williams questioned 'a new and strange world' that had emerged (quoted in Bennett et al. 2005: xx). But, at the ending of the Cold War, there was a particular kind of irony both in the moment and in the seemingly endless – or was that pointless? – scratching around for the means to explain the way forward.

This was because, for all their dramatic expansion in the years after the Second World War (Calhoun 2010), the modern social sciences had largely failed to predict the ending of the Cold War. How was this possible when their very purpose was the same as it had been a century earlier when they were conceived, namely, to engage with social issues mostly in the hope of making a better world? Understandably, prediction was seen as an important element in this. But anger was added to the irony because international (and area) studies, which were 'prominent foci' (Calhoun's 2010: 55) for the social sciences in the post-Second World War period, had failed, and absolutely so. As already noted, the bridge between Cold War certainty, the desultory interregnum and the new place, would be paved with words that would – perhaps, we should use *could* – both carry understandings and ensure a safe destination. Yet, as every academic worth their disciplinary salt knows, words are seldom – if ever – neutral. If this is one complication of academic work, another is that 'words can reveal but a tiny fraction of an incredibly complex life-world...about us' (Young and Arrigo 1999: viii). This has great salience for this essay and for SANORD's work because, as natural scientists know – or, at least with the Harvard Entomologist EO Wilson, should know – 'We live in a little known world' (Wilson 2005: 156). The professional way to this unknown world is, as suggested in the foregoing pages, through the power of words.

So, words weigh – or *should* weigh – heavily in the deepest deliberative moments when the academic profession is called to exercise its greatest creativity, and its intellectual twin, the greatest care. However, and understanding this point is essential, if academics know this, why have they been so slapdash in the way that they interrogate the poisonous and socially controlling language that is used to manage the institutions, universities, to which we have devoted our careers and – all too often our very lives – in the post-Cold War period?

So much has been written about the hollowing out of the university in recent years, that the question, 'who or what are universities for?' scarcely raises an eyebrow in the proverbial common room these days. This is in sharp contrast to an age when all in the university – not only those in the social sciences and humanities – were both intimately linked to the social issues of the day and constantly wrestled with the language that made those times. At this point, the full technique of the argument is revealed: using established perspectives drawn from critical theory, it looks to the regimes of control that underpin higher education. As all good critical theorists know, the past is always a good place to start understanding the present.

Many biographies written by academics and others attest to the vibrancy, the heat and the intensity of the questions asked in the various ages in which they were written. Paradoxically, one of the best South African biographies is also probably the least known, and for this reason alone it deserves a few dedicated paragraphs.

Born in 1903 to an English-speaking mother and a father who spoke Afrikaans, Eddie Roux joined the Communist Party of South Africa (CPSA), founding the Young Communist League when he was a student in Johannesburg. After taking an honours degree, he was awarded a studentship to Cambridge where he took a doctorate in plant physiology. On returning to South Africa, Roux chose first a life in politics and political journalism but left the CPSA in 1936, following the purge of his mentor, Sidney Bunting. He then resumed his academic life, and by 1962 was professor of Botany at his alma mater, the University of the Witwatersrand. He published academically and, at the same time, wrote Bunting's biography as well as the acclaimed book, *Time Longer Than Rope: A History of the Black Man's Struggle for Freedom in South Africa* (1948), which was reprinted several times. A recent study has brought to light Roux's considerable additional skills, one of which was a political cartoonist (Pretorius 2011).

With few exceptions, today's university is a very different place from that in which a well-trained scientist – even with a social conscience – could devote considerable time and energy to community life outside the academy. These days, we are drawn into the dulling routines of what is called (in university-speak) 'community outreach' – which, as all academics know, is one corner of what one might call a golden triangle – the other corners being teaching and research.

What has shaped this triangle – within which Eddie Roux would arguably have been constantly called to account before a dean (or someone higher up the managerialist totem-pole) – is an approach to managing the university that is largely alien to its underlying purpose, namely, 'for happy scholars...[to follow]...their studies, searching only for truth...unworried by the passage of time or the world outside' (MacMillan 2009: 84). Despite this change in direction, the purpose of this chapter is not to trace the emergence of the cult of managerialism that has almost turned universities – not only in SANORD but elsewhere too – into business corporations in which excellence is judged less by the quality of scholarship than by the capacity to turn a profit. As has been plainly established, I am interested in looking at one aspect of this, namely, the kinds of words that make academics believe that the university is a place where social control is not only inevitable but correct.

Weasel words

It was of course the English writer, George Orwell that first alerted the world to the deception and deceit of language, and its grubby political use. For Orwell, words, like ways of seeing the world, were always for something and someone.

South Africa was (as it remains) a country replete with words that fashioned a pre-selected series of social options by pretending to present – in objective ways – another world entirely. In a largely neglected (but undoubtedly important) text on the old South Africa, published in apartheid's final years, Emile Boonzaaier and John Sharp argue that the words analysed in their book, *South African Keywords; The Uses and Abuses of Political Concepts*, 'constitute a discourse about the nature of South African society, which reveals the logic and serves the interests of those who wield power' (1988: 6). But if the keywords used by apartheid reinforced the meta-narrative of race and charted the course of its highly bifurcated university system, what keywords reinforce the meta-narrative that has built a 'society of universal commerce', to use Emma Rothschild's (2002: 250) compelling term for the times in which we live? Are these the same words – and ideas – that have charted a university system that has engaged with, rather than critiqued, the globalised economic system that has further empowered the rich and driven the poor to its margins and, if this were not enough, imperilled the survival of the very planet?

What does this mean for SANORD, an organisation born from the success of international co-operation in ending a system whose essential features mirrored the discrimination that marked South Africa's apartheid past, as acclaimed cartoonist, Zapiro, shows in the cartoon on the next page.

The language that has built this world, as did apartheid-speak, exercises a form of social control. Today's academic speak is deeply embedded in discourses which, like those around race, have captured a range of intellectual interests which they inform and with which they intersect. Of these, certainly, economics with its assumptions that human nature is essentially driven by the rational pursuit of self-interest is in the vanguard; it is supported, however, by management studies with its closed understandings of society, its Taylorist logic and management fads such as the 'balanced scorecard' which has all but crippled higher education (Head 2011). Through these developments, universities throughout the world have been corporatised, and important forms of knowledge have been commodified and forced to live in the shadow of market ideology. As in apartheid South Africa, the university has become an 'administered society' and serves particular interests.

But, as we have seen, language alone cannot capture the entire complexity of the life-world; particular words have been drafted to serve the interests and the purposes of universal commerce. Through their constant circulation by think-tankers, the press and the political class, the particular language they have made has been incorporated into what Don Watson calls 'the machine of business and politics' (2004: 3). Watson's frank and refreshing take on the use of language in the construction of the market-centred world of the twenty-first century turns to America's twenty-sixth president, Theodore Roosevelt, to explain the title of his 2004 book. For 'Teddy' Roosevelt, 'weasel words' were those which have had the meaning sucked out of them in much the same way that a weasel sucks the content out of eggs (Watson 2004: 1, 3). In the book, Watson provides definitions of weasel words and, interestingly, provides examples of their use in contemporary English. Let me illustrate this by turning to a word that we have already identified: innovation.

Some months ago a senior academic manager at South Africa's largest university invited me to participate on the opening panel of a week-long series of events at the university under the theme 'Research and Innovation'. The intent of the series of discussions was clear from the sub-title of the programme which read, 'Excellence, Innovation, Leadership'. The programme itself suggested that the university was keen, not only to highlight its own 'research and innovation' but also to bring home to the university community how important breakthroughs in 'innovation' had been in other places and countries. Hovering over the keynote panel on which I served, was the idea of 'commercialisation'. One of my fellow panellists was clear about the importance of this: all innovations should be brought to 'the market'; indeed, he seemed to suggest that this was the only possible measure of the success of innovation and, by implication, of the university.

It struck me on that day, as I have written elsewhere (Vale 2011), exactly how ideological the idea of innovation has become in higher education and, to draw the thought closer to both Watson and Roosevelt, what a powerful weasel word it has become in the contemporary university. For one thing, and largely unquestioningly, senior university managers who are charged with promoting the research function are now called 'Deputy Vice-Chancellors for Research and Innovation'. This reflects, and reinforces, the fact that South Africa's research system is constructed around what the official literature calls, 'a national system of innovation'. South Africa is not alone in this, of course. Research thrusts in many countries have innovation at their respective centres: the Nordic system included. Indeed, the OECD's (Organisation for Economic Co-operation and Development) Guidelines for Collecting and Interpreting Technological Innovation Data, a key tool for both policy-makers and scholars in innovation studies, is known colloquially as the 'Oslo Manual' (OECD 2005).

But, like any effective weasel word, innovation lives far beyond its dictionary definition. South Africa, along with many other countries, has established government-funded agencies devoted to improving innovation. Indeed, my co-panellist who was determined that all innovations, including the suggestion that South Africa's political settlement, should be brought to market, was from the newly established Technology Innovation Agency which boasts a budget of R410 million (see Claasen 2010). And, in further evidence of how international fashion is followed, the minister responsible for science and technology in South Africa regularly appoints blue-ribbon panels to look into the country's progress on this front. A recent one, chaired by a senior vice-chancellor, included a number of serving and retired senior academic administrators, a regular consultant to government and a prominent business-intellectual known for his decades-long forceful support for market-driven economics (DST 2012). The group offered a doormat definition which reads as follows: 'Innovation is the capacity to generate, acquire and apply knowledge to advance economic and social purposes' (DST 2012: 4).

Used this way, innovation has become a cypher for the university engaging, not so much with society, but with the economic system – often (and this is implied) through the modernisation processes of globalisation. Unsurprisingly, then, this version of innovation reinforces the idea of the knowledge economy, and is propelled into public consciousness by celebratory rhetoric as this snippet drawn randomly from the world-wide web suggests:

> Ours is a future to innovate. Change is inevitable...and constructive change is innovation. Knowledge is the asset to be harnessed. Innovation is the process where knowledge is created, converted into products and services and commercialized in a worldwide market all enabled by unprecedented advances in technology. In the 21st century the most successful nations will be those that best harness the intellectual capital of people and all of these thinkers will not necessarily be citizens of those nations (*Arab News* 2005).

This view of innovation is premised on the endless promise of modernity offered by the power of technology, and, as such, innovation is, 'overwhelmingly predicated on a metaphor of diffusion or adaption' (Michelsen 2009: 65). In this form, the idea of innovation draws the university away from its traditional setting as a space for free and unfettered enquiry into the association that knowledge should serve only the business community. In a benign interpretation, this association began with the need to generate what was initially called 'third-stream income' but which, especially in the US, has reached the offensive point where individual academics are managed as 'cost-centres' (on this, see Head 2011: 9). The accelerating intrusion of business into the university has not only eroded the sacred trust between society and scholarship, often reduced to the idea of 'academic freedom', it has commodified all forms of knowledge. So, and to put the issue as plainly possible, in this setting no form of knowing can exist independent of a particular regime of economics – and this regime is associated with the market.

But, for all the celebratory language around the idea of innovation, it can hardly be considered a neutral word. Its location is within a cluster of terms that celebrate the 'knowledge economy' and reinforce the ideological appeal of the free-market system (Marginson 2009: 10). In other words, terms like innovation are little more than proxy words for an economic system that essentially explain and lend legitimacy to particular actions and beliefs that they support.

So, is innovation, as it is used in the discourse on contemporary higher education, an ideology? The answer is yes, if we accept that ideology is a network of ideas that stabilise the values on which society builds its everyday existence, help to perpetuate the routines that determine everyday lives, and set the compass within which citizens (or professionals) place their hopes for the future. But this is not all that an ideology does. The dangerous part is what the late Tony Judt wrote in his last piece: 'the thrall in which ideology holds a people is best measured by their collective inability to imagine alternatives' (Judt 2010). The conclusion is unavoidable: the association between science policy and economic growth that lies at the base of the National System of Innovation – the centrepiece of South Africa's research policy – is an ideology.

The core problem is not the word itself but the ahistorical use to which it has been put. There is little doubt that innovation – as defined outside of its modern market-centric setting – played an important role in, say, Britain's rise to global power in the eighteenth and nineteenth centuries (see Chang, 2010). But the value of innovation – the act, that is, not the use to which word the word has been put in the contemporary juncture, is not clear-cut as it suggests. So, innovation is closely associated with the USA (Ive 2012), where culture is not as readily associated with the achievements of modernity as once was the case. This has been shown through the processes of financial 'innovation' which have proven highly complex and very destructive of the very purpose for which they were intended. As Ha-Joon Chang notes, innovation has produced markets that are too efficient – and this has resulted in quite the opposite – because 'many complex financial instruments were created that even financial experts themselves did not fully understand...unless they specialised in them – and sometimes not even then' (2010: 231, 177).

So, the problem with innovation, as it is currently used, is that it is emptied of history and this encourages those who use it to believe that it can deliver more than it is capable of. If this were not enough, it is linked to a chain of exhortatory language which essentially draws from the same empty well around knowledge as a commodity, technology as an essential and – and, as importantly – neutral force in society, and reinforces the idea that economic growth is a force that benefits all in society even-handedly. The underlying chain of evangelistic-type logic draws international organisations and states towards the idea that science, technology and innovation play an *economic* role in securing 'successful' societies. This is utopian-type thinking that most involved in innovation studies would eschew if they were to reflect on what they were saying rather than endlessly celebrate the limited achievements of the field.

And yet, serious scholarship, even in the narrow field that has grown up around the idea of 'innovation studies', suggests that the 'poor hardly feature in innovation studies' (Lorentzen and Mohamed 2010). This, to twist Hannah Arendt's thinking, only confirms the notion that as words – in this case, innovation – become empty, deeds become brutal. But what of the much-vaunted idea that 'social innovation' offers a palliative – or even a counter-narrative – to the high-level (read technical) end of innovation? Essentially this fails because bringing about fundamental social change requires interventions that lie beyond the parameters of market-driven thinking – the idea of innovation stabilises this thinking, proposing that all social relations are mediated by money. If truth be told, was not the most successful social innovation in modern times – certainly the 'innovation' that benefitted the most lives – the implementation of the National Health System in the United Kingdom in 1948? Decidedly, this lay beyond the market.

Imagination

Rather than the mindless repetition of weasel words, the exercise of imagination should be integral to how academics approach both their own labour and the labour that governs them. But, sadly, John Dewey's truism that 'every great advance in science has issued from a new audacity of imagination', has been almost lost to the professional academic calling.

Instead of allowing scholars to fully explore what lies beyond 'our little known world', to use EO Wilson (2005) again, the rituals of individual disciplines, the routines of higher education management, and the current ideological moment have arrested understanding in the same way that the Lilliputians chained Gulliver on his famous journey to their country. At first, the citizens of Lilliput saw Gulliver as a resource: certainly he was seen as helpful in dissolving various hurdles they faced. But, with time, this faded and they turned on him forcing him to escape. The lesson surely is this: the harnessing of scholarship to serve the goals either of the state or the dominant ideological fashion is invariably fleeting. But the deeper danger is that it is counter-productive and destructive of the very purposes of scholarship itself. This is what Nordic and other scholars throughout the world said of the kinds of knowledge that made apartheid.

In this struggle, as this chapter has been at pains to show, words play a crucial role. They awaken us to the limits of what it is that we know, and they can promote ends and purposes in much the way apartheid did. Understanding this may force imaginative minds to search out explanations and meanings which lie beyond the low horizon provided by economics.

For me, this charts the challenge for SANORD. Can the organisation rise to the hopes of its founders and imagine that a new world is possible? Or will it follow the knowledge economy towards the barren fields and the emptiness of weasel words.

References

Arab News. 2005. 'Innovation builds knowledge economy'. 15 April. Available online.

Calhoun C (2010) 'Social sciences in North America', in *World Social Science Report*. Paris: UNESCO.

Chang H (2010) *23 Things They Didn't Tell You About Capitalism*. London: Allen Lane.

Claasen L (2010) 'Mixing a new techno tune', *Financial Mail*. Available online.

Bennett T, L Grossberg and M Morris (2005) *New Keywords: A Revised Vocabulary of Culture and Society*. Oxford: Blackwell.

Boonzaaier E and J Sharp (1988) *South African Keywords: The Uses and Abuses of Political Concepts*. Cape Town: David Philip.

Booth K (1991) 'Security and emancipation', *Review of International Studies* 17: 313–326.

DST (Department of Science and Technology) (2012) *Final Report of the Ministerial Review Committee on the Science, Technology and Innovation Landscape in South Africa*. Pretoria.

Fukuyama F (1989) 'The End of History?' *The National Interest* 16 (Summer): 3–18.

Head S (2011) 'The grim threat to British universities', *New York Review of Books*. 16 December. Available online.

Hoare Q and G Nowell-Smith (eds) (1971) *Antonio Gramsci: Selections from the Prison Notebooks*. London: Lawrence & Wishart.

Huntington SP (1993) *The Third Wave: Democratization in the Late Twentieth Century*. Oklahoma: University of Oklahoma Press.

Ive J (2012) 'Apple's invisible aesthete emerging from Jobs' shadow'. *Financial Times* (London), 10–11 March, p. 9.

Judt T (2010) 'Captive minds, then and now', *New York Review of Books*. 13 July. Available online.

Lorentzen J and R Mohamed (2010) '...to each according to his (or her) needs. Where are the poor in Innovation Studies?', paper prepared for NickFest, Sussex University, United Kingdom, March 2010.

MacMillan M (2009) *Stephen Leacock*. Toronto: Penguin.

Marginson S (2009) 'Open source knowledge and university rankings' *Thesis Eleven* 96: 9–39.

Michelsen A (2009) 'Innovation and creativity: Beyond diffusion – On ordered (thus determinable) action and creative organisation', *Thesis Eleven* 96: 64–82.

OECD (Organisation for Economic Co-operation and Development) (2005) *Guidelines for Collecting and Interpreting Technological Innovation Data* (third edition). Paris.

Pretorius JD (2011) Ideology and Identities: Printed Graphic Propaganda of the Communist Party of South Africa 1921–1950. PhD thesis presented, University of Johannesburg.

Rothschild E (2002) *Economic Sentiments: Adam Smith, Condorcet and the Enlightenment*. Cambridge: Harvard University Press.

Roux E (1948/1967) *Time Longer Than Rope: A History of the Black Man's Struggle for Freedom in South Africa* (second edition). Madison: University of Wisconsin Press.

Sellström T (1999) *Sweden and National Liberation in Southern Africa, Volume I: Formation of a Popular Opinion 1950–1970*. Uppsala: Nordiska Afrikainstitutet.

Sellström T (2002) *Sweden and National Liberation in Sothern Africa Volume II: Solidarity and Assistance 1970–1994*. Uppsala: Nordiska Afrikainstitutet.

Tambo O (1985) 'Address by Oliver Tambo to the nation on Radio Freedom', African National Congress Archives. Available online.

Vale P (2011) 'What has happened to the humanities?' *Transactions of the Royal Society of South Africa* 66 (1): 25–31.

Watson D (2004) *Watson's Dictionary of Weasel Words, Contemporary Clichés, Cant and Management Jargon*. Sydney: Knopf.

Wilson EO (2005) 'Biodiversity' in J Stangroom (ed.) *What Scientists Think*. London: Routledge.

Young TR and BA Arrigo (1999) *The Dictionary of Critical Social Sciences*. Boulder: Westview Press.

Contributors

Saleem Badat is Vice-Chancellor, Rhodes University, South Africa.

Anne Bang is Senior Researcher, Christian Michelsen Institute, Norway.

Bernhard Bleibinger is Associate Professor of Music, University of Fort Hare, South Africa.

Mignonne Breier is Research Development Manager, University of Cape Town, South Africa.

Tor Halvorsen is Associate Professor, Department of Administration and Organisation Theory, University of Bergen, Norway.

Albino Jopela is Lecturer, Department of Archaeology and Anthropology, Eduardo Mondlane University, Mozambique.

Seke Katsamudanga is Lecturer in the Archaeology Unit of the History Department, University of Zimbabwe.

Pieter le Roux was Director, Institute of Social Development, University of the Western Cape, South Africa.

Lucas Magongwa is Head of Deaf Education, Centre for Deaf Studies and Studies in Education, University of the Witwatersrand, South Africa.

Ancila Nhamo is in the Department of History, University of Zimbabwe.

Stanley Ridge is Professor Emeritus, University of the Western Cape, South Africa.

Risto Rinne is Professor of Education at the Centre for Research on Lifelong Learning and Education University of Turku, Finland.

Tore Sætersdal is Senior Advisor, Department of Research Management, University of Bergen, Norway.

Anne Sørensen is Vice-Chairperson, Danish Development Research Network, Denmark.

Gabriel Tati is Senior Lecturer, Department of Statistics, University of the Western Cape, South Africa.

Peter Vale is Professor of Humanities, University of Johannesburg, South Africa.

Lightning Source UK Ltd.
Milton Keynes UK
UKOW04f2126030716

277532UK00019B/601/P